TWAYNE'S WORLD AUTHORS SERIES
A Survey of the World's Literature

FRANCE

Maxwell A. Smith
Guerry Professor of French, Emeritus
The University of Chattanooga
Former Visiting Professor in Modern Languages
The Florida State University

EDITOR

Jules Michelet

TWAS 638

JULES MICHELET

By OSCAR A. HAAC

State University of New York at Stony Brook

TWAYNE PUBLISHERS
A DIVISION OF G.K. HALL & CO., BOSTON

Photo of Jules Michelet by Nadar
Courtesy of the French Cultural Services

Library of Congress Cataloging in Publication Data

Haac, Oscar A.
Jules Michelet.

(Twayne's world authors series ; TWAS 638)
Bibliography: pp. 185–89
Includes index.
1. Michelet, Jules, 1798–1874.   2. France—Historiography.
I. Title.   II. Series.
DC36.98.M5H27   907'.2024 [B]   81–4230
ISBN 0–8057–6482–8   AACR2

To Gunilla

Contents

About the Author

Oscar A. Haac is a professor of French and has taught at the State University of New York at Stony Brook since 1965. He earned doctorates at Yale University and at the University of Paris. His teaching appointments include Yale, the Pennsylvania State University, Emory University, and several summer schools. He directed language institutes at Emory and in France. His publications include studies on eighteenth- and nineteenth-century French literature as well as editions, translations, bibliographical contributions, textbooks, and professional articles. He has contributed the *Marivaux* volume to the Twayne series and has written a book, *Les Principes inspirateurs,* and a number of articles on Michelet. He has edited Michelet's course of 1839 at the Collège de France, and is currently at work on those following. He has received fellowships and grants from the John Simon Guggenheim Foundation, the American Philosophical Society, the American Council of Learned Societies, the French government, and from the research funds of the universities at which he has taught. In 1963, he was made Chevalier des Palmes Académiques.

Preface

Some critics have assigned Michelet to the "lyrical school" of nineteenth-century historiography, along with Carlyle, as a master of style and on account of his remarkable feeling for the past—an ability to identify with his subject. This classification also indicates that his account is discursive, for he departed from the prevailing abstract and analytical trend when he began his work. As a genius of words, the creator of striking images which have attracted generations of readers, he is also known as the great romantic historian of France, just as Delacroix is the great master of romantic painting, and this in spite of his classical principles of aesthetics. Michelet was anxious to dissociate himself from romanticism, for his objective was neither artistic nor rhetorical. Even while he aimed at describing the truth in the past, progressive or regressive as it might be, he accused contemporary novelists of overemphasizing decadence. He believed in the French people. In the face of the many failures of past reforms and revolutions, he saw his own task as one of encouragement, as a sustainer of faith. This is why his work is so moving, but for us he also remains one of the outstanding creators of French prose.

His emphathy for the actors of the past was matched by his unshakable conviction that the French people can shape their destiny. He is a democratic idealist who celebrates the triumphs of freedom and feels compassion for suffering and defeat. He visualizes these struggles with moral overtones. As a professor, not only of history, but of ethics at the Collège de France, he felt it to be his mission to inspire students and readers. He saw himself increasingly as the educator and guide of the people at large, the wider public for whom he composed a series of popular books on religion, education and the family, and on natural science, while continuing his *History of France*. He hoped to reach as large a segment of the population as possible and held so fervently to his role as an educator, that he refused the opportunity, when offered in 1848, to enter politics.

Today we have a clearer picture of the historian than could have been presented before the remarkable renewal of studies since World War II. The manuscripts gathered at the Bibliothèque Historique de la Ville de Paris have been supplemented by the Dumesnil legacy, papers handed down by Michelet's daughter and son-in-law, all of which are now cataloged; those at the Institut have become available to the public. The publication of the early writings *(Ecrits de jeunesse)* and the *Journal* by Paul Viallaneix and Claude Digeon have revealed the author intimately. Michelet's courses are being edited, and the first critical edition of his works is appearing under the direction of Paul Viallaneix of the University of Clermont-Ferrand. Much has been learned since Gabriel Monod's admirable *Life and Thought of Jules Michelet* (1923). My own study of his *Principes inspirateurs* [Guiding Principles] was followed by the basic work of Paul Viallaneix, *La Voie royale* [The Royal Road] and many others, especially the picture of Michelet's religious concerns by Jeanlouis Cornuz and the numerous contributions honoring the anniversary of Michelet's death (in 1874). Further, the Dumesnil property at Vascoeuil (between Rouen and Beauvais) has been transformed into a Michelet museum by Maître Papillard.

My brief account can only provide glimpses of Michelet's vast work. It is not a biography but rather the history of this work and his ideas, a reader's guide to what is most original and striking. In attempting to do justice to the historian, teacher, author of popular books, and to the inspired spokesman for a new France, I have included, in summary form, material still unpublished, especially from the courses from 1840 to 1851. In brief, I have tried to show what makes his text memorable, why Michelet remains a great classic of literature, and history.

My presentation is essentially chronological, though some of the popular books are grouped together. I interrupt the account in twenty-six volumes of French history, since Michelet described the French Revolution before he told of the Renaissance, but my method has the advantage of following his changing interpretation, his discovery and application of scientific theories in the popular books and the *History of France*. My arrangement provides meaningful parallels between his various efforts.

The greatest problem was that of choice. By focusing the discussion of the Revolution on Robespierre, we can define Michelet's position favoring Danton and compare his approach to that of other historians, but we sacrifice a multiplicity of other themes. In this respect, I can do no more than provide a meaningful introduction to reading Michelet, and this, even today, remains a moving experience. His style, his images, above all his generosity and idealism are outstanding qualities which anyone can appreciate.

I wish to add my deep appreciation to those who have suggested ideas and revisions, to those whose work preceded my own, especially Paul Viallaneix, to researchers like E. Fauquet, W. Kusters, M. Magó, and above all to Edward Kaplan and Jeanlouis Cornuz, who made precious suggestions after reading my manuscript, and to those whose careful correction has proved so valuable: Kay Wilkins, Linette Brugmans, and my wife, Gunilla.

My deep appreciation also to the American Council of Learned Societies that provided support for my research in France, to the State University of New York for a sabbatical, and to colleagues whose advice was essential, especially to Elof Carlson, professor of biology and genetics, who elucidated some of the issues.

Oscar A. Haac

State University of New York at Stony Brook

Chronology

	Principes de la philosophie de l'histoire. Professor of history and philosophy at the Ecole Normale Supérieure (1827–1829).
1827–1828	*Précis de l'histoire moderne*.
1828	Trip to Germany; Michelet named to teach Louise-Marie-Thérèse, Princess of Berry, granddaughter of Charles X.
1829	Professor of history at the Ecole Normale. Charles is born.
1830	Trip to Italy. Named to teach Clémentine, fifth child of Louis-Philippe. Head of the historical section, National Archives.
1831	*Introduction à l'histoire universelle; Histoire de la République romaine*.
1832	Trip to Belgium.
1833	*Précis d'histoire de France; Histoire de France*, volumes 1–2.
1834	Named to replace Guizot at the Sorbonne. Trip to England.
1835	*Oeuvres choisies de Vico*. Trip to Aquitaine with report on the libraries. End of instruction at the Sorbonne. *Mémoires de Luther*.
1836–1838	Michelet replaced by substitutes at the Ecole Normale.
1837	*Histoire de France*, volume 3; *Origines du droit français*. Trip to Belgium and Holland with report on the libraries.
1838	Named professor of ethics and history at the Collège de France. Elected to the Académie des Sciences Morales et Politiques. Trip to Venice.
1839	Trip to Lyons. Death of Pauline.
1840	*Histoire de France*, volume 4. Meets Mme. Dumesnil and her son, Alfred. Trip to Belgium.
1841	*Procès des Templiers*, volume 1; *Histoire de France*, volume 5.
1842	Fatal sickness and death of Mme. Dumesnil. Trip to Germany with Adèle and Alfred.
1843	*Des Jésuites*. End of instruction of Princess Clémentine. Marriage of Adèle to Alfred Dumesnil.
1844	*Histoire de France*, volume 6.
1845	*Du Prêtre, de la femme et de la famille*.
1846	*Le Peuple*. Trip to Belgium.
1847	*Histoire de la Révolution*, volumes 1–2. Trip to Holland.
1848	Course at the Collège de France suspended by Salvandy (January) and reopened (March) after the February Revolution.

1849	*Histoire de la Révolution,* volume 3. Marries Athénaïs Mialaret.
1850	*Histoire de la Révolution,* volume 4. Yves-Jean-Lazare born (2 July) and dies (24 August).
1851	Definitive suspension at the Collège de France. *Histoire de la Révolution,* volume 5; *Pologne et Russie; Kosciusko; Les Soldats de la Révolution* (published 1878); *Procès des Templiers,* volume 2.
1852	Termination at the Collège de France at the National Archives. Departure for Nantes into "exile." Revision of *Histoire de France,* volumes 1–6.
1853	*Histoire de la Révolution,* volumes 6–7. Return to Paris; trip to Italy. *Principautés danubiennes, Mme. Rosetti.* Winter at Nervi, east of Genoa. Slow recovery from exhaustion.
1854	*Les Femmes de la Révolution; Le Banquet* (published 1879). Travels to Genoa, Turin, Acqui, Paris.
1855	*Histoire de France,* volumes 7–8. Trip to Belgium and Holland. Death of Adèle of consumption.
1856	*Histoire de France,* volumes 9–10; *L'Oiseau.* Travels to Switzerland.
1857	*Histoire de France,* volume 11; *L'Insecte.* Winter at Hyères.
1858	*Histoire de France,* volume 12; *L'Amour.*
1859	*La Femme.*
1860	*Histoire de France,* volume 13.
1861	*La Mer; Sylvine* (unfinished novel); *Histoire de France,* new revision of volumes 1–6 (many changes already in the 1852 edition).
1862	*Histoire de France,* volume 14. Charles dies of tuberculosis. *La Sorcière* (published in Brussels after some changes).
1863	*Légendes démocratiques du Nord; Histoire de France,* volume 15.
1864	*La Bible de l'humanité.*
1865	Trip to Switzerland, visit with Quinet; winter at Hyères.
1866	*Histoire de France,* volume 16; "Le Collège de France" for *Paris Guide.*
1867	*Histoire de France,* volume 17.
1868	*La Montagne;* prefaces for the *Histoire de la Révolution,* to appear (new edition) 1869.
1869	Preface to the *Histoire de France; Nos Fils.* Travels to Italy.
1871	*La France devant l'Europe;* chapter: "L'Expiation," for *La Nature* (by Athénaïs). Suffers stroke. Trip to Switzerland, then to Hyères.

CHAPTER 1

Ambitions

I *The virile joy of youth*

THE beginnings were difficult. Michelet renders the atmosphere in his famous letter to Edgar Quinet which serves as a preface to his book, *Le Peuple* [The People, 1846]. He pictures the obstacles but also his determination in a dramatic testimony to their bond of friendship:

I remember that in the dire misfortunes of daily deprivation and fears for the future, which the enemy but two steps away (in 1814!) . . . we were without fire, the snow covered all. Unsure of just where our bread for the evening was to come from, with life apparently at dead end, all I felt in me was the stoic acceptance of life without religious hope, but even then, dead with cold, I struck down my hand on the oak table I still possess, and felt the virile joy of youth and of the future. (*PE*, 70)[1]

He shared the sensitivity of his contemporaries of the great romantic generation—Lamartine, Vigny, Balzac, and Hugo—but much like Rousseau, in his *Confessions*,[2] he rejected the literary imagination in favor of life and truth: he was to be an intensely personal historian, "literary" in spite of himself.

Jules Michelet was born in Paris on 21 August 1798, in the disaffected church where his father, Jean-Furcy, had set up his ill-fated printshop. It was a harsh existence. At an early age the boy had to help running the press, as did his uncle, Narcisse, and in 1808, when the father was cast in prison for debt, the uncle and the boy carried on. Jules did not attend school until he was sent to the Latin school of the picturesque M. Mélot (*EJ*, 189–91), so that, albeit with difficulty, he was admitted to the Collège Charlemagne two years later. All this time he continued as a printer's helper, if only to satisfy the claims of the "horrible Vatard," the usurer pressing for payments (1812). He tells of a book of children's games, *Le Savant de société* [The Social Expert], being printed to satisfy these claims:[3] "It was I who did most of the composition. When we lived on Boulevard St.–Martin [1809] I had already learned our family profession and could have earned a living at it. So, the minute I returned from Mélot and completed my bit of homework, I put on my apron and unflinchingly composed thirteen or fifteen pages" (*EJ*, 199). Jean-Furcy kept the family together. He had unlimited confidence in his son. Jules recalls how in earlier years his father would take him into his bed and sing a song of his own invention: "How happy I am to be a father, my son provides my consolation, / To my last hour, my son will be my happiness" (*EJ*, 186). Jules justified this trust. Inadequately prepared, awkward, introverted, he had to repeat his first year (the third class) at Charlemagne, but so avidly did he work that he soon became the most distinguished pupil of his class.

In 1811 debts led to the seizure of the family possessions; in 1812 the printshop was closed by Napoleon's decree reducing the number of authorized presses. Undeterred, Jean-Furcy found a new position (1814) at the sanatorium of Dr. Duchemin and, when Michelet's mother died (1815), was able to install his family on the premises. Three years later, when the sanatorium closed, he established a boardinghouse, rue de la Roquette, accompanied by three important residents: Mme. Fourcy, the administrator of the sanatorium, who had begun to exercise great influence over Jules as his "second mother," Pauline Rousseau, the companion of one of the infirm who was to become his wife, and Paul Poinsot, his closest friend since their common studies with Mélot. They came to share their hopes and intellectual concerns. For a while Paul was away at Melun as a pharmacist's apprentice, but he returned in 1816 to serve, with Mme. Fourcy, as a witness to Michelet's baptism, an overpowering experience following Jules's conversion after reading the *Imitation of Christ* (*EJ*, 187).

By contrast, his parents were republicans and freethinkers who looked upon priests as the representatives of wealth and power. Michelet explains: "I knew the name of Jupiter long before that of Jesus" (*EJ*, 183). The reaction against the Voltairian orientation at home might have pitted Jules against his father, except for their continued close affection. Jules admitted that his father was at times harsh in manner, but "express before him a tender feeling, a generous thought, you could see a tear shining in his eyes. . . . His poor education and [the abuse of] his fellowmen were not able to stifle his admirable good nature" (*EJ*, 212). Father and son were to share the same roof for close to fifty years, to Jean-Furcy's death in 1846. In Jules's memory, the father's simple faith, the hope of "Old France," was transmuted into the faith of Voltaire and Rousseau (*J* 1,657), but judging by their correspondence,[4] Jean-Furcy could hardly have aspired that high. It is true that he printed at least one dangerous tract by Babeuf (*VR*, 398), but he was no intellectual.

Poinsot returned to live with the family from 1817 to 1820. He studied pharmacy, then medicine, and finally became an intern at the Bicêtre hospital. His closeness to Jules is attested by their correspondence. One day Jules writes, in a melancoly mood: "The weather bursts with rain and somehow a ray of sunshine penetrates under the clouds to spread its cheerless light. The green of nature is drowned more than refreshed. The sadness of all I see takes me back to my favorite thoughts. When natúre no longer attracts our eyes, we lose self-examination" (*EJ*, 259). It is a supreme example of pathetic fallacy, testimony to the intimacy of their relations. This is evident also in the following letter, reacting to Paul's suggestion that he marry Pauline (1820):

Right now I love Pauline and greatly so, even physically, lively as she is, always changing. Besides her heart is constituted more or less like mine. She is compassionate, she loves me as much as she is able to love, perhaps as much as any woman can. She likes what I like. She is easy to get along with. She is gay but even though she likes amusement, she is not much of a spendthrift. So the obstacle to our marriage is not in her but in my unsurmountable hesitation. (*EJ*, 105)

He explains that marriage would give Mme. Fourcy the second place in the household, an unacceptable position, and here lies the secret, touched upon only in a reference to the love of older women in *Nos Fils* [Our Sons, 1869]: when Mme. Fourcy's daughter committed suicide, sympathy had brought her together with Jules and she initiated him to love.[5] Their affection remained even after he became intimate with Pauline (1818); indeed, he did not marry (1824) until after Mme. Fourcy's death in 1823.

By that time Pauline was pregnant. Jules did his best to argue for the marriage in most practical terms in letters to his aunt in the Ardennes who expected a more distinguished alliance. However, Pauline never entered into his professional life and thought. In spite of Michelet's kindness, she became alienated and, by the time she died in 1839, had turned to drink. The historian blamed himself bitterly for her unhappiness.[6] The pattern was already established at the boardinghouse, rue de la Roquette, with Michelet's closeness to Poinsot on the intellectual level, separate from his love, as he understood it, for Pauline.

The shock of Poinsot's death, in 1821, just as he was about to realize his dream and become a doctor, was overwhelming. Jules rushed to Bicêtre but arrived too late: "My friend was no more. I only saw a body still warm and seemingly asleep. . . . He was strikingly beautiful. His skin, whiter than it had ever been and his black hair formed a contrast which without the calm and angelic softness of his face would have had something frightening about it" (*EJ*, 134). The realism of this description recalls others, that of his grandfather dying of cancer in 1814. Gangrene had set in: "Horrible to say but a week before his death, worms were already in the wound" (*EJ*, 215). A year later Michelet describes his mother stoically waiting for death, advising that her bedsheets might serve as a shroud (*EJ*, 216). Poinsot's death was the most gripping of these experiences.[7] It prompted Michelet to compose his *Mémorial*, a tribute to their friendship, the best account we have of his early years (*EJ*, 183–218). Poinsot had been part of his most intense life, that of the intellect, as were his books. They provided consolation in the face of a harsh life.

At the Collège Charlemagne, his schoolmates—mocking, rowdy, inconsiderate—used to terrify him, perhaps even call forth the death wish he speaks of in *Our Sons* (*NF*, 86–88); thus

as soon as I had escaped from the school and fled through the most deserted streets of the Marais, I took up my homework. Then I relaxed with my books. There I found feelings which corresponded to mine, and never had to fear that cruel derision which pursued me at school, which made me sink right through the floor, and which I seemed to rediscover on the face of all those who passed by me. (*EJ*, 206)

We can just see the fourteen-year-old boy choosing back streets to avoid strangers, turning to his beloved classics. It was his way to fight back. He became a star pupil in order to earn respect.

As opposed to the more melodramatic account in *The People*, cited earlier, the *Mémorial* makes no reference to foreign troops, to the Restoration, to his striking his fist on the oak table. In its more genuine simplicity it subordinates everything to his consuming thirst for knowledge.[8]

II *The heroic spirit*

In 1817, Michelet passed the Baccalauréat with high honors. At Charlemagne he had distinguished himself, earned prizes, and above all the lasting friendship of two outstanding professors, Villemain and Leclerc. They would precede him to the Ecole Normale Supérieure and attain important positions. Villemain was to teach literature at the Sorbonne and become minister of education, and secretary of the French Academy; Leclerc, in classics, would eventually become dean of faculty at the Sorbonne.

Michelet's first teaching assignment was that of tutor at the Briand Institute, a private Catholic school that provided useful contacts and income needed while pursuing advanced degrees. It was a time for arduous preparation as we can judge from the *Journal de mes lectures* [List of my Readings] and *Journal des idées* [List of Ideas], where he records his multiple projects and the universality of his interests. He kept these diaries until 1829 when he lost his teaching assignment in philosophy and concentrated on his work as a professional historian (*EJ*, 219–48, 301–31). For some of these years we also have his *Journal* (1820–23: *EJ*, 73–177) which is far more complete and explicit. Here we find comments on Poinsot and Pauline, here we read meditations on death, here we discover Michelet's passion for Byron, and the record of his friendship with Poret, a fellow student and future colleague. Their contacts lasted until Poret died in 1864. The three diaries reflect a veritable explosion of knowledge in literature, philosophy, and history, as yet unchanneled and without a set objective.

Michelet's two theses for the Doctorat (1819; in *OC*, 1:21–59) are, in keeping with the time, elegant, brief essays, one in French on the moral philosophy of Plutarch, the other in Latin examining Locke's idea of infinity. Most interesting is the way Michelet associates the two authors to his own idealism. Plutarch's models of virtue appear as the antithesis of "the sad system of fatalism," for there would be no point honoring the great men of the past "if all our acts were predetermined" (*OC*, 1:36). It is an ode to free will, to the free human spirit.

The Latin essay claims that, according to Locke, man can conceive of eternity and, therefore, of God. This interpretation contradicts the interpretation of Victor Cousin, who saw infinity in Locke merely as a negative concept, for it bore no relation to space and time, the locus of all human thought.[9] It is uncertain whether Michelet realized that he was contradicting the famous professor at the Sorbonne—he was to meet him five years later, in 1824—and that he was translating a peripheral issue in Locke into transcendental terms. By analogy to Descartes's "I think, therefore I am," Michelet held that man's soul conceives of infinity and God, and that therefore they exist. It is clear that such proof mattered most to Michelet himself, convinced as he was of the transcendence of the human spirit. Actually such problems were unimportant. These theses were exercises in Latin and French style and, as such, they were brilliantly successful. Similarly, no one objected to the admittedly controversial assertion that "the most sublime accomplishment" of Plutarch was his education of the Emperor Trajanus.[10]

Michelet continued to teach at the Briand Institute until he passed the Agrégation in 1821, the first year the examination was given. It was a success, but the committee objected to his style. His friend, Poret, obtained first place; Michelet was third. As a result and since he declined an appointment outside of Paris, he had to be content with a position as substitute at Charlemagne for a year. Poret obtained a regular appointment there. The following year, however, Michelet was appointed to teach history at the Collège Sainte-Barbe, rue des Postes (today, Lhomond; this is not the present institution next to the Sainte-Geneviève Library). It was a fashionable, conservative, Catholic school where his references from Briand were appreciated. Of course he had to conceal his unorthodox tendencies, a feat he could scarcely have accomplished in later years! His instruction was an immediate success.

He held the position for six years, increasingly restless, not on account of the school, but because history was taught only to relatively young pupils. It was a field only recently added to the curriculum and still distrusted by the government. In 1826 the instruction was pushed back one more year so as to exclude pupils not only in the last two, but in the last three years. Furthermore, modern history was offered only in the last of these years and was limited, again by government decree, to the period from 1453 to 1648 or possibly to 1789 but excluding the Revolution. Thus controversy was to be avoided. Michelet was the author of an unsuccessful petition against the decree of 1826. He concluded that the only way to have access to a more mature audience was to request a transfer to the newly reconstituted Ecole Normale Supérieure. He was appointed there in 1827 to teach history and philosophy, at least until 1829 when, much to his regret, he was asked to devote himself entirely to history.

He had undertaken to publish in both areas simultaneously. By 1826, he had already composed two textbooks to suit the history curriculum, the *Chronological Tables of Modern History* (1825), a brief summary of European history from 1453 to 1789, and the *Synchronic Tables* (1826), charts in parallel columns, one for each important country, recording events from 1453 to 1648. The reorganization of 1826 made both books obsolete. Undeterred, Michelet composed his *Précis de l'histoire moderne* [Outline of Modern History, 1828] to take their place. It was a far more detailed work, again beginning with the fall of Constantinople to the Turks and ending just before the Revolution.

He managed to include a number of original views and topics, e.g., the development of trade, the erosion of royal power in England, the "English Revolution" which pointed toward 1688,[11] the discovery of America, and colonial policy in England, Spain, and Portugal. No word, though, about the United States. The insights include the conception of a European balance of power, such as Michelet found it exposed in the work of Heeren.[12] In this perspective he analyzes the intervention of France on the side of the Protestants in the Thirty Years' War, to oppose Hapsburg power, and accords the French victory at Rocroi (1643) special significance: it represented a social revolution, the first major success of a national infantry. Then he stresses the "revolution of the Fronde" as an all-important aftermath of the war and the Treaty of Westphalia (1648), for the collapse of the Fronde set the stage for absolute royal power in France. Even in so restricted a framework, Michelet was able to portray new and original views.

The approach of this précis foreshadows the basic method of all of his historical work. It is discursive and narrative, not epigrammatic or abstract. It focuses on key events "so as to leave a lasting impression" in the minds of students; it emphasizes "representative data which might take hold of their young imagination, limited in number but chosen so well that they remind them of all others" (*OC*, 2:24). History will be a series of vivid pictures chosen so as to evoke major trends and "serve as a symbol" for an entire period, a key to understanding. This was indeed Michelet's purpose. He avoided the philosophical abstractions of a Guizot, or Mignet, as well as the style of a simple chronicle without comment, adopted by Barante.

The task was complicated by the fact that the text had to conform to the official program and furthermore could not infringe on other manuals, e.g., the précis of the Middle Ages by Michiels or the outline of modern history by Ragon. This led to delicate negotiations with these colleagues. We cannot therefore be overly critical in judging Michelet's results. They do constitute a valuable preparation for his *History of France* and adopt a broad, European orientation which will remain evident throughout his work.

Simultaneously he pursued his philosophical interests. The study of Rousseau, Condillac, and Locke—and Michelet's reaction to the sensationalism of the last two—led him to seek the true origins of institutions and language. One project, eventually abandoned, concerned the "history of peoples and their customs discovered in their vocabulary" (1823); other projects proposed to deal with Greek literature and philosophy (1824; *EJ*, 227, 232). Michelet's fundamental idealism quite naturally directed him to the Scottish philosophers of "common sense," to Thomas Reid and Dugald Stewart, who seemed to provide an answer to the obstacle of historical determinism.

One day he made an important discovery. While reading the third volume of Stewart's *Brief History of Metaphysical, Moral, and Political Sciences* in the Buchon translation, he came upon two critical appendixes: Victor Cousin's essay on the philosophy of history, and a note by Buchon concerning Vico; Buchon expressed surprise that Stewart's ideas were so close to Vico and yet failed to mention him. This experience of January 1824 (*EJ*, 231, 318) was so pertinent because just a month before, Michelet had become interested in Vico's *De Antiquissima Italorum sapientia* [Roman Wisdom from the Earliest Days, *EJ*, 227] in which Vico interpreted early inscriptions and etymologies as monuments of still earlier customs and tried to reconstruct the original institutions of Rome. Vico's method placed Michelet's own research in an exciting new perspective.

Reading Cousin's essay in the Buchon volume made Michelet anxious to meet the philosopher. Poret introduced him in 1824, and in 1825 Michelet met Edgar Quinet at the home of Cousin. By that time Michelet had decided to translate Vico into French, and meeting Quinet, who was similarly engaged in translating Herder, was an important event. Cousin encouraged Michelet and Quinet to proceed with their translations. His support was essential to both. Only the fact that Cousin later turned conservative and seemed to speak for a repressive government, prevented Michelet and Quinet from acknowledging their debt in future years.

The focus of these studies and concerns was the universality of knowledge made meaningful by moral philosophy, i.e., the need to expand one's interests in all disciplines in order to encompass the progress of civilizations. This was admirably expressed in Michelet's *Discours sur l'unité de la science* [Discourse on the Unity of Science, 1825; *EJ*, 289–99], delivered to the students of Sainte-Barbe but intended for a much wider audience.[13] He appealed to them to choose a broad curriculum of general studies and to keep in mind the universal principles without which the individual disciplines lacked meaning, for such a humanistic approach mattered far more than the study of sense impressions as practiced by Condillac or Locke. It was the great "lesson" to be derived from the examination of human progress, the condition for creating new institutions and making history. Once again Michelet found confirmation in Vico. His summary of Vico's discourse, *De Mente eroica* [On the Heroic Spirit] reads like the conclusion to his own address: "The heroism he speaks about is that of the great soul, the courageous genius who does not fear to encompass universal knowledge in his studies and who will develop his natural potential to the highest degree" (1826; *OC*, 1:347). This is also the essence of Michelet's *Discourse*, the basis of the humanistic idealism he tried to transmit to his students.

III *Cousin and Quinet*

A brief view of the two men so closely associated with Michelet's enterprise is called for. Although only six years his elder, Victor Cousin was the leader and hope of liberal youth. In 1815 he began teaching philosophy at Paris as an associate of Royer-Collard. In 1817 he met Schelling and Hegel in Germany. In 1821 he was suspended from teaching for being too radical, philosophically (as a partisan of the German idealists) and politically. Back in Germany, he was arrested as a suspected liberal and freed only on Hegel's personal intervention. When his essay appeared in 1824, he was the well-known spokesman of the new "eclectic" school, and favored by Michelet because he espoused the Scottish school of "common sense" with its emphasis on innate spiritual powers, as well as on German idealism. Reid, Stewart, Kant, and Hegel were his guides.

In 1828 Cousin was reinstated as a professor, along with Guizot.
The liberal revolution of 1830 was on the horizon. Unbounded en-
thusiasm greeted Cousin's course on "Truth, Beauty, and the Moral
Good."

The solidarity, however, did not last. Cousin was elected to the
French Academy in 1830 and to the Academy of Moral and Political
Sciences in 1832; he became director of studies at the Ecole Normale
Supérieure and, in 1840, minister of education. In short, he became
part of the system while Michelet and Quinet turned against it.
Quinet was furious when, in 1830, Cousin could not provide him
with a teaching position in Paris—Quinet lacked the qualifications,
the Doctorat and Agrégation—and Michelet was outraged by Cousin's criticism of his performance at the Ecole Normale in 1838; it
was partly to avoid Cousin that Michelet requested an appointment
to the Collège de France. It is suggestive that while, in 1828, Michelet admitted his debt to Cousin and expressed his enthusiasm in
a letter to his cousin, Célestine Lefebvre (Gabriel Monod, *La Vie
et la pensée de Jules Michelet,* 1:70; hereafter cited as *JM*.), he
claimed in 1869 that Cousin had not guided him in any way (*JM*,
1:55, 124). Cousin changed as much as he did. Cousin even revised
his famous course on "Truth, Beauty, and the Good" and explained
that "spiritualism," not "eclecticism," was henceforth his philosophy
(in his Preface and Opening Discourse of 1853).

Edgar Quinet, like Michelet, moved in the opposite direction.
Born in Bourg in 1803 from rather well-to-do, Protestant parents,
he came to Paris to study law, but soon merged into the literary
scene and developed his passion for Herder's *Ideen* [Ideas]. His
German was still poor, so he translated the book from T. O. Church-
ill's English version, *Outlines of a Philosophy of the History of Man*.
Later Quinet compared his work with the original. There were
strong resemblances between Herder and Vico. Many critics assumed that Herder knew his Italian precursor. Herder also studied
the growth of civilizations, but his view of culture was far broader
than that of Vico, and his interests ranged more widely, including,
e.g., China and India. Even so, Michelet felt that "his" Vico was
the original mind and that Quinet's Herder was a "fatalist," i.e., a
determinist, a conclusion which betrays ignorance of Herder's en-
lightened view of human progress.

Quinet remained Michelet's closest friend for many years, even
though there were some disagreements. Quinet moved to Germany
and, after his long struggle to marry Minna Moré in spite of the

objections of her nationalistic family, he warned of the threat to France of this new German spirit. [14] Michelet did not see it that way before 1870. Besides, Quinet reacted more radically against Napoleon III and remained abroad, in exile, while Michelet soon returned to Paris. Still, their common start, their common battles of 1843 against the Jesuits, strengthened their bond. It was only in 1868, after Quinet, in his *Révolution*, failed to express appreciation for Michelet's work and, more seriously, saw the French Revolution as an extension of Christianity, [15] that their friendship diminished. Even then Quinet's widow, Hermione Asaki, was justified in publishing much of their correspondence under the title, *Fifty Years of Friendship*. Their rapport continued the fervent intellectual comradeship Michelet had entertained in his youth with Poinsot.

IV *Man is his own Prometheus: the Vico translations*

Giambattista Vico wrote his *New Science* to parallel Bacon's "new method" *(Novum organum)*, to analyze man and his social institutions. Michelet's translation appeared in 1827 preceded by an essay on Vico based on his *Autobiography*. In 1835 Michelet added translations of the *Autobiography* and *De Antiquissima* [Roman Wisdom from the Earliest Days], along with selections from other works, entitling the volume *Oeuvres choisies de Vico* [Selected Works of Vico]. This was to remain the standard edition for over one hundred years, until supplanted by more modern translations. [16] Michelet did not meet our standards of accuracy, either in his translation or in abridging the *New Science*, but his objective, to make Vico readable by avoiding the multiple repetitions—Vico's methodical approach made him relate each basic aspect to every other—was commendable and successful. His version was an instant success and most everyone interested in Vico henceforth approached him through Michelet. The complete translation of the *New Science* by Princess Belgiojoso (1844) passed almost unnoticed.

Michelet had worked with feverish speed to prepare the 1827 edition, for a rival translation by A. Allier had been announced. The main problem was to acquire enough Italian to master the difficult text, but Michelet did surprisingly well. He made a few errors, e.g., when he substitutes "freedom" for Vico's "free will" or "freedom of choice," but on the whole it was a remarkable achievement. [17] He did have the help of De Angelis, an Italian refugee in France, and Ballanche seems to have sent him a partial translation of *Roman*

Wisdom in manuscript, but he successfully resolved most problems on his own.

Vico wanted to discover the principles behind the process of history. Therefore he concentrated on early documents like the Twelve Table Law of Rome, interpreted as the result of even earlier customs, which he also saw reflected in (often imaginary) etymologies. Thus he arrived at the idea of three stages of man: (1) the era of gods, the primitive period when all powers and events were identified with divine action; (2) the era of heroes like those of Homer or Virgil's *Aeneid;* and (3) the age of rational man and analysis. In this context Vico distinguished between the *verum* (truth in the form of mathematical logic) and the *certum* (certainty in a social or historical frame of reference). Thus he abandoned Descartes's exclusive reliance on abstract, antihistorical logic: *verum quod factum* (the truth is in the deed). Vico was adamantly opposed to Cartesian geometricians bent on explaining history in terms of logic, for the unfolding of the human spirit followed different rules. Michelet agreed wholeheartedly. Vico's battle against rationalistic historians was also his own.

Vico exempted the chosen people, the Hebrews of sacred history, from his law of three ages, from the need to rise from a savage state to civilization. He distinguished divine and profane history because he was anxious to safeguard the biblical tradition. Michelet ignored this: his translation renders only the historical relativist, not the orthodox Vico who wanted to shield church doctrine. Our historian realized that in spite of his orthodoxy, Vico advanced historical relativism, a radically new theory of man's development.

Another difficulty was created by Vico's cycles in history. He postulated a return to barbarism after the collapse of civilizations, e.g., after the fall of Rome. He was more pessimistic than Michelet, who had inherited ideas of progress from Turgot, Condorcet, and other Enlightenment thinkers. Originally Michelet questioned this theory of cycles, and the idea of a return to barbarism. In 1828 he explained that if these cycles occur, they become constantly larger. Thus he tried to combine Vico's cycles with his idea of progress; he would not accept the idea that history repeated itself.[18] However, he speaks of Vico with growing approval: in 1833 he still rejected this "symbolism" of Vico and considered it fatalistic, like the pantheism of Schelling, Hegel's philosophy of history, and theories of race-determined history as proposed by Barante: "They may disagree with each other in every other respect, but they agree in opposing man's freedom!" (*OC*, 4:662) This passage from the *History of France* was deleted in 1852. A manuscript note of 1854 showed that he had absolved Vico, if not Hegel and the others, from the reproach of fatalistic determinism. This text concludes:

Virgil and Vico are non-Christians, perhaps super-Christians. . . . When I was translating Vico, I still hoped to reconcile science and religion, but after 1833 I laid it down that Christianity was temporarily dead, and in 1848 I asserted that all religions die. . . . My masters were Virgil, Vico, and [Roman] law. I spent ten years, from 1830 to 1840, reconstructing the tradition of the Middle Ages; I showed how empty this tradition is. It took me ten more years, from 1840 to 1850, to reconstruct the anti-Christian, antimessianic tradition.[19]

How surprised the devout Vico would have been to read these lines, dictated by Michelet's later battles with Christianity, but Michelet was correct in recognizing a kindred spirit in Vico, radically innovative in spite of himself, potentially unorthodox, and frequently obliged to hide his views.

When Michelet applied for the position at the Ecole Normale, he wrote to Mgr. Frayssinous, the conservative minister of education, that his Vico translation was "illuminated by a philosophy along religious lines" (*JM*, 1:30, 76). He was as anxious to impress the authorities with his orthodoxy as Vico had been when he dedicated the *New Science* to Pope Clement XII, and wisely so, says Michelet (*OC*, 2:341).

The importance of Vico, to Michelet, is above all, that of an idealist convinced, as he was, that man's creative spirit is the essential driving force in history. Translating Vico's concept of free will into a will to be free and to create a better destiny, Michelet draws from him his preferred motto: "Man is his own Prometheus."[20] While, to safeguard his originality, he refused to admit that anyone had ever influenced him, he would frequently sign letters "Jules Michelet, translator of Vico." Our historian liked to consider himself as Vico's continuator and interpreter.

CHAPTER 2

The Historian Established

I *History or philosophy?*

MICHELET'S passionate interest in Vico was part of his attempt to develop a moral basis of history. This is why he welcomed the opportunity at the Ecole Normale to teach both philosophy and history (1827–1829).[1] His courses in philosophy concern themselves with the condition of man, broadly conceived, but their application to history is evident. The course of 1827 insists on the "invincible faith" of Stewart and Reid, Kant and Schelling, on the transcendent ideal philosophers defined and poets felt, the concepts of the immortality of the soul and the divine. "As Bacon said, I would rather believe in principles which are totally absurd, than surrender the fundamental truths immanent in these shapes," i.e., their transcendence. Michelet credits Condillac's sensationalism with having founded modern psychology and defined its method, but "Condillac's foundations are deficient and all he will erect on them will collapse," since the faculties of our immortal soul escape him; and so Michelet would build a new psychology on the voice of conscience, that window to God as Rousseau had conceived it in the "Profession of Faith of the Vicar from Savoy," in *Emile*, and which Dugald Stewart had made his central principle. On this basis Michelet constructs his analysis of the self, in its relationship to the nonself, that of the soul to the world around it, in a system explaining our mental processes, e.g., the association of ideas, imagination, logic, language and its symbols. Vico's *certum* of the soul and the human self in history, and *verum* of abstract logic, are very much involved. It is an interesting course, the most basic and philosophical, a "method" for the idealist which Michelet always remained.

Meanwhile his courses in history alternate between classical antiquity and the Middle Ages, in preparation for his *Roman History* and the *History of France*. A common element will be found early in both works, a "geography of the spirit" that relates Italy and France to the genius of the inhabitants.[2] In a way this kind of psychology may appear as an abstraction, but it was documented and developed on the first two journeys that Michelet made outside of France. In 1828 he proceeded to Germany in search of the spirit of the Middle Ages and the Renaissance; in 1830 he went to Italy to study Roman archeology. In each case he established contact with scholars in these fields and combed libraries for sources. He returned from Germany having purchased some of the works of greatest interest. We have the record of his diaries (*J*,1); he made use of every opportunity to prepare his publications.

It is instructive to follow his travels more closely. In 1828 he spent two weeks in Heidelberg, one in Bonn, and a few days, mostly to buy books, in Frankfurt and Mainz. Ten additional days were spent in stage coaches. In Heidelberg he found his friend, Edgar Quinet, and Friedrich Creuzer, whose *Symbolik* was to guide him to the early practices and beliefs of the Indo-European peoples, especially once it appeared in Guigniaut's French adaptation (beginning in 1837). Unfortunately he could not join Grimm in Göttingen, the other scholar whose work was essential in reconstructing the customs of medieval Europe, much as Vico's was for Rome; he could contact Grimm only by letter. Tieck and Goerres were other significant encounters in Heidelberg, while in Bonn Michelet met the historian Hüllmann and the romance philologist Diez. Only the critic Wilhelm Schlegel refused to make himself available.[3] Among the authors he could not meet, but whose works he looked up in libraries and then bought at Frankfurt, we find Hammer, the historian of the Ottoman empire, Marheinecke, who wrote on the Reformation, and Spittler, a specialist on European history. In his program of readings Michelet was looking far ahead!

The trip to Italy in 1830 was very different in nature. Four days at Turin, three at Genoa, one at Pisa, three in Florence, eleven in Rome, two in Bologna, and three in Milan, with twenty-two spent in stage coaches. His interest focused on historical sites and archeology as well as on art, mostly since Raphael. In Rome he met William Gell, a British archeologist, and Eduard Gerhard, the director of the archeological institute. He was also introduced to an important cultural salon, that of Vieusseux in Florence, and met Manzoni in Milan—the two could find nothing to agree upon—but most of his contacts were in preparation for the *Roman History* and its interpretation of Italy (*J*, 1:56–73).

On 1 May 1830 Michelet returned to Paris; on 27–29 July the long awaited liberal revolution placed Louis-Philippe on the throne. Michelet, who had been the tutor of nine-year-old Princess Louise-Marie-Thérèse de Berry, granddaughter of Charles X (1828–1830), passed on, like the crown, to the new ruling house, to tutor Princess Clémentine, age thirteen, the fifth child of the new king. The new regime favored him. In October he obtained the directorship of the historical section of the National Archives. He also solicited an appointment to the Collège de France; however, this did not materialize until 1838. Even so, the favor of Guizot, minister of the interior in 1830 and of education in 1832, was to propel him beyond the horizons of the Ecole Normale; in 1834 Guizot asked Michelet to replace him as a professor of history at the Sorbonne. Surprisingly, if we think of his more radical stance in later years, Michelet was considered in those days to be one of the "doctrinaires," i.e., a conservative partisan of Guizot and the new regime. Michelet's daughter, Adèle, was born in 1824, his son, Charles, in 1829; now he had assured himself of a comfortable income to provide for them. He was ready to embark on his first major publication as an historian; it would further establish him in his career.

II *A framework:* Introduction à l'histoire universelle *(1831)*

The *Introduction* stands as a cornerstone to Michelet's life work. It defines the grand movement of history, the progress of civilization. He follows its torch from the fatalistic pantheism of the Orient to the germination of freedom in Persia, Egypt, and India (*OC*, 2:230–31), thence to Rome, the key to the development of Europe and guide to the future. Greece appears only in a subsidiary role as the "most beautiful among the beautiful," while Rome fertilized Europe, by the spread of Latin, through the influence of the church. In 1864 his *Bible of Humanity* was to draw an analogous picture but the agencies of progress will have been revised, e.g., by a new view of the Orient and the originality of Greek thought, and by a critique of Christianity. However, the basic concept of the historic sweep of freedom and civilization will remain unchanged.

The nations of Europe are analyzed in their great diversity. Italy is characterized by the individualism of its Renaissance artists,[4] while Germany seems steeped in the romantic dream of its Middle Ages, an "India in Europe" (*OC*, 2:238–40). This image reflects the interest of Tieck and Brentano, and especially of Grimm, Creuzer, and

Goerres in the German Middle Ages, its institutions and literature, but also the studies of India by German scholars: Friedrich Schlegel, *On the Languages and Wisdom of India,* Creuzer's *Symbolik,* Grimm's theory of Indo-European languages. Michelet's association of India and Germany was further strengthened by the parallel between Indian "fatalism" and Luther's Augustinian reliance on divine grace. There emerges a view of Germany far less self-reliant than Italy, and less able to realize freedom. Even so, Michelet admired the Indian and German civilizations.

A side light on European development is provided by England, seen as the haughty incarnation of industrial progress (*OC,* 2:252). Michelet is reacting to the bitter rivalry with France. England is the antithesis of France, for England lacks the force of reason of a Pascal, Bossuet, Montesquieu, and Voltaire, and the maturity of France, the land of "prose," in terms of Vico's three ages (of gods, heroes, and prose). Only in France do equality and social genius dominate (*OC* 2:248–53, 344). In later years our historian would not list Pascal and Bossuet in this context, but he will still adhere to the concept of national psychologies, and he will continue to base his view of progress on the geography of the spirit of nations.

Psychological associations, derived from Michelet's experience, especially from his reading, dictate his image of humanity "creating itself," as set forth in the *Introduction* and again in the *Roman History* (*OC,* 2:341). The forces of freedom must oppose the proponents of "fatalism." In this context he accuses Hegel of subordinating man to the system of his *Philosophy of History,* of "petrifying" man's efforts to attain freedom. Schelling's pantheism is criticized in the same light: it stifles progress and puts Germany to sleep. These hasty judgments show that Michelet did not understand how closely Hegel's three epochs of history parallel those of Vico. He came to reject the phrase "philosophy of history"—even though he had used it himself in the 1827 edition of Vico—as a "fatal opium" which obscured the progressive triumph of freedom (*OC,* 2:255). By analogy, he will oppose any systematic philosophy, or theory of race, as an abridgment of man's free development: "Man is his own Prometheus!"

He admits that in their primitive and relatively pure state, races may have had definite characteristics, but now that they are infinitely mixed, especially in modern France, freedom, i.e., the denial of determinism, should be the historian's first concern, man's unending struggle against "fatalism" (*OC,* 2:229).

Individuality in unity, such is his ideal. Everywhere he emphasizes European unity. It was the goal of Charlemagne, and modern
France is dedicated to its accomplishment. Michelet upholds France
because it serves humanity best. In all this, he tells us, the historian
is two-faced, Janus-like, "seeing the ancient world end and the
modern world rise, with France leading it on its mysterious road
to the future" (OC, 2:258). He assigns to France the same focal role
that Rome held in antiquity.

A fascinating detail concerning how the *Introduction* was published is furnished by Gabriel Monod (*JM*, 1:228). Michelet came
to an understanding with L. Hachette, publisher and graduate of
the Ecole Normale Supérieure, whereby the works were printed
at the author's expense, then turned over to Hachette for sale and
distribution. Intimately familiar with the printer's trade, Michelet
was able to strike a hard and profitable bargain. He maintained this
procedure (with different publishers) all his life.

III   Histoire romaine *(1831)*

Begun in 1828, completed in 1831, two volumes took the story
from the origins of Rome to the death of Caesar and Cleopatra; the
successor volume on the Empire was planned, but only sketches of
individual emperors remain. Inspired by Vico, Michelet was most
intent on unraveling the earliest days of the monarchy. He found
an admirable guide in Berthold Niebuhr, whose *Roman History,*
translated by Golbéry into French (1830), traced Rome from its
origins to the Punic War, and shed light on what Vico could only
guess at (OC, 2:340). First in the course of 1830, and now here,
Michelet draws on Niebuhr to develop a picture of the Pelasgians,
the pre-Indo-European inhabitants of Italy originating in Asia Minor—Homer called Troy a Pelasgian city— who came to control the
northeastern Mediterranean as far as the domain of the Etruscans.
He realizes that the last word on these "races" has not been spoken
and adds a "Note on the Uncertainties of the First Centuries of
Roman History" (OC, 2:641–54). Theories of race had haunted
French historians since Mably and Boulainvilliers, the first favoring
the Celts, the second the Frankish invaders—as did Michelet's contemporary, Henri Martin. In view of the confusion between the
concepts of race and language groups, and the rudimentary stage
of research concerning all of them, including the Etruscans, no
wonder that Michelet asserts the right to add his interpretation.

His foreword contains a glowing tribute to Niebuhr, but it is strangely conceived: Michelet notes that in Niebuhr's Denmark there never had been serfs and that he shares his own love of freedom. He praises him further for having tackled the problem of race twelve years before Augustin Thierry raised it in the *History of the Conquest of England by the Normans* (1825), as if the races involved were the same and as if race had not been discussed for many years before that. One cannot help but feel that Michelet expresses some jealousy in dealing with the immensely popular work of Thierry that had appealed to his generation. He prefers to grant priority to Niebuhr who died in 1831, while Thierry remained a rival on Michelet's own ground, France in the Middle Ages.[5] Needless to say, the detail of all these theories of primitive races in Europe, whether in Niebuhr, Thierry, or Michelet, is hopelessly out of date. It was a topic of fascinating debate at the time, but now seems hardly important. What we read about the Pelasgians, the Osci, the Tusci (*OC*, 2:354–58), or even the Etruscans—here Michelet drew on Karl Otfried Müller's *The Etruscans* (1828)—is of lesser interest compared to the analysis of institutions, the city and the family (*OC*, 2:396), or its decline when slaves were imported (*OC*, 2:516).

Most impressive is the account of later developments where sources were more reliable: the Samnite and Etruscan wars mentioned by Tacitus (*OC*, 2:428–35), the Punic wars against Hannibal, that great general of Carthage, "the Wallenstein of antiquity," with Polybius, writing under the sponsorship of Scipio, as an essential source. There are moving moments, as when Michelet tells of the Romans, defeated at Cannae but not demoralized, who "forbade their women to weep" (*OC*, 2:471). The portrait of Julius Caesar is equally memorable. Brutus stabs the tyrant, but Caesar lives on greater than life (*OC*, 2:602). The image reminds us of Shakespeare's Brutus, who says on seeing Titinius slain:

> O Julius Caesar, thou art mighty yet.
> Thy spirit walks abroad, and turns
> Our swords in our proper entrails.
>
> (V, 3)

Michelet could not help expressing his admiration of great men, even though his intent was to write a history of the people at large, even though he will protest, in the preface of 1866, against those historians who tie the progress of civilizations to legends of great men (*OC*, 2:335). His talent for images and portraits wins out and carries the reader along.

IV *A new kind of history*

Michelet had made the momentous decision to write the history of France. It was an ambitious undertaking, more so even than he imagined, for he initially announced five volumes to cover not only political, but also cultural history from the Middle Ages to Napoleon (*OC*, 4:626); it would take him twenty-six volumes and a lifetime to accomplish this task.

Notable precedents were few for a documented, critical history told with commitment and enthusiasm. What was available? After the famous but fanciful work of Mezeray in the seventeenth century, two histories of France were written which were still being read: one by the Abbé Velly (1755) carried to 1819 by Dufau, and Mably's *Observations on French History* (1765), still important enough to be honored by Guizot, in the preface to his *Essai sur l'histoire de France* [Essay on French History, 1823]. The objection to Velly and Mably was not only that the accounts were secondhand, but that they lacked the style of Chateaubriand, whose *Génie du christianisme* [Spirit of Christianity, 1807] and *Martyrs* (1809) had become models for the new generation. Besides, the influential group of young liberals at the Sorbonne in the years 1828–1830, Guizot, Villemain, Victor Cousin, called for new approaches, and original documents were being reprinted in great number, beginning in 1823 with the large collection of chronicles (*Collection des mémoires relatifs à l'histoire de France*) edited by Guizot.

Few of Michelet's contemporaries dared rival his enterprise. Augustin Thierry gathered brilliant, if fragmentary contributions in *Dix Ans d'études historiques* [Ten Years of Historical Studies, 1817–1827] and *Lettres sur l'histoire de France* [Letters on French History, 1820–1828]; his greatest success was a history of the Norman conquest of England (1825). Another resounding success was Barante's *Histoire des ducs de Bourgogne* [History of the Dukes of Burgundy, 1824–1825], a modern version of chronicles hostile to Louis XI.

The work closest in scope to that of Michelet was the *Histoire des Français* [History of the French, 31 vols., 1821–1844], by the Swiss author Sismonde de Sismondi, a straight, simple narrative which, by 1831, had reached volume 15 and Louis XII. It followed chronicles at length, and contained summary judgments: Chilpéric was "the French Nero" (1:359); Louis I was "pious and beloved" but a "shameful ruler" (3:46). Finally, in 1841 Sismondi apologized (26:3) because, in spite of the great length of his account, economic developments, art, and literature were not even touched upon. He was a limited historian, but an honest republican, an appealing person, and a perceptive critic of Michelet's work, astounded by what he found there.

There were other contributions—intelligent, analytical, concise— infinitely more limited in scope than Michelet's work, such as Mignet's *History of the French Revolution* (1824), brief, well written, constantly reprinted—it accepted even the Reign of Terror as an historical necessity—and the rival history by Thiers, no match in either analysis or conciseness (1823–1827). Finally we must mention Guizot's lectures, published under the title *Histoire de la civilisation en Europe et en France* [History of French and European Civilization], philosophical, reflective, a mere framework, undeveloped because Guizot was propelled into politics and remained in positions of influence until 1848.

No question then that there was a place for the work of Michelet. He combined narrative talent with love for documents; he had the broad background and the compassion needed to make his subject live. The courses at the Ecole Normale served as a preparation, and so did his travels which, eventually, were to take him to all parts of France and most of its neighbors. Here we are well informed, since the *Journal*, fragmentary for the early years—he destroyed much of it—is complete for his travels. Remarkable among these brief, strenuous, and intensely lived tours is his description of Brittany of 1831, the basis for what may seem a disproportionately long sketch in his "Tableau" of France (*OC*, 4:33–40).

It was not his custom to let his family accompany him, but for once he took Pauline and Adèle with him as far as Normandy. We find him in Le Havre meditating at the water's edge, watching his daughter, now seven years old:

Perceiving this terrifying perspective of infinity on the one hand, my daughter on the other, and that force attracting man back to the abyss of nature, I felt my fiber of individuality tearing apart: the general, the universal, the eternal, that is man's home!

It is you, my noble country, that I shall ask for help. You have to take the place of God who is escaping us and fill in us the incommensurate void left by Christianity when it died. You must become our equivalent of the infinite. . . . Then perhaps shall we ascend again toward God. (*J*, 1:83)

Many passages of the *History of France* written two years later express the idea that the Christian religion has become part of the medieval past which he will piously explore. Rarely can we find such statements in this early period that Christianity has already died for him, but ten years later, speaking of Joan of Arc, he will return to the idea that patriotism has taken its place, that the Virgin has become Joan, and Marianne.

There are other revealing passages concerning religion—the description of the ritual stones at Carnac, the rounded dolmens of the Druids: "Their circle is God," says Michelet, their arcades point to heaven but rest firmly on the ground (*J*, 1:94). He evokes Druid rites at Lok-Maria-Ker and Carnac, the gigantic stones seen through the fog, rose-colored heather and yellow blossoms which suggest the crown of Hamlet's Ophelia gone mad (*OC*, 4:338). His sensitivity carries him far beyond the philosophizing of Cousin or Guizot. Above all Michelet's religious awareness is clear. While his rejection of Christianity remains guarded, his sympathy extends to all aspirations. He is ready to interpret the Middle Ages!

V   Histoire de France, *volumes 1–2 (1833)*

The first volume of the *History* begins with Gaul in Roman times and leads to the Capetians, from Eudes, count of Paris (888) disputing the authority of Frankish kings, to Hugues, whom Michelet sees as the first truly French ruler (987). The year 1000 is taken as symbol. Michelet makes much, too much, of fears in the popular mind that the world was about to end.

As in the case of Rome, the question of the original population, i.e., of "races," was not easily resolved. With Wilhelm von Humboldt, Michelet traces the origins to the pre-Celtic Basques in France and Spain.[6] Then he speaks of the Celts, also called Kymris or Galls, finally of the Germanic aristocracy that ruled under the Frankish kings, the Merovingians and Karolingians. Fortunately Michelet did not take sides in the long standing battle of preferences, where Boulainvilliers, then Mably, finally Guizot praised the creative leadership of the Germanic Franks, while others, like Thierry and Henri Martin, favored the underdog, the Celts. We have seen Michelet's sympathy for the Celts of Brittany. He mentions their legends, the "Breton cycle" of epics, the tales of Marie de France, which are part of his "comparative mythology" (*JM*, 1:278), while he interprets the rule of "the Germans," his title for book 2, as merely a step toward national independence under Hugues Capet. He sees the races and traditions melting together. All along his great merit lies in superb evocations, e.g., Europe fighting Africa and Asia as Charles Martel defeats the Moors (*OC*, 4:272, 704). He quotes chroniclers like Gregory of Tours to great effect and puts aside professional rivalries to include a long passage concerning Eudes from Augustin Thierry.[7]

The second volume of the *History* contains the famous "Tableau of France" (bk. 3), the psychological geography of the French provinces, then goes on to the end of the "Christian Middle Ages," i.e., to the death of Louis IX on the last crusade (bk. 4). The death of Christianity, suggested in the *Journal*, is implied here.

Having foresworn the exclusive dominance of race, Michelet proves himself nonetheless tied to it: in the "Tableau," Breton as a Celtic language suggests the idea of the strong Celtic "front" which France—with Pelagius, Abelard, and Descartes—opposes to England (*OC*, 4:334). It provides an example of fortuitous associations which determine Michelet's image of a province, with bizarre results. Of the three men mentioned, only Abelard, born in Nantes, comes even close to originating from Brittany. Pelagius is a Welsh monk who was active in Rome, a heretic who denied that man was born in sin as St. Augustine proclaimed and, therefore, did not consider man totally dependent on divine grace for his salvation. Michelet's sympathy for Pelagius as a heretic draws Wales into the anti-English front of Celts, but what is his relationship to France and Brittany? As for Descartes, he was born in Touraine, a fact unknown at the time. What the three have in common is "French" rationalism, an independence of thought Michelet likes to oppose to the haughty materialism of England, as well as to the clouds of spiritualism in Germany. He would not accept the industrial capitalism of England, which had outstripped France during the Napoleonic era; he had more sympathy for Germany, the "India of Europe," with its Augustinian "fatalism" from Godescalc, a monk condemned for his doctrine of predestination, to Luther.[8]

When Michelet discusses Flanders, he returns to his image of a hostile England; he suffers from the defeat at Waterloo:

Oh England, England, you did not fight alone that day; you had the entire world on your side. So why do you claim all the glory for yourself? What is the meaning of Waterloo bridge? Is there any reason to be so proud that the mutilated remnants of one hundred battles, the last draft of young Frenchmen, a motley crew who had barely completed the lycée and just left their mothers' kisses, disintegrated in the face of your army of mercenaries? (*OC*, 4:376)

To Michelet England seems "odious" in its moments of triumph, or any time; a catalog of his comments on English pride would be a grotesque sample from his work. Fortunately his antagonism is mitigated by his cordial friendships with individual Englishmen, many of them scientists.

It is fairer to judge Michelet by his commentary on other provinces, by his account of Lyons, for instance, seen as the great center of communication since the Celts and the Romans, in recent times the home of the silk industry. He feels that the sedentary life of the weavers of Lyons made them prone to visions. He traces a long tradition of mysticism and heresy from the Waldenses—intent on restoring primitive Christianity—to Saint-Martin and Ballanche. Piously he also recalls Gerson (*OC*, 4:367), for Gerson retired to Lyons and died there; he is important to our historian because the *Imitation of Christ* was attributed to him. Gerson's name is tied to Michelet's conversion of 1816. Such associations and historical coincidences, like Gerson's residence in Lyons, contribute to Michelet's definition of regional characteristics, but the "Tableau" concludes that the greatness of France stems from the harmony of its parts, from the amalgamation of their various traits, from the unity of France as a nation (*OC*, 4:383–84).

The historical account which follows in book 4 stresses religious developments. Striking scenes describe the sharp contrast between the authoritarian Dominicans, the backbone of the Inquisition, and the humble Franciscans who abandon themselves wantonly to their inspiration, propelled from orthodoxy to heresy and back again. Abelard, on the contrary, is the voice of the future: when he was teaching in Paris "it seemed that for the first time a free voice was heard. . . . It was as if, up to his time, the church had merely stammered, while Abelard spoke" (*OC*, 4:453). This scared even St. Bernard, not Abelard's equal in logic, but a persuasive leader who had organized a crusade, and now turned against him, and Heloïse: "That was the end of the restoration of philosophy in the Middle

Ages . . . , the end of the intrusion of logic into religion, the end of the victory of prose and reason over faith!" It had been a short-lived but glorious moment (*OC*, 4:455–57).

The way Michelet saw it in 1833, the "dry logic" of Abelard was simply not suitable for this age of visions and inspiration (*OC*, 4:663) which was likely to welcome the heretical thought of fervent mystics like Joachim of Flores: his view of the end of the world and the dream of a better one was reflected in the *Eternal Gospel* of John of Parma, a general of the Franciscan order who spoke of Joachim. This transfiguration of reality through faith was a noble utopia which expressed itself also in the architecture of the great cathedrals, for "these stones are not stones but pulsing life." Just as it was said that a stone might become bread, they are symbols of transubstantiation, the representation of the passion and aspirations of the age.[9]

These comments are greatly modified in 1852 when Michelet feels that the poetic spirit of this architecture must be overcome by the spirit of prose, by the new faith of freedom. Nonetheless he will continue to honor Joachim of Flores and the *Eternal Gospel* (*OC*, 7:72–74) along with other heresies that fought against a petrified orthodoxy. Pierre de Vaux from Lyons is described with great sympathy; his Waldenses, as well as the Albigensians, appear as valiant heirs to the Pelagian heresy and forerunners of a man-centered faith of action (*OC*, 4:499–504).

By contrast, Germany slumbers in myth and sentiment. Michelet finds the German spirit mirrored in the Rhine:

Indeed, the Rhine is a sacred river, replete with tales and mystery. I do not speak only of its heroic passage from Mainz to Cologne, where it pierces its way through basalt and granite. To the south and to the north of this feudal passage . . . it mellows. . . . An immense poetry hovers over the river. It is not easy to define. It is a vague impression of nature, vast, calm, and soft, perhaps a mother's voice calling for man's return to nature. . . , perhaps the poetic appeal of the Virgin, whose churches rise all along the Rhine.[10]

The mysticism which rules Germany extends westward until it meets Flemish sensuality as illustrated by Rubens,[11] or comes up against the industrious Dutch. Michelet's "geography" of the spirit of nations extends well beyond the "Tableau."

The Albigensian crusade horrifies him. Vividly he depicts the cruelty of Simon de Montfort, acting for the king of France, Philippe II Auguste, but under instructions from Pope Innocent III. A culture was destroyed, one castle after another. Michelet would exonerate the king, saying he fought primarily to extend his lands, but not the pope, at the pinnacle of papal power, bent on exterminating a progressive, rational faith.

The Albigensians were vanquished, but did Innocent triumph? Here Michelet adds a startling afterthought. Innocent did not believe it himself and, the year before his death (1215), was beset by doubt. He no longer trusted his methods, the efficacy of persecution. "It is not with impunity that one sacrifices humanity to an idea" (OC, 4:546). Somehow the historian imagines Innocent repentant, a secret ally of freedom.

Equally strange is the idea that Louis IX felt similar doubts and questioned the value of his crusades. Michelet concludes: "If even Saint Louis is troubled, how many other souls must have doubted and suffered in silence!" (OC, 4:560, 592). How can this be true? Louis IX is known for his piety; he organized two crusades and died on the last, in Tunis (1270). From the fact that there were no further crusades, Michelet simply infers that doubts beset those who animated them. He gives a psychological explanation for changes in the making and may not be far from the truth, except in reading doubt into Innocent III and Louis IX personally.

At the end of this second volume Michelet takes credit for having told much that was unknown before, buried in those "catacombs of manuscripts" of the National Archives, that "necropolis" of the nation. His history had "dusted off" old documents and "brought them back to life" (OC, 4:613). Thus he describes the process which, in 1869, he will call "the resurrection of total life" (OC, 4:12). His use of original documents will be even more successful in the volumes to follow, but his greatest originality lies in recreating the spirit of the past in a vivid interpretation.

The critics reacted with admiration and surprise, often along ideological or religious lines. The large number of reviews is in itself the greatest tribute (OC, 4:728–851). Sismondi, whom Michelet had indicated as an essential source (OC, 3:911–14), was astounded by the difference in perspective which taught him a great deal (OC, 4:96). Victor Hugo is cordial and understanding (OC, 4:97, 605). Others, like Nisard, who felt that he had spoken well of what he considered a great work, implied reservations which annoyed Michelet. He was most disappointed that Sainte-Beuve refused to discuss his work; their temperaments were just too different (OC, 4:101–5, 738–52).

Guizot was so impressed that he named Michelet to replace him at the Sorbonne for three semesters (January 1834 to March 1835). The news was conveyed by Villemain who complimented Michelet publicly on his success, but privately objected to the grand conclusions drawn from minor events and to the "mysticism" inherent in his interpretations.[12] The important fact for us is that Michelet, even at the risk of errors in judgment, subordinated the detail of history to fundamental issues and kept them before the reader.

Admittedly this method had its dangers. The rigorous opposition between France, cradle of freedom, Germany, land of fatalistic dreams, and England, home of materialism and pride, is a strange "geography." Traveling to England in 1834 with Victor Duruy, his student, he observed the effects of industrialization and found that nowhere did wealth and poverty stand in such stark contrast. "The new feudalism," with its poor laws and workhouses, reduced the worker to a slave of the machine, while industry flourished. This in turn contributed to the humiliation of France.[13] The English seemed all too proud of themselves! Such was his impression not only in the centers of manufacture, but at Warwick castle, a monument of English domination in the Hundred Years' War. When he met Talleyrand in England, he was horrified that the famous diplomat, the representative of France, accepted and even glibly justified British policy (*J*, 1:125). These observations confirmed Michelet's preconceptions, just as his subsequent experience in Germany in 1842 strengthened those convictions. It took the war of 1870 to prove to him that Quinet's warning concerning the new German nationalism had to be taken seriously.

Truly, Michelet is an interpreter, not a chronicler of events. His sensitivity responds to the conditions he observes, just as it gives meaning to the documents he utilizes. He introduces order into history, deeply felt, not without bias. No wonder his contemporaries were startled.

VI *Documents of the past:* Mémoires de Luther *(1835) and* Origines du droit français *(1837)*

Michelet's first lecture to a university audience, at the Sorbonne in January 1834, was proudly published (*OC*, 3:211–23). The spring semester was devoted to the Middle Ages; the following course took up the Renaissance, but by March 1835 fatigue and illness forced him to give up this instruction. He had tried his best to reduce his two-course load at the Ecole Normale. Even if one course was confined to providing the bibliographical background to the other, it was too much, for he was also preparing the additional translations for *Vico's Selected Works* (1835), and planning two extensive collections of documents in translation, the first an analogous volume on Luther, the second a compendium of medieval law. Besides, the third volume of the *History of France* was advancing. His regular position at the Ecole Normale had priority; the more desirable but temporary assignment at the Sorbonne had to give way. Another victim of these circumstances was a critical evaluation and introduction to his Luther texts. When *Luther's Memoirs* appeared in 1835, the volumes were numbered two and three; the first was never to appear (*OC*, 3:275).

One might ask why Michelet passed on so rapidly beyond the Middle Ages to a study of the Reformation. The answer: he had been fascinated by Luther ever since Heidelberg in 1828. He had visited the Luther house, then, in Frankfurt, bought Aurifaber's *Table Talk*, and rapidly read this account of daily life around the reformer (*EJ*, 330–31). Right there and then he had large sections translated by Adolphe Müntz, a German instructor.[14]

Luther's Memoirs Written by Himself and Put in Order by Jules Michelet was the first major publication in French sympathetic to Luther since the Reformation. Charles de Villiers' *Essay on the Spirit and Influence of Luther's Reformation* (1804, 1820) had attempted to rehabilitate his memory. Mme. de Staël, Sismondi, and Guizot, all three of Protestant background, had mentioned him with understanding, but the general tone of discussions in Catholic France had been hostile. Prudently, by letting the reformer speak for himself, and by abstaining from adding the introductory volume, Michelet, as "editor," was rarely forced to defend him. Still, he does introduce himself frequently into the book where the first person, in spite of the title, does not always dominate.

Michelet's texts stem largely from Aurifaber, but also render Luther's Latin works and correspondence, which he could read easily. The result was a slanted view, for Aurifaber had been unable to explain Luther as a religious leader. Thus Luther the man dominates the last two of five sections, composed almost exclusively of fragments from Aurifaber (*OC*, 3:502–7). Instead of a Protestant theologian, Michelet discovered a kindred spirit, like himself dedicated to the life of the spirit and haunted by the temptations of the flesh. As Luther put it: "The more I macerated my body . . . the more

I burned. . . . If you want a beautiful, pious, wealthy wife, well dear, you can find one in a painting, with rosy cheeks and snow white legs. These are also the most pious, but they are no good in the kitchen or in bed" (*OC*, 3:356–57). It is amusing to find Adolphe Müntz wishing to replace "in bed" with "making beds and cleaning house," because otherwise there were "obscene" implications which could not have been in Luther's mind.[15] Michelet understood Luther far better than his secretary-translator, though even he censored some vulgar expressions.

Michelet wrestled with an apparent paradox. Luther freed the church from the domination and corruption of Rome, but at the same time rejected free will and insisted on man's absolute dependence on divine grace. When student objections—his course was also devoted to Luther—and a penetrating critique by Pauline Roland in *Le Temps* questioned this point, Michelet added a brief preface in which he merely restates the paradox: "If Luther denied liberty in theory, he established it in practice" (*OC*, 3:257). The historian never understood why the doctrine of justification by faith alone, which denies free will, produced the revolt against Rome of Luther and Calvin, and not a "fatalistic" acceptance of the status quo. Luther's Augustinian principle did away with the need for an intermediary who intercedes for man, i.e., with the traditional role of the Catholic Church and the sale of indulgences.

Michelet held to his association of free will and freedom until 1842, when the abuses of the rationalist, free will position of the Jesuits changed his outlook. Thereafter his Luther became the brother-in-arms of the revolutionary heroes of mankind from Socrates, Erasmus, and Rabelais to Danton, many of whom Luther would have disclaimed. In developing this position in 1855,[16] Michelet blamed himself for having presented Luther in theological terms. This of course was untrue. Michelet had not even consulted theologians on Luther. What he meant was that he now considered the debate between free will and divine grace to be irrelevant. Actually Michelet's shift was less contradictory than it might seem, for he had from the start honored Luther, the man, the humble and strong leader, a compassionate friend[17] but also a brave reformer calling for the return to pure Christianity in his heroic act of independence.

In all this, Luther's rough forthrightness is emphasized, but the portrait is incomplete: Luther's debates with Carlstadt and his battles with Münzer and the Anabaptists are discussed in detail, but his ruthless opposition to the peasants is ignored.[18] The reformer's indebtedness to the princes who protected him from Rome produced a complex interplay of forces which Michelet prefers not to judge, in spite of his own commitment to the people. Luther's famous pamphlet, *Against the Thieving and Murderous Hordes of Peasants* (1525), is not even mentioned. Furthermore, Michelet knew too little German to appreciate the importance of the Bible translation. In spite of such weaknesses, the *Memoirs* constitute a remarkable book, startlingly new at the time, and an appealing interpretation by a kindred spirit.

The two volumes did not sell as well as expected[19] but they aroused many comments, attacks as well as praise, from Protestant and Catholic points of view. Michelet's sympathy for Luther was evident, and this was not an easy position in a country where the dominant view remained Bossuet's defense of the Catholic Church in the *Histoire des variations* [History of Differences]. Even Protestants questioned Michelet's orientation. It is important to note that his view of 1855, expressing disillusionment with the church, did not bring him closer to the Protestant position. His preference for the mother church was never in doubt.

The best appreciation of the *Memoirs* was that of Sismondi (*OC*, 2:234–35), who clearly perceives what separates his own rational Protestantism from Michelet's intense and committed view. It would seem that with all his omissions and lack of theological background, Michelet was closer to Luther than the Protestant, Sismondi, and certainly closer than his critics. Quite rightly our historian upheld his duty to present his subject with sympathy and compassion.

After *Luther's Memoirs*, Michelet devoted his energies to adapting Grimm's *Rechtsaltertümer* [Antiquities of Law] to France, i.e., he gathered a collection of documents that might illustrate the customs and institutions of the French Middle Ages. In preparation he searched the libraries of southwestern France (1835) and of Holland and Belgium (1837). On the first trip he wrote a report to Guizot, then minister of education;[20] on the second, two letters to Daunou, the director of the National Archives.[21] Considering the habitual rush of our historian to return to his family, the information is remarkably detailed.

The Origins of French Law Sought in the Symbols and Formulation of Universal Law (1837) ought to have been a collection of documents from the archives of Paris and the provinces, of laws and statutes analogous to those in Grimm's *Antiquities of Law*. Instead,

it is above all a translation of documents presented by Grimm—
again Adolphe Müntz was Michelet's principal assistant and translator—along with selections from a number of other sources such
as the glossaries of Ducange and Laurière (*OC*, 3:605), the *Laws of
Manou* from India (edited in 1833 by Loiseleur-Deslongchamps),
Colebrooke's *Digest of Hindu Law* (1801), and authors of antiquity
from Homer and Aristophanes to Pliny, Varro, and Plutarch.[22] The
question arises: How many of these sources contribute to French
law? The "universal" perspective and the assumption of Germanic
influences through the Frankish kings provides a partial answer.
Besides, the conceptions of Vico and especially those of Creuzer's
Symbolik postulate stages of development which seemed applicable
to France. Michelet explains:

I believe that one of the essential tasks of French law was to find out
whether our law did not also have its poetic age. Our primitive codes of
law, Salic and Ripuarian [i.e., Frankish from the Rhine], contain a certain
number of poetic formulations, though these are less French than Germanic. The Capitularies [ordinances of the Franks in France] . . . contain
almost no such formulations or symbols, and our books of law written in
French during the Middle Ages are nothing less than poetic. Under the
apparant naiveté of their language, one constantly senses logic and the
capacity of abstract thinking of doctors in Roman law. (*OC*, 3:604)

In other words, French rationalism stands in contrast to Germanic
symbols. The attempt is made to identify a distinctly French spirit
in documents which Michelet arranges according to the life cycle,
from birth to marriage to death. There are examples to illustrate
feudal authority, knighthood, serfdom, property, flags, heraldry,
battle cries, all from widely dispersed sources. The collection is
admittedly fragmentary (*OC*, 3:605) but it points the way to comparative law. Jacob Grimm himself wrote that Michelet had admirably supplemented the *Antiquities* and adapted his own materials
to medieval France (*OC*, 3:587).

How remote and primitive—in Vico's terminology: how naive and
poetic—were the statutes of medieval France? When Alfred Nettement called the third volume of the *History of France* overly poetic,[23] Michelet wrote to explain:

As poetic as the shape [of history] might appear in my books, I have stripped
numerous events of the romanesque quality with which other historians
endowed them. Thus Mr. Guizot sees only the miracle of individual genius

in Charlemagne's rule while I explain it quite naturally and from documents,
by the influence of the church and a civilization imbued with religion. Mr.
Thierry talked a lot about race; I added the factors of geography and climate
which shape and determine race. . . . I called your attention to the commercial and nonheroic character of the wars of the fourteenth century; Mr.
Barante had not judged them that way.

The *Origins* was a collection of these "documents" that permitted
the historical emphasis to shift from the individual to the institutions
which shape him "quite naturally." They constitute the "material"
base of the progressive thought of France, its nonheroic spirit of
prose and reason.

Still, if we examine the body of these documents, all of which are
supposed to shed some light on medieval France one way or another,
we find much that is "poetic." Their scope is surprising:

Nowhere does India consider humanity with more pleasant approval than
in its view of women, this charming symbol of nature which is the sum of
its beauty.

In Persia, by contrast with India, the state dominates nature. The state
is the world, the king the symbol of the state.

Roman law . . . is above all *real* law, a law of property. As such it survives
in our laws and still rules us. *Personal* law is no longer confined to the city
as it had been in Greece, but free as a bird in the forest; it developed in
the Germanic world.[24]

If nature is unkind to man in the North, fraternity is all the more de-
veloped there. The idea of paternal authority dominates India and ancient
Italy while the fraternal spirit dominates the heroic peoples . . . , [e.g.,]
Orestes and Pylades.

German law is material [i.e., nonpoetic] in form only.

[For the Gauls] rhythm is a need. . . . The Celtic poems are rhymed,
while alliteration rules those of Scandinavia. (*OC*, 3:629–33)

From these representative excerpts—and I consider them typical—
we get the impression of a groping miscellany with a substantial
emphasis not only on the "poetic" times of early history but on
poetry and literature, with such sweeping generalizations as the
idea of a fraternity extending from Greece to Scandinavia.

Even so the collection is valuable. No one questioned its useful-
ness. Much was left to the reader who had to supply observations
from other areas to arrive at what the title announces, an understanding of French medieval law. Not many readers would be capable of that. In his critique, which was favorable, Nisard said that

the title was imposed by Michelet's editor (*OC*, 3:575). The *Origins* did illustrate the development of law and institutions. Everyone was impressed, including Daunou, Michelet's superior at the National Archives.

VII *The Middle Ages continued:* History of France, volumes 3–6 (1837–1844)

The all-important third volume of the *History of France* appeared at the same time as the *Origins*. The same spirit prevails. The preface emphasizes that, in the period to be studied (1270–1380), chronicles have become the primary source of the historian; they have replaced the "heroic" epic. This means that France has reached Vico's third stage of development, the era of prose and reason: "Our early laws contained a few symbols, a few poetic formulations [but] all in all, French law has at all times been less fettered by symbolism than that of any other nation. . . . In order to appreciate the austere genius and the maturity of our law, we had to establish the contrast between it and the poetic law of other nations and show the difference between France and the world" (*OC*, 5:39). This passage reads like an introduction to the *Origins*. We can in fact consider the third volume of the *History of France* as the missing part of the *Origins*, the direct application of its principles to France. It not only portrays the break between the earlier, "poetic," religious, mystical Middle Ages and the age of "prose" when a new rationalism conflicts with an outdated and unchanging hierarchy of the church, but here Michelet begins to use original documents; it represents not only new principles but a new method.

The volume traces the rise of royal power. Its most dramatic moments are the condemnation and dissolution of the Knights Templar—with their wealth flowing into the coffers of Philippe IV le Bel—and the account of the king's struggle with Boniface VIII. Philippe rejects the censure of the pope, sends Nogaret to attack him in his palace so that Boniface dies of the shock soon thereafter, and has a French pope elected, Clement V (Bertrand de Gott). Once established at Avignon, Clement institutes heresy proceedings against Boniface. Michelet adds with relish that Dante relegates Boniface to hell. To our historian, these events spell out the suicide of the papacy and the triumph of the modern age (*OC*, 5:84, 94).

Not that Michelet finds Philippe le Bel virtuous. He points to his greed, plunder, and theft. Philippe profited from the "captivity" of the pope at Avignon. He confiscated not only the property of the Templars, but that of the Jews. Many of them fled; those who returned suffered a fate worse than lepers (*OC*, 5:493). As for the Knights Templar, Philippe staged the spectacular trial of their grand master, Jean de Molay, and had him condemned and burned at the stake. The trial is covered in great detail (*OC*, 5:88–134); Michelet later edited the Latin transcript in two large folio volumes (1841, 1851).

Gold had become lord, money the new religion (*OC*, 5:88, 162). By analogy, the *Roman de la rose* [The Rose] by Jean de Meun kills the idealism of his precursor, Guillaume de Loris. Thus prose replaces poetry (*OC*, 5:134). The historian does not applaud; he will be just and stern, even in dealing with inevitable progress. This becomes even more evident under Philippe le Bel's successor, as Edward V of England contests the French crown of Philippe V de Valois. It is the beginning of the Hundred Years' War with catastrophic French defeats at Crécy (1346) and Poitiers (1356). The days of knights in armor are numbered. King Jean le Bon is taken prisoner by the English and the Dauphin, the future Charles V, faces a revolt of Paris merchants under Etienne Marcel.

The result, the Grand Ordinance of 1357, was a model of sensible reform, but it was bound to be ineffective: "The Ordinance destroyed abuses, but the monarchy hardly lived on anything else. To kill them was to kill royal power, to dissolve the state, to disarm France" (*OC*, 5:217). And so Marcel will be assassinated, while the king is freed, at a price: the Treaty of London forces him to give up a good part of France. Again the historian does not exult; he emphasizes, possibly overemphasizes, the spirit of each age. In the preceding volume he had stressed the power of the church; now it is the turn of kings. For all that, the modern age does not create utopia.

The sympathies of the historian are with the people. He admires the good sense of the citizens of Paris and honors Rienzi, spokesman for the people of Rome. Petrarch is praised less for his poems to Laura than for his support of Rienzi and of his plan to reform Italy, even if it had no more chance for success than that of Marcel in Paris (*OC*, 5:200–203). The course of 1840 will return to Petrarch and Rienzi in glowing terms.[25] The heroes of freedom are symbols of hope even in defeat. Even in the face of darkness, i.e., in the face of English power over France, Michelet celebrates the spark of hope where he finds it.

The fourth volume of the *History of France* describes the death of France, the victory of the British. The fifth will portray the resurrection with Joan of Arc. Michelet's wife, Pauline, had died in 1839, and the preface to the fourth volume evokes the experience with renewed intensity, but of course by transferring the anguish to the national plane (*OC*, 5:281). The volume ends, fittingly, with the haunting symbol of the *Dance of Death* as portrayed in painting and on the stage (*OC*, 5:467), in anticipation of a brighter period to follow.

The decline of France is dramatic. One memorable scene shows the mad King Charles VI meeting with Emperor Wenceslaus who is quite drunk (*OC*, 5:324, in 1398). The nadir is the battle of Agincourt (1415), the slaughter of a good part of the French nobility on their horses mired in the mud, weighed down by armor, and impeded by the traditional close formation, twelve deep, while the English archers take their toll (*OC*, 5:420–24). Charles d'Orléans was captured there. Michelet is moved; he cites some of Charles's poetry, along with a violent anti-British piece by Eustache Deschamps "who seems to understand the titanic, satanic character of the country of Byron" (*OC*, 5:427–29).

Agincourt left Paris in the hands of Henry V of England. France needed a savior and she was saved. The account of Joan of Arc in volume 5 of the *History* is a masterpiece, especially the description of her trial based on manuscripts from the National Archives.[26] The church finds itself on the side of reaction whereas Joan incarnates the *Imitation of Christ* (*OC*, 6:39–47). She is the link between the image of the Virgin and modern France, somewhat like Clotilde and Geneviève before her, but in a new spirit, for while she is still the Virgin *(la Pucelle)*, she is already Marianne, i.e., France herself.

Her replies during interrogation show her virtue, her good sense, her purity, and above all her faith. "The doctors see only the letter, not the spirit," while her inspiration comes not from the church hierarchy, "the church militant," but from God, and his "church triumphant" (*OC*, 6:100). In the face of trickery and deceit, she was bound to be condemned. The forces facing her have English qualities according to Michelet, who finds them somber, skeptical, and satanic like characters in Shakespeare, Milton, or Byron (*OC*, 6:111). Frenchmen serving the English, such as her prosecutor, Cauchon, are as bad as they. The account ends with a prayer: "Now let the new France not forget that word of the old: 'Only great hearts know the glory of being good.' "[27]

Charles VII, crowned by Joan, would not lift a finger for her, once the monarchy was restored. Its centralized power would be established by his son, Louis XI, who already as a Dauphin showed his impatient independence. Charles understood him better than he could control him: when Louis was the guest of his great rival, the duke of Burgundy, Philippe le Bon, Charles said: "The duke is harboring the fox who will eat his chickens" (OC, 6:222). Indeed, as soon as Charles died (1461), Louis took charge and when Philippe came to Paris to hold a tourney, he played him a trick: "An unknown knight appeared in the ring, well paid [by Louis] for the occasion, and threw all the others. Hidden in a corner, Louis enjoyed the spectacle. . . . This restless genius was born with all the modern instincts, good and bad, but above all with the impatience to destroy, the disrespect for the past" (OC, 6:229). The modern spirit of Louis, who reads and fosters the art of printing, is compared to the pomp of Burgundy and the Order of the Golden Fleece (OC, 6:229–32). Thus the stage was set for "the grand comedy," the inevitable destruction of Burgundy by a strong, centralized France. This will be the subject of the sixth and last volume of the history of the Middle Ages.

The volume was published in 1844, but much of it was prepared earlier; the course of 1839 proves it. Striking and often moving scenes, some from the chronicles of Châtelain, Olivier de la Marche, and Commines, introduce the protagonists, Louis XI and Charles le Téméraire (the Bold), the latter the son of Philippe le Bon. The devious attitude of Louis is emphasized, e.g., when he weeps for public effect because his father assumes the right to name bishops (by the Pragmatic Sanction of Bourges, 1438), but retains this right when he becomes king (though officially abrogating the Sanction, OC, 6:242–43). In his admirable portrait of Louis, Michelet shows that the days of heroic chivalry were past. Louis realized that the power of France depended on his person, on staying alive; it was better to hire mercenaries and remain safely away from battle. He often won by treachery and poison, with an iron determination, formed when Charles forced him to witness the burning of Liège, a city which had fought for France against Burgundy. Michelet adds comments on the French spirit of Liège and its most famous son, the musician, Grétry (OC, 6:363–67).

The Swiss, paid by Louis, defeated Burgundy; soon thereafter the troops of René de Lorraine killed Charles le Téméraire. The gruesome details, the dismembering of his body, are included (OC,

6:427–28). Then the aftermath: Louis incites Liège against Marie, the duke's daughter and heir; he also corrupts or does away with her lieutenants. Thus modern France is born, ruthlessly, without pity. Michelet's sympathy goes out to the idealistic feudal lords, the losers: "That decrepit old tyrant, feudalism, gains much for having died at the hands of a tyrant" (*OC*, 6:464).

Some of the most dramatic moments, e.g., the death of Charles le Téméraire, are drawn from the chronicles and had also been used by other historians, including Sismondi and Barante. What is new in Michelet is his attempt to penetrate behind the facts, to define the spirit of regions and the meaning of events. Flanders, observed in 1832, 1837, and 1840, called opulent and sensuous in the *Journal*, is depicted again in volume 5 of the *History* where our historian speaks of the Golden Fleece and the lust for pleasure of the dukes of Burgundy, who derived their strength and wealth from Flanders.[28] In volume 6, Flanders becomes the essential element in the struggle between Charles and Louis. In the same manner, Michelet uses his observations in Switzerland. The *Journal* of 1838 tells us that he "finally understood" the key role of the Swiss who gradually rose from providing mercenaries to attain the state of a modern, cosmopolitan nation. In 1843 he returns to Switzerland, following the footsteps of Charles le Téméraire.[29] Geography, art, architecture, literature, as well as the documents studied in archives (the report to Daunou, *JM*, 2:24), all contribute to his critical interpretation. His documentation for volume 6 was particularly thorough. The work progressed slowly enough for Michelet to discover and use the Burgundian archives at Lille,[30] to cite but one example.

New perspectives emerged, of which Barante, in his *History of the Dukes of Burgundy*, had not dreamed—as one review put it. The difference was critical distance. Michelet perceived not only the parsimony of Louis XI, his deceit, his using money to corrupt, but his function as the founder of a modern state. Opposite him there is the magnificence of the duke of Burgundy, of his great cities, Ghent, Bruges, and Liège. Michelet also made superb use of traditions and lore. An excellent example is the death of Charles de Berry, duc de Guyenne, the powerful brother of Louis XI: as titular head of the League of the Public Weal, organized to resist the king, he held his brother in check. Louis had only one way out, Michelet tells us, the death of his brother, and his brother died. He was said to have been ravished by the devil one stormy night; it was also rumored that he ate poisoned fruit, and Louis was not beyond arranging for this.[31] It is a story well told. We witness the creation of modern France, a state strong enough to invade Italy and return with the spirit of the Renaissance.

CHAPTER 3

The Professor at the Collège de France

I   *The first courses*

A T THE Ecole Normale Michelet had last taught the Middle Ages.[1] In 1836 he asked Duruy to replace him; the following year he asked Filon, convinced now that the time had come for a promotion. Villemain and Leclerc had used the Ecole as a stepping stone; why could not he? Besides, Victor Cousin, from whom he was estranged, had become the director of studies at the Ecole Normale. The long sought appointment at the Collège de France materialized, but only after Guizot had been replaced by Salvandy as minister of education. No longer favorable to Michelet as he had been in 1834 when he asked for him as a replacement, Guizot must have sensed the vast differences between their approaches to the past. In later years, under the impact of religious debates, Salvandy would also turn hostile.

Michelet was installed as a professor of "History and Moral Sciences" in February 1838. A month later he was elected to the Academy of Moral and Political Sciences. Michelet was gratified. He felt so at home in this distinguished body that he never stood as a candidate for the French Academy.

At the Collège, he became the colleague of some of the great scholars of his time: the orientalist, Eugène Burnouf; the geologist, Elie de Beaumont; the literary critic, J.-J. Ampère—all were personal friends who provided information when his work required it.[2] Michelet's courses, consisting of two, later of one lecture a week, soon became popular and attracted a growing audience of all ages. Mme. Dumesnil and her son, Alfred, were first known to him in 1839, seated week after week in the first row. Alfred Dumesnil, who took faithful notes of the lectures, came from near Rouen. He was to be Michelet's son-in-law, a man of letters of note, secretary of the Lamartine society.

The courses remained centered on France in the Middle Ages until the end of the first semester of 1843.[3] He devoted his first course to his native Paris, a sociopsychological history, fully reported in the *Journal général de l'instruction publique* [General Review of Public Education].[4] The first eight lessons speak of Paris from the fourth to the ninth centuries and then discuss Abelard. Paris is pictured as a center of civilization since the construction of the Roman baths of Cluny. With St. Denis and St. Marcel the city assumed a position of religious leadership. Such it was when Ste. Geneviève saved the city from Attila and from famine:

Gregory of Tours, being a bishop, says nothing of this, but there was doubtless need for seers more than for bishops and politicians, or at least for saintly women to tame the savage beasts, more corrupt and perverted in their thought than savages. Never could the Armagnac brigands have been reduced to order without Joan of Arc, and the legend of Ste. Geneviève [facing the Huns] is far more credible than that of Joan. Childeric venerated her, that mistress of Paris. . . . One day he was intent on killing some prisoners and bolted his doors, but submissively these doors opened of their own accord at the touch of Geneviève. Her charity is admirable in these times, a compensation for the ills of the world. Such was the beginning of France.[5]

In the *History of France,* Attila did not threaten Paris but only pursued Theodoric, and Ste. Geneviève was not mentioned (*OC* 4:214). There is less difference between the course and the *History* in the accounts of Brunehaut and Frédégonde (*OC,* 4:228–29), but in the course the romanized Brunehaut stands for culture against her violent rival. The Abelard of the *History* was a Breton, the spokesman of a rational Christianity (*OC,* 4:452); in the course he appears more as a man of method, the Descartes of his time. However, the basic interpretation of France as a force for maturity and reason remains the same. In both instances France is opposed to a poetic, childlike Germany. Michelet compares the Chapter of Notre-Dame, the Sainte Chapelle founded by Louis XI, and even the Jesuits of later times, with the Augustinians and Luther whose motto is: "May law perish; long live divine grace!"[6] The compliment to the Jesuits is remarkable, coming just five years before his bitter attacks. The remaining nine lessons move on to the Renaissance and modern France, to the gradual unfolding of humanism and reason.

The course of 1839 stands far closer in spirit to the account of events in the *History,* because it corresponds to volumes 5 and 6 that appeared, or were planned, soon thereafter. Chivalry and feudalism decline with the power of the church which, torn by schism, is no match for royalty. A centralized France will arise under Louis XI and so the stage is set for the Renaissance, conceived not only as a rebirth of classical knowledge but as the shining light *(la grande clarté)* of humanism which is to guide Europe. In the last lesson there occurs the first use of the French term, *renaissance.*[7]

Once again Gerson appears as the author of the *Imitation* and as the inspired leader from Lyons—Michelet had visited Lyons again (*J,* 1:297–98)—while the city is seen divided by its two elevations: Fourvières, with its cathedral, is the symbol of love and mystical faith; Croix-Rousse, with its weaving looms, represents the city at work (lesson 2).

The assassination of Louis of Orléans by the duke of Burgundy (1407) calls forth a warning against "the methods of Robespierre" (lesson 3). The Grand Ordinance is called "a truly national monument" which favors the cause of the people (1357, lesson 5), while after telling of the calamitous defeat at Agincourt, Michelet adds: "We shall not repeat the cold comment of Bossuet: 'So what?' " (1415, lesson 6). Salvation came through Joan of Arc, "still the Virgin but already France *(la patrie):* humanity was reborn in the death of the virgin of Orléans" (lessons 6–9).

The most original parts of the course are its evocations, first of Flanders, its industry, its art, the head of Christ by Van Eyck (admired at Bruges in 1837), the great city of Ghent, which is compared to Lyons and Florence (lessons 13–14). A special development concerns Liège, that outpost of France and ally in the drama which pits Louis XI against Charles the Bold, that "comedy" in which, as we have seen, the modern spirit must triumph. Warwick castle is also described in an evocation of English power (lessons 16–18). In 1453, the fall of Constantinople will send scholars fleeing to Italy, spreading knowledge, much like the invention of printing, taken as a religious act of enlightenment. "We have arrived at the Renaissance through the return to life! I unravel what so long has been enigma."[8] We can understand with what enthusiasm Alfred Dumesnil and his mother listened to these lectures. To them the professor was "acting, fighting, enthusiastic, sympathizing with his audience." It is amusing to learn that Michelet would add a comment "if he saw a priest shake his head."[9]

II *Death and anguish*

Soon after the last lesson, his wife, Pauline, died. She had become increasingly despondent and taken to alcohol. It was a serious crisis in which he accused himself of having neglected her and favored his mistress, history: he had indeed shared his father's room and let her sleep alone (*J*, 1:316, 801). As after Poinsot's death, the *Journal* vows a veritable cult to death and to the Père Lachaise cemetery: "With its roses and honeysuckle, this cemetery seems paradise, but oh what terrible ugliness lies beneath! . . . We must learn to die. After our personal life we must begin another, universal if that be possible." Death appears as a remedy for the profound evil in our nature. Every generation must start over with new efforts, but ultimately death inspires an immense charity, even for the priests who attack his ideas. He will include them in his love, "for benefit accrues to the one who loves most." He vows to describe the suffering of the past in all its anguishing detail, not to gloss over it in an abstract analysis like that of Mignet (*J*, 1:314–18). In 1841 he will elaborate in even more striking terms: "I must prove to myself and to humanity whose ephemeral manifestations I depict, that one is born again, that one does not die. . . . [So when] my wife died . . . I plunged with somber joy into the death of France [suffering with] my brothers [of the past whose] living shadow I was" (*J*, 1:359–62). For him, compassion is the key to understanding. This is what he means by saying that history is a "moral chemistry." In *The People* of 1846 he will for the first time see history as a resurrection (*PE*, 73).

No wonder that the course of 1840, devoted to the history of Rome, is centered around death.[10] Ruins of successive cities are piled one upon the other, the waters babble *(gazouillent)* in the aqueducts while below the skeletons from another era form a city of their own, the subterranean city of death *(mors)* beneath the city subject to current fate *(fors)*. Janus-like, the historian must look in both directions. These considerations cause him to evoke *The Prisons,* engravings by Piranesi, "hallucinations" in underground vaults with stairs without end, visions of frustration which recall Grainville's prose poem, *The Last Man,* thoughts of the end of the world, thoughts of Aeneas imprisoned by Dido.

Michelet documented himself carefully on the history of Rome. He knew the studies of Roman antiquities by Bosio, Artaud, and

Ampère. For another series of lessons, where he develops the meaning of the Renaissance in Italian art, he studied Rio's interpretation of Rumohr, two critics whose Catholic point of view did not coincide with his, but who helped him develop his own. He compares the religiosity of Raphael with the "realism" of Giorgione and Titian. In Renaissance art, as in the Renaissance in general, he finds a return to nature which he calls "naturalism," the representation not only of the body, but of landscape and the material world. To him this "naturalism" signifies the triumph of man over religious abstraction, a victory of life over death. He places Michelangelo in a category by himself, transcending all schools, the greatest representative of the Italian Renaissance.

In similar terms he celebrates the invention of printing. As before, he welcomes knowledge made available to all, but this time he adds detailed comments on print making, on techniques of engraving, and the historical conditions favoring them.

Thus the course of 1840, like its predecessor and for that matter its successor, moves from death to life, from darkness to enlightenment. Meanwhile our historian experienced a profound transformation. "Everything has died in me," he notes, "antiquity, the Middle Ages. I feel profoundly modern at this moment" (*J*, 1:364). "Action, action!" he added, commitment in the present to a better future. Political events were to contribute to this. The future Napoleon III tried to exploit the patriotic fervor created by a Franco-British crisis which led close to war (and the Treaty of London between England, Prussia, and Russia, of July 1840). He landed at Boulogne in a frustrated attempt to seize power (August 1840). The tension rose again when Napoleon's ashes were returned from St. Helena (December 1840). Michelet, who had exalted the genius of Napoleon a year before (at the beginning of the course of 1840), called the return of his ashes the "last irony" (*J*, 1:355) and projected a brochure defending his memory, though eventually he gave it up. We have seen how proud he had been in 1833 of Napoleon's victories, how deeply he suffered from his defeat at Waterloo; only he felt that Napoleon's name was being abused, especially by Louis Bonaparte trying to take advantage of the popular enthusiasm aroused by the return of his uncle's ashes. Michelet maintained little critical distance toward Napoleon whom later he will condemn as a tyrant.[11]

He returned to the inspiration of the past when he began "the course of 1841" in December 1840, to the "seekers for truth" and a new faith, e.g., Bernardo Ochino, who discarded his Franciscan robe and left both Italy and the Catholic Church:

Alas, to leave the infant Jesus, no longer to praise the son of God; alas, to leave the holy Virgin at whose feet he had lived, to renounce her consolation. . . . He felt something breaking inside him and could not help but say: "I follow you, divine reason wherever you lead me; I shall follow you onto death!" . . .

Gentlemen, let us feel for his pain, this cruel separation! . . . Ah, why do we always search further? I shall tell you. To search is to be human. . . . It is not our fault, it is the irony of nature which created us infinite in will and desire. . . . This irony, we compensate for it in our way by attempting to become infinite in places [we wish] to reach, in thought, in time. Alas, how can we extend our individual sojourn? By absorbing the past and breathing with our weak lungs the breath of the future.

This is the function of the historian. Michelet adds that life would be meaningless without this faith in the infinite, for "the world lives by faith." He continues: "There is one sure way to obscure these events, that is, to make them incidental to the Reformation, to tie the eternal history of freedom to the incidental concerns of Geneva and Calvin, to make free minds depend on the fatalism of a theologian" like Luther. The heroes of freedom include Servetus, burned by Calvin, as much as Giordano Bruno, burned by the Inquisition. He exalts the independent humanism of the heretics.

Of course, the Catholic press disapproved of both these lectures and the *History of France*. When Cochut criticized his presentation of Joan of Arc in volume 5, Michelet felt called upon to reassess his method even further. He now sees himself as a seer *(vates)* who brings the past to life with his "golden bough" and whose suffering enables him to make the terrible silence of history speak out (*J*, 1:376–78). Michelet remained an historian, but he will also be a prophet; he redefines his role.

Several passages in the *Journal* continue this process and prepare for the course of 1842 on philosophy and method. The *Journal* describes the past as

a crowd weeping and lamenting . . . , a crowd that aspires to live again. . . . But then, when you, [souls of the past,] still shared our mellow light, when you had your brief moment to live, love, and suffer as we do, why did you not try to make last what you held so dear? [The spirits of the past cannot answer and want the historian to step in:] Someone must come who knows us better than we did ourselves, to whom God gave a heart and an ear to hear. . . . [Someone is needed] who loves the dead, who finds for them and says in their stead the word they never uttered. . . . Yes, they are asking not just for an urn . . . , a dirge, one to weep for them, but for a prophet, a seer. . . . They need an Oedipus who can explain their own riddles to them . . . , a Prometheus, so that their voices which went out and froze in midair will melt by the fire he stole, so that their voices will sound again and once more begin to speak. (*J*, 1:377–78)

Michelet opposes this method to the approach of Hegel who "formulates" and of Quinet who examines and analyzes (*J*, 1:382). He would literally enter into the spirit of the past, e.g., of Renaissance art, religion, and law, in order to "de-symbolize" medieval traditions and make them part of the history of freedom.

This is what Michelet means when he says in his course of 1842: "I will force my science to yield a *vita nuova*," a new life. His models are Vico and Leibniz, whose monads appear as particles of an omnipresent vital force. They make up life just as the individual facts of history constitute the elements of ideas that he wants to describe. He is also indebted to Pierre Leroux's *Of Humanity, its Principle, and its Future* (*J*, 1:386) but keeps a critical distance. He cannot accept Leibniz's optimism any more than the idea of Leroux that the individual will be absorbed by the crowd. Like Leroux he conceives of history as a kind of transmigration of souls, but he insists on starting out from individual experience.

It was not just a theory; it was his life's story. He met Mme. Dumesnil in 1839, came to love her, found an intellectual companionship such as he had not previously experienced, but soon she fell ill. Her husband was most accommodating. He stayed in Normandy and was glad when, in view of her worsening condition, Michelet moved her into his home and had Adèle care for her. All too soon their hopes faded. The foremost physicians were helpless in the face of "a malignant tumor" (uterine cancer). Eventually Mme. Dumesnil retreated into the religion of her childhood and began to confide only in her confessor, the Abbé Coeur. He was a respected colleague who taught at the Sorbonne, a Jesuit, whom Michelet never criticized; he even appealed in his favor to protesting students (*J*, 1:593). Still, the ascendency of the abbé could not help but be resented. Michelet felt increasingly excluded from her sick room, her thoughts, even from her will, for he wrote: "She will not leave me even a metal ring. I am cruelly hurt" (*J*, 1:374). I suspect that the transformation of Michelet's religious views and his violent

attack on the Jesuits were impelled by this experience and by the
tragic death of Mme. Dumesnil.

In January 1842 he asked a former student, Yanoski, to replace
him at the Collège de France, only to see him fall gravely ill after
just one lecture. Unable to cancel his course, he was forced to teach
seven lessons (April–May) before Mme. Dumesnil's death. The
pressure of events contributed to the crisis. He tried the best he
could to draw strength from his own heart, to live by his new faith
which was by now far removed from the Christian view: "I would
draw the various religions from the inside as from a movement of
my heart. I would reinvent them as a cure for my soul, leaving them
behind as I found that they did not contain the balm which I was
seeking" (J, 1:381–82). Indeed, the course surveyed many religions.[12] Michelet traces the birth of freedom in Indian thought, in
the Mahabharata and other epics, then in the rise of the city states
of Greece; he compares them to David vanquishing Goliath. The
approach resembles that of the *Bible of Humanity* (1864) with its
new emphasis on Greece. The Christian tradition is also examined;
it seems largely opposed to the ideals of freedom and universal love,
especially when the Middle Ages shouted "Peace, peace!" in their
search for otherworldly solutions. Christianity, Michelet feels, simply did not love man enough, and sacrificed freedom to a tyrannical
and forced unity. He prefers the "seekers" who "serve the future,"
like Abelard and Heloise, but lest it be said that he lacks compassion,
he adds: "Let us not claim that the Middle Ages never loved as we
do." Still, his way is not that of "the saints who weep in their niches
of stone," but rather a belief in life: "For in this lies our salvation,
that creation has made us creators. Otherwise how could we fight
the blight of death? That is our purpose in living *(causa vivendi)*."
What is required is an inversion of the dogma of the Trinity so that
the cult of the Virgin becomes that of universal motherhood, of
fertility and regeneration, to be reconciled with the faith in Christ
and the Holy Spirit.

To illustrate his approach, Michelet rewrites the book of Genesis.
He merges the various myths of creation and, proceeding from small
creatures to the large, arrives at the "colossal elephant" taken to be
"the definitive being" as he "walks, grave and strong, through forests
less high than he. He seems to be the king, the pope of animals."
Later comes man, his leaders first looked upon as divine, then as
heroes, finally as human, equals in a democracy. As to the sexes,
woman appears as the earth mother, man as its creative genius, the

creator, e.g., of Greek sculpture or of the Roman empire. This picture may appear as a parody of the Bible but to Michelet it is an expression of faith in universal, if popular terms, a way to the renewal he needed if only to combat his own despair.

He was teaching what he calls "my philosophy, my method," in an attempt to find strength in the past to face the present; and the inspired moral tone was very much part of his new mode. In this he was not alone. Since 1841 Mickiewicz and Quinet had been his colleagues at the Collège de France. Mickewicz concerned himself with the literary and religious history of the Slavic peoples, first to 1648 (1841), then to the partitions of Poland (1842), while Quinet's courses discussed Italy in the Middle Ages (1841), then religion in Southern Europe (1842). The three professors came to be known as "the trinity of the Collège de France." They were deeply religious but radically unorthodox and aroused widespread criticism. Indeed, Michelet wondered how long he could continue to teach Princess Clémentine and the ladies of the court, but they encouraged him in spite of the uproar.[13]

III *The need for rebirth*

After the death of Mme. Dumesnil, Michelet undertook a nostalgic trip to see her husband in Normandy, then, in company of Alfred, Adéle, and Charles, he left for Germany in search of consolation (19 June–31 July, 1842). This time he traveled by way of Tübingen and Stuttgart to Munich, with a return via Nuremberg and Frankfurt.[14] "Action, action, and again action" is the solution, he exclaims (*J*, 1:431), as he finds himself in strong contrast to the sentimental, philosophizing Germans whose essential quality is *Gemüt* (feeling, soul, *J*, 1:452). What the Germans cannot understand, he explains, is that "in Paris 10,000 men are ready to die for an idea!" (*J*, 1:458).

Travel made him feel strong and active, but soon after his return he found himself depressed again (*J*, 1:427, 429, 834); "how much more I traveled in Jules Michelet than in Germany." The painful afterthought was: why had he not met Mme. Dumesnil earlier in his life, the first and only woman who had realized herself with him? "Too late, too far: these two expressions sum up the tragedy of the world" (*J*, 1:447, 457).

He found the Germans to be good workers, but lacking the spark of the extraordinary (*J*, 1:455). There were few liberals like Hegel and Schelling;[15] nearly everyone seemed conservative or apolitical, steeped in the past: Uhland, in Tübingen, was working on the history of the folksong; Gustav Schwab, from his pious point of view, spoke of the dangerous ideas of Hegel, Schelling, and of the *Life of Jesus* by Strauss (*J*, 1:427, 431). Goerres, whom he met again in Munich, seemed all too Catholic. Michelet unjustly held him responsible for the censorship that forced the departure of Schelling, Rückert, and Oken from the city.[16]

Everywhere Michelet describes the cathedrals in detail: the sanctuary at Augsburg by Syrlin, for instance (*J*, 1:434–36). He dwells on the work of early German artists like Adam Krafft and Peter Vischer, Dürer, Hans Sachs, and Cranach (*J*, 1:451–53). He also admires the Rubens collection at Munich (*J*, 1:442–46). He seems unconcerned with contemporary developments. Trier gives rise only to comments on its Roman background (*J*, 1:462–63).

To explain these reactions we must realize how little Michelet knew of the German languages. He read German only with difficulty, with the help of a dictionary. We find him proud of having translated one stanza of a poem by Rückert all by himself;[17] when Alfred and he undertook to translate a letter, they began with the last paragraph and were disappointed to find only polite greetings. Inevitably this limited contacts, but reactions to art, architecture, and landscape (viewed in human terms) are striking. He speaks, e.g., of the admirable "gravity" of the Danube at the Valhalla in Regensburg (*J*, 1:449).

The course (of 1843, first semester) he will teach upon his return is the most personal. The search for allies in his battle against mechanistic and scholastic values animates his lectures. His is a transcendental faith. No wonder that the account in the *Journal des étudiants* [Student News] seems unsatisfactory. Michelet protests and seeks a new solidarity with his audience:

I speak to you in confidence and to you alone, not to those outside. I entrust you not only with my science, but with my inmost thought on the most vital of subjects. Precisely because this audience is large and inclusive in age, sex, regional and national origin, I feel that I am facing humanity here, i.e., man, myself. From me to you, for man to man, anything can be said. It seems that there is only one speaker here. Mistake! You too are speaking. I act and you react, I teach and you teach me. Your objections, your opinions touch me closely.

Michelet is sure that his portrait of "the true spirit of the Middle Ages" cannot be summarized. If he knew that someone (like us) might attempt it, if his "winged words" frozen in midair could be recaptured, he would discontinue the course!

He speaks about Roman Gaul at the end of the Frankish rule, or rather, its people, the lowly serf, "animal-man" and "slave," and his naive but sustaining faith, "religion below" *(la religion d'en bas)*. Inevitably he had to yield to the rich and the powerful, at least until the people learned to associate and stand together. The magic word is "association." The process of attaining it may be a long one, but France teaches its people brotherhood: "France is an education, . . . an initiation."

The image is reinforced by the analogy of the family protecting the child. The family appears as the foundation of morality, as the basic cell that gives strength to the nation, just as it will later in *The People* and *Love*. Furthermore, the parent-child relationship is the symbol of the life cycle, of eternal rebirth: "The savior is not the giant, it is the child. The one who saves is not the rich, it is the poor. . . . The one who gives of himself in the Middle Ages is the poor man, the humble. Life always rises from below." An apocalyptic passage evokes Grainville's vision of *The Last Man* and the terror of death, but goes on to show that death leads to new life. Michelet approaches the idea of resurrection. When the Roman empire died, he tells us, its law and institutions remained; the church did much to safeguard Roman culture. However, only "the law of love" can assure permanence, only fraternity, never repression.

He vividly depicts the barbarism of early Gaul. Often men were beaten to death in punishment for an infraction, yet civilization grew in the shelter of the monastery, protected by the faith of the people: witness Ste. Geneviève, born of peasants, or St. Eloi, a simple artisan.[18] Salvation could come only from the meek, perhaps from some local saint, not from "the bearded Christ." Some listeners must have been shocked by this sacrilegious language used to qualify the revolutionary rise of the people from serfdom.

Was Christianity then doomed? To survive, Michelet explains, it must learn "the art of dying," i.e., the church hierarchy must give way to the truly Christian family, to civil liberty, and to "the Christian republic of Europe." Christianity had to be reborn, just as he himself was reborn after the deaths of Mme. Dumesnil and of the duke of Orléans. This prince had been the hope of all French liberals; his passing in July 1842 caused consternation.

When did the rise of the people to solidarity and influence finally materialize? Under the Capetians? In the Renaissance? Or only at the time of the French Revolution? Michelet does not say but his meaning is clear: the nation progressed by faith, the faith of simple people expressed in myths and legends. These were not pious frauds as some have called them, but the truth told so that children could understand. The spirit of the people was bound to triumph once it became conscious of itself and unified.

Finally, the historian analyzes his "method" of universal compassion. I grew up, he tells us—as he will later in *The People*—"like a blade of grass among the paving stones of Paris, like the moss on a wall," and came to love the early ages of France at the historical museum of A. Lenoir,[19] and so he dedicates this course "to you, beloved France, loved by God," for France is not just a nation but "a second fatherland to all (Jefferson), a place of universal initiation where all peoples enter into the spirit of the world, a complete Europe in microcosm, . . . an initiation which gave me the idea of the life to come." Unlike Sismondi, who speaks as a liberal Protestant and writes to document the mistakes of the monarchy and the church, Michelet will embrace "the totality of the past" in his sympathy. His love for France extends to all its parts. It is a humanism.

He concludes: "I come to kindle the hearth of the modern family." The ideal of "association" is also the model for the rebirth of the nation in his own day, a passage from darkness to light. The theme of education and moral reform is the link, be it a tenuous one, to the second semester which follows, the course on the Jesuits taught jointly with Quinet.[20]

IV *Years of crisis:* Des Jésuites *(1843)*

Battles against Jesuit influence were not new. Let us recall Pascal and his *Provincial Letters* (1656–1657), the dissolution of the order in France (1762), and its interdiction by the pope (1773). The Jesuits were secretly reinstated in 1800 and officially sanctioned again by Clement XIV in 1814. In France "the fathers of the faith" were authorized in 1815 and founded colleges that were to be closed again in 1828. Even so, their influence as confessors and directors of conscience increased rapidly, especially after 1833. In 1842 we find Villemain, the minister of education, formally warning the Chamber of Deputies that they constitute a great danger. Mignet, as secretary of the Academy of Moral and Political Sciences, took an equally strong stand. In 1844–1845 the prime minister, Guizot, attempted to have Rome disband the order and reached a compromise whereby most Jesuits were moved from the large cities; in exchange, the minister of education, Salvandy, ordered an end to the attacks on Jesuits in state institutions and at the Collège de France.[21]

This shows that Michelet and Quinet could count on considerable support when they decided on their parallel courses against the Jesuits. They were responding to an intensive campaign against the unorthodox teaching at the University, launched by the Abbé Garat in 1840 and carried on by the Catholic press ever since. When they began their courses, they had not even learned of the sharpest and most extensive attack, Desgaret's anonymous *Monopole universitaire, destructeur de la religion* [The University Monopoly Destroys Religion, 1843], a large volume in which Michelet and others were quoted out of context, or misquoted, to "reveal to the country the sum of abominable untruths broadcast from our lecture halls" by professors supported and "fattened up" by "the sweat of the people," i.e., paid by the state.[22]

For Michelet and Quinet it was a matter of academic freedom. All through their courses[23] they emphasized their right to free speech which stood at the antipodes of Jesuit obedience and principles. They blamed Jesuit thought control for the fact that since Ignatius of Loyola there had not been a single creative genius in their fold. The order seemed to foster death and sterility by upholding its right to discipline its members and others in the name of the very document which guaranteed free speech in France, the Charter of 1830. For the two professors this was a crusade and a matter of faith, for Jesuit thought control seemed to preclude true religion.

"My teaching springs from my unending trust in the young," Michelet told his students, for "history is the progressive victory of freedom" (*JS*, 53–55). It was theirs to earn and to continue building as the "true successors of others who built" God's eternal church (*JS*, 78). Our historian evokes the tradition of Ste. Geneviève from the previous course, the rise of a living faith against Jesuit obedience. In a grotesque analogy, he compares Jesuits killing the will of the individual with the artifice of training race horses, breeding skeletonlike animals to be ridden by dwarfs (*JS*, 84). For him, religious freedom goes hand in hand with political liberty, social "association," and solidarity. The free groupings he had described in the Middle

Ages are the antidote to a controlled militia like that of the Jesuits
(*JS*, 97, 102–3, 190).

Quinet's analysis includes a striking portrait of Loyola. The Jesuits
were organized to combat the Reformation, but, he asks: Who is
their enemy today? It is the Revolution, and 1789 for Quinet is a
return to pure Christianity (*JS*, 159), which he sees threatened by
the Jesuit hierarchy emanating from Rome. This threat from Rome
(*l'ultramontanisme*) will be the title of his course for 1844. The
Jesuits are a force foreign to the genius of France and to the nation-
states of Europe (*JS*, 223).

The historical perspective matters, especially to Quinet, but the
call to action dominates, a call to oppose Jesuit control of the masses
through the press and the confessional. When the priest gains the
confidence of the mother, he also captures the child (*JS*, 115). This
will become Michelet's principal theme. To him, such control denies
true religion. Who are the believers today? he asks; not the clerics,
for the most fervent priest (Lamennais) is outside the church (*JS*,
104, 218). In Quinet's view the Pharisees have taken over the church
(*JS*, 185) and Michelet agrees.

The Jesuits was a popular success. A sixth edition appeared in
1844; by that time there had been one hundred published responses
(*JS*, 32). The liberal press was plainly favorable, except for a much
discussed article by Lerminier in the *Revue des deux mondes*.
Among the religious newspapers, only the Protestant *Semeur*
showed any sympathy and noted the genuine religious concern of
the authors. The Catholic press—especially Veuillot and his *Uni-
vers*—reacted with violence. Desgarets returned to the attack in
L'Université jugée par elle-même [The University Condemns It-
self].To them, the idea of replacing the official church seemed preposterous (*JS*, 21–24).

The story of these battles would be incomplete without Adam
Mickiewicz, the Polish poet. His courses, entitled "The Official
Church and Messianism" (1843) and "The Church and the Messiah"
(1844),[24] also call for the rebirth of the nation, but from a different
point of view. The Lithuanian mystic, André Towianski, who is
never mentioned, had cured a mental illness of Mickiewicz's wife
and earned his undying gratitude. Under Towianski's influence,
Mickiewicz turned into an inspired mystic and announced a return
of Napoleon.[25] The coming of "the man" would restore justice and
the glory of Poland. He convinced himself that Napoleon was an
incarnation of the Christian message, that he understood the needs

of Poland better than anyone else, that a new prophet would arise. He taught his last course (1844) under a picture of Napoleon weeping for France.

Mickiewicz's courses were poetic and lyrical. They contained moving interpretations of Polish authors and asserted that "only the Slavs are privileged for having conserved the original [Christian] tradition and their native sense of the Godhead."[26] This vision is not so different from Quinet's view of the French Revolution as the rebirth of original Christianity,[27] and even close to Michelet's call for a religious renaissance. All three saw France as the agent of renewal capable of overcoming national antagonisms and war. Their friendship bridged their different views of Napoleon.

In 1849 Mickiewicz was a witness, with Béranger, at Michelet's second marriage. The image of their solidarity, "the trinity of the Collège de France," was reinforced when all three were suspended by a hostile government—Mickiewicz in 1844, Quinet in 1846, Michelet in 1848; the last two were reinstated after the Revolution of 1848 until 1851. When Michelet and Quinet reopened their courses jointly in March 1848, an empty chair was placed on the podium in honor of Mickiewicz, and a medal struck in memory of their common resistance to the previous regime. The "trinity" was not forgotten.

The courses of Michelet and Quinet attacked only the Jesuits, not the church as a whole, but the *Journal* of Michelet's August 1843 trip to Switzerland shows how universal the obstacle he saw in Christianity really was. At Lyons he mentions a girl seduced by her confessor and quotes a friend: "Wherever there are Jesuits, parish priests are cuckolds in spirit" (*J*, 1:518). In Geneva he is disappointed that Adert, a publisher, does not speak against the Jesuits; at Fribourg he discovers his own hatred of Jesuits in the city's youths; at Strasbourg his negative impression of the cathedral becomes clear to him when he finds "the Jesuit monogram" on the main altar (*JS*, 521, 525, 532). At Meaux he visits the study of Bossuet, convinced that the triumph of his pulpit led to the defeats of Louis XIV: no question that "France is going down under the Jesuits" (*JS*, 535). In his eyes, Bossuet had been perverted by the Jesuits who taught him.

There were some moments of consolation. On 3 August 1843, Adèle was married to Alfred Dumesnil. Both had felt that Michelet and Alfred's mother were entitled to their brief happiness. There was a dinner with friends, then loneliness, a last "adieu" to the past (*J*, 1:515).

V   *Years of crisis:* Du Prêtre, de la femme et de la famille *(1845)*

Michelet had been haunted by Jesuits, now the circle widens. In *Du Prêtre* [The Priest], the first of two books he planned to draw from the course of 1844, a bishop is quoted saying: "We are all Jesuits" (*PR*, 8). Calumny is called "the Jesuit art,"[28] and directors of conscience all seem to resemble Molière's Tartuffe attempting to seduce Elmire, except that true Jesuits would be more successful: Michelet outlines their craftier strategy (*PR*, 89–92). He does not actually accuse them of physical seduction, but of the kind of moral and psychological dominance that disrupts a marriage and threatens the very marrow of national strength (*PR*, pts. 2–3).

As for the course of 1844, there remain only two groups of fragments: one entitled, "the great monks," honors the solitary creators of the modern spirit from Descartes and Galileo to Newton and Montesquieu, finally Voltaire, "lay priests" whose mission was not unlike his own at the Collège de France. The second fragment depicts France, the "land of enlightenment," as much the center of the modern world as Rome had been earlier. This was to be the theme of the second volume which was never written, *Rome et la France* [Rome and France, *PR*, 15; *PE*, 228].

The attack had shifted to the church as a whole. Jesuit influence still seems pervasive, but the objective has become to reform priesthood as a whole, to bring the priest back to nature, to enable him for his own good to understand and emulate the holy order of thinkers outside the church *(la sainteté laïque)* on whom progress now depends (*PR*, 16).

The first part of *The Priest*, which makes up two thirds of the book, is devoted to the Jesuit perversion of the seventeenth century, which would otherwise have been the age of French glory. Much is made of the Jesuit, Possevino. He organized the persecution of the Waldenses in which 400 children were burned (*PR*, 24), planned the St. Bartholomew massacre while calmly arguing the difference between "those who died of love" and "those dead in [divine] love" (*PR*, 58), and trained St. François de Sales. Thus even the inspired activities of this remarkable man and of Mme. de Chantal fit into the nefarious pattern, for the convents they founded increased the numbers of men and women ready to surrender their will to directors of conscience, most of whom were Jesuits (*PR*, 34–46).

Michelet only regrets that Pascal's *Provincial Letters* did not include the historical detail of Jesuit schemes (*PR*, 63–64). Our historian describes them converting noblemen by bribes, fomenting alliances responsible for the Thirty Years' War (*PR*, 55–56), hypocritically arguing both sides of a question, ready to recommend, depending on the situation, either the austere life of Gonzales, or an easy forgiveness of sins according to Escobar (*PR*, 79). They were the Tartuffes of real life (*PR*, 89–97).

A surprising conclusion is that their determined activism led others to fatalistic inaction, which Michelet ascribes to Hobbes in politics, to Spinoza in philosophy,[29] and to Molinos and his *Spiritual Guide* in religion. Even though condemned for heresy, this book spread its poison, quietism (*PR*, 99–100). Quietism, in turn, is seen as a "method of dying" to life and nature, intransigent in Molinos (*PR*, 99, 134–40), more subtle in Fénelon and Mme. Guyon. Her passionate *Torrents* are compared to a gorge of the wild river Reuss in Switzerland (*PR*, 103–10). Here Michelet returns to the paradox he had already discovered in St. François de Sales and Mme. Guyon: Fénelon and Mme. Guyon display active leadership but kill the will to act in their disciples. Fénelon and Mme. de Maintenon are, for instance, held responsible for the sad fate of Mme. de Maisonfort, a girl without religious calling who was practically forced to take vows at St.-Cyr, and then was cast out by a Lettre de Cachet for betraying her feelings (*PR*, 122). A parallel case is Bossuet's "direction" of sister Cornuau who collected his correspondence. She was reduced to an automaton. Michelet calls this a method of putting the will to sleep (*assoupissement*, *PR*, 130–32), a "quietist" technique adopted by Bossuet (*PR*, 123, 139), all this in spite of the fact that Boussuet was an activist and a determined opponent of quietism. In his rigidity, Bossuet appears as a tool of those he combated!

Equally startling is Michelet's image of Marie Alacoque, a mystic whose cult of the Sacred Heart of Jesus may have been a form of folly, but who made a dangerous disciple in the Jesuit, La Colombière, for he proceeded to England and so antagonized the Protestants that he assured the bloodless Revolution of William of Orange (1688). A Protestant victory of a Jesuit's doing is the bizarre result of such logic (*PR*, 149–59).

In every one of these instances Michelet pities the victims. He accuses the directors of conscience of having established a dangerous state within a state, much like Rousseau who, in the *Social Contract* (IV, 8), accused the church of demanding loyalties which alienate the citizens from the nation. Rousseau had concluded: "Whoever dares say: 'Outside the church no salvation!' ought to be driven from the state." Michelet would agree but his emphasis is different; he is less concerned with the disruption of the state than with brainwashing by priests who destroy the independent will of women, and make them into mere shadows of themselves.[30]

This is precisely the theme of the second part of *The Priest*. The director renders the husband powerless in his home; he catches him like a fly in his net (*PR*, 198), and rules the "trembling herd" of women like a tyrant, *à la* Bonaparte. Wives and their children are subjected to what Dante called "transhumanation," i.e., they come to adopt the will and purposes of their director. Thus Rome rules them with greater power than any emperor ever possessed (*PR*, 210–17). Michelet draws a haunting picture of this process:

The horror of being observed day and night is bound to trouble the powers of the soul in strange ways. The darkest hallucinations will appear, all the nightmares that poor reason in its eclipse can dream in broad daylight, while fully awake. You know the visions engraved by Piranesi: vast underground prisons, deep wells without air, stairs which climb for ever without end, bridges to the abyss. (*PR*, 204–5)

Since directors of conscience see the Virgin Mary only as the chaste Virgin, and not as a symbol of fertility, of woman who is an initiation for man, Michelet accuses them of perverting a symbol of life into a tool serving their own power and threatening the future of the nation (*PR*, 209–10).

The third part of *The Priest* sums up the present danger: 600,000 girls are being educated in convents while their fathers are isolated in their homes by the rule of a director (*PR*, 48, 233–40). As a result the mother loses her personality, is seized by *ennui*, frustration, and boredom. This leaves her unable to function as a wife and mother (chaps. 2–3). The love which must permeate the home has fled (chap. 4) Michelet admits that the family has always lived by sacrifice: Griseldis served a cruelly jealous husband (*PR*, 225). However the priest who stands between wife and husband demands too much (*PR*, 229)! The universal spirit of love must not be sacrificed to the limitless power of Rome (*PR*, 274–75).

It would seem that Michelet has broken with Christianity, but an afterthought shows that this is not quite true. The suffering of sincere, lonely priests weighs heavily on him. His heart, he tells us, goes out to all who are unfortunate. All he is trying to do is to restore the priest to his role in life and nature. Ideally he envisions him as an elder who has learned much and "in his heart has found words which lead to the world of the future" (*PR*, 275–76, 16).

Such words of reconciliation notwithstanding, a former student of Michelet, Emile Saisset, published a rigorous critique under the title, "The Renaissance of Voltairianism."[31] Saisset admits that the confessional has been abused, but accuses Michelet of wanting to abolish the priesthood altogether and substitute a cult of Voltaire. It was the definitive break which separated Michelet from the *Revue des deux mondes* and its editors who had supported him. The course of 1845 and the following book, *The People*, accented this separation from former allies and colleagues. In that course Michelet emphasized a theme already implicit in *The Priest:* if the church cannot guide modern man to solidarity and love, then this becomes the function of public education, of "lay priests" like himself, inspired by the *Philosophes* and by the French Revolution. For the first time, 1789 appears as the "foundation" of the new faith.

The task of such an education will not be an easy one. The course of 1845 realistically assesses the difficulty of teaching the masses. Illiterate and untaught, they do not know their past and cannot anticipate their future, but freedom requires knowledge. The Revolution tried to find a solution. It did all it could for higher education. It founded the Ecole Normale Supérieure and the Ecole Polytechnique. It planned a nation-wide system of Ecoles Centrales for higher education. Still the problem remained how to reach the people at large and advance their condition. Here Michelet touches on a very personal problem. He had never been able to interest Pauline in his work. Now, in his loneliness, he engaged in sexual relations with two maids, first Marie, whom he called "*barbara rustica,*" then Victoire, "*barbara,*" but his determined efforts to educate them proved largely fruitless.[32]

More than ever before, he was aware that he could not reach those who needed education most. As an historian he forcibly spoke to an elite. *The Jesuits* and *The Priest* sought a wider audience. More popular books were needed and, above all, other links, perhaps through his students. His course of 1848, *The Student*, will explore this further. Meanwhile, the tone of his instruction had changed. Since the "crisis" of 1842–1845, he felt a new sense of urgency. Out of the ideal of "lay sainthood" arose Michelet, the prophet, the professor in search of his humble origins, the spokesman for the people.

VI   A *free society:* Le Peuple *(1846)*

The People appeared, as planned, exactly one year after *The Priest*, in January 1846. After two negative books, one directed against the Jesuits, the other against priests and directors of conscience, it was time for a restatement in the affirmative of his plan for social reform through association and patriotic spirit. As was his custom, Michelet's lectures anticipate the book. The course of 1845 states the essential themes: France is the Revolution, heroic in its perseverance, anticlerical, antimaterialistic, above all determined to bridge the gulf between the two parts of the nation, one educated, the other illiterate, those he calls "barbarians," like his maids. The term is not pejorative. The historian's heart goes out to the simple and lowly who, with their fundamental good nature and good sense, are the backbone of France. The chapters he will devote to them in *The People* he will hold in special esteem (*PE,* 165–86, 247). The course stresses the theme of brotherhood and "association," the common enthusiasm manifest at the taking of the Bastille. He ends with a call for education (within the limits we discussed) and for solidarity among the different classes, especially farmers whom he will place first in *The People.*

The books begins with the remarkable letter to Edgar Quinet (*PE,* 57–75) in which Michelet tells of his youth, of the great inspiration he found in the Museum of French Monuments of A. Lenoir to which he attributes his passion for the past (*PE,* 67), of the dramatic moment on a cold winter day when he struck down his fist on the oak table, determined to overcome all obstacles (*PE,* 70). We have noted that the *Mémorial* of his early days avoids such melodrama, but in 1846 the relative well-being which separated the historian from his humble origins transmuted these into the myth of the people and called for the heroic gesture. It is amusing to find that his aunts in the Ardennes were deeply shocked because he admitted his humble origins (*PE,* 64); Aunt Hyacinthe at Renwez was all too proud that the family had progressed and wanted to hear none of this. Finally, the letter to Quinet turns to historical method. It is here (*PE,* 73) that Michelet defines it for the first time as "resurrection" and opposes it to Guizot's "analysis," or Thierry's "narrative." He then restates his involvement, his suffering when he views the decline of France, his undying hope for harmony and peace with France in the forefront of Europe under the eternal banner of Revolution.

The book is divided into three parts, the first of which, "Of Slavery and Hate," is outstanding. It traces the divisions between classes but postulates that Frenchmen are sociable and hate only when taught to hate. The last two parts seek a solution to present ills, the liberation through love (pt. 2) and patriotic solidarity (pt. 3).

The first part begins with a tribute to the farmer. These valiant men go out even on Sundays to visit their "mistress, the land." Michelet strongly objects to Balzac's novel, *The Peasants,* which, he feels, views the farmer's condition as hopeless and decadent (*PE,* 61), and upbraids others for seeing the dirt farmer only for his dung, when he is actually happier and more independent than the city dweller (*PE,* 87, 93).

Then he turns to the laborer (chaps. 2–3), once independent as an artisan, now the slave of the machine. It sets his pace and takes his leisure to think and dream. He is the victim of "machinism," of the industrial system and its pressures.[33] These leave the entrepreneur equally frustrated, short-tempered, likely to beat his apprentice. It is not human nature that is at fault for even the mass (*la foule*) of the people is of good will; it is the system, the market conditions which dictate prices and rates of production, uncontrollable factors pitting the worker against the owner. Michelet would convince the manufacturer not to fear his workers, for they depend, as he does, on financial success (chap. 4). Everyone wishes to be a creative member of the group in which he lives, his immediate "small family," and of the larger family of France (*PE,* 110). It is to everyone's interest to uphold the right of property. Proudhon may have said, "Property is theft!" but he himself added that if this be true, there are 25,000,000 thieves in France unwilling to surrender (*PE,* 136).

Our historian addresses himself to all groups, though there is less emphasis on the white collar class. In his peculiar way he finds storekeepers and merchants thriving on deception, for to them bankruptcy, not dishonesty, is the true dishonor (*PE,* 121). Government employees are described as sadly underpaid but overwhelmingly honest (chap. 6). He even pictures the tribulations of the rich bourgeois with generosity (chap. 7). He senses an icy cold of egoism among the wealthy (*PE,* 141), but does his best to sympathize and see them as "the poor of yesterday" (*PE*, 137). There is no question, however, that he feels closest to the popular classes and to the city worker in particular. He compares him to a captive bird singing to the setting sun, wishing for "more light" like the dying Goethe (*P*, 112–13).

What is notable in this first part are keen observations of working conditions with meaningful statistics, e. g., for the increases in salary, more rapid in the city than in rural areas (*PE*, 106–7). The weavers of Lyons are studied—he observed them in 1839 and 1843—and the poor at Amiens, where he visited in 1846 (*J*, 1:645). *The People* is a valuable document, more perceptive and realistic than observations by Fourier—Michelet respects him (*PE*, 210–11)—or other social reformers.

Inevitably he becomes more vague as he turns to solutions for society's ills. He expresses confidence in human nature, in the natural "instinct" which leads to social harmony (pt. 2, chaps. 1–3) and exalts the spirit of the simple and childlike (chaps. 4–7). All will be guided by the heart. The wealthy will have to change their perspective, for they have been studying the masses only in prisons or in the gutter, and have based their conclusions on a small, unfortunate minority (*PE*, 152). They will have to learn that we need, not religious cults to preserve order, but the rules of nature and love. There is a utopian dimension in all this, but the warning to the upper classes to remember their popular origins is pertinent (*PE*, 192–93). Michelet's hope is focused on the simple, on the common people and their unerring intuition (*PE*, 182–86).

The third part is a paean of praise for solidarity, for association, especially in marriage and the family (chaps. 1–3), and for a humanitarian patriotism which is an object of faith (chaps. 4–9). Hans Kohn's definition of a nineteenth-century nationalist certainly applies: it is a person who has made an objective survey of the spirit of nations and has found that his country best represents the cause of humanity.[34] Michelet's ideal of France is that of a creative harmony which transcends and, at the same time, serves as an antidote for the "medieval" doctrines of the church and the conservative aberrations of philosophers like Victor Cousin (the attack is veiled). He hopes to restructure society in the spirit of nationalism, sacrifice, and devotion. Familiar with the ideas proposed by Pierre Leroux and Jean Reynaud in the *Encyclopédie nouvelle* (*PE*, 182), Michelet recoils before grandiose schemes and prefers to begin his reform within the family. He speaks of the father teaching the son, and of the son teaching the father. He turns to the young in particular as the creators of the future (*PE*, 243–46). Reform will proceed from the family to the wider group of the city, of the nation, propelled not by Christianity but by the idealism of the Revolution. It will be a labor of sacrifice and devotion, but the object is clear: "My country, my country alone can save the world"—and it will do so by relying on the individual and the solidarity of friendship.

VII   *Toward 1789*

The pattern of the two previous years repeats itself: the day after publication, Michelet begins the course which, in turn, anticipates the next book, this time the *History of the French Revolution*. The course of 1846 forms a transition. The first semester continues to elaborate on the theme of 1845, the national spirit, while the second provides an historical outline to explain the personality of France and its Revolution.

The historian begins by developing a theory also expressed the year before: spontaneity is life, imitation is death. It leads him to strange appraisals. Seventeenth-century French art should be rejected as an imitation of classical models. The Italianized landscapes of Poussin and Lebrun are contrary to the French spirit. So is the Catholic hierarchy; he considers it a form of tyranny at home in Italy, Spain, and Austria, but he adds an entire lesson on the Protestant tyranny in England which he considers no better. A six word summary of Hobbes—"Nature is war, despotism the remedy!"— seems to sum up the character of the English nation. England stands for materialism and mediocrity while France prepares the world for freedom, with Voltaire, Rousseau, and the doctrine of its Revolution. Montesquieu appears as an anglomaniac for praising the English system in his *Spirit of Law*, and, worse than that, picturing a "mad" France in the *Persian Letters*.

All ideas contrary to those of 1789 seem henceforth to be foreign, or French imitations of foreign models. At times his new intransigence borders on xenophobia. He reproaches Mme. de Staël for having been beguiled by the German dream—he even accuses himself of this—and now prefers the literature of death, Sénancour, and Grainville, to the explosions of color in romanticism. He is proud that Chateaubriand resisted the German temptation, and salutes Lamartine, Béranger, George Sand, and Lamennais as authors in the national tradition.[35] He welcomes them on ideological more than on literary grounds. They too believe in 1789 when France became herself, i.e., resisted foreign models which for too long had abridged her freedom.

An original lecture is devoted to the national costume. The machine age brought great changes, as he noted in *The People*, and such change is welcome as long as industry will provide a sufficient diversity of colors and styles to permit self-expression. In another lesson he pays an enthusiastic tribute to Géricault as an interpreter of character, in his *Carabinier* [Rifleman], and of death, in *The Raft of the Medusa*. Michelet likes these paintings so much that he never accuses him of abusing color like the romantics, or rather, he realizes that Géricault is not opposed to his revolutionary ideology like the authors he blamed for romantic excess. The painter David repels him, however; David's *Marat* seems "flabby and weak," or could it be that it is too flattering a portrait of a man whom our historian hates? Michelet's generalizing spirit organizes history and painting into friend and foe! His view of literature is no different.

The final lecture of the first semester deals with law and justice; it also introduces the great sweep of the spirit which shaped the Revolution. Michelet begins with the popular movements of Marcel and Lecoq (1302, 1357), contrasts Rabelais and the freedom of the Renaissance to the Italian-inspired massacre of St. Bartholomew (1572), finds the bankrupt authoritarianism of Louis XIV overcome by Voltaire and Rousseau, and sees the French people becoming a nation in 1789. The greatest day will be 14 July 1790, the General Federation with the provinces and classes side by side on the Champ de Mars, strong in their association.

The course is less a history than a juxtaposition, a collection of strongly partisan judgments designed to provide an orientation for his students, a manifesto in favor of the French Revolution, directed against the church still steeped in the Middle Ages. It was a startling series of lectures addressed to an overflow audience of 1,000 or more, with intense applause that likened it to a demonstration.[36] 1848 was on the horizon! Michelet's stand is clear: he opposes the extremes on the right, e.g., de Maistre and his apology for the St. Bartholomew massacre, with as much vigor as the partisans of Robespierre and the Reign of Terror; he favors the middle road of Danton. Michelet's resolute position and personal appeals, like one favoring a free Krakow,[37] brought notoriety and correspondence. Not everyone would accept that "France was saved in spite of the Terror."

The *Journal* confirms how vital his reorientation was to him. He can hardly understand his former self: "What was I doing when I embroidered on the ideal of the Middle Ages and hid the truth? I worked against myself and universal progress" (*J*, 1:658). He is now ready to fight the "religion of slaves . . . which produced, justified, and exalted the rule by the grace of God," i.e., the divine right of kings which he sums up as the regime of "favoritism and injustice" (*J*, 1:654). He is equally opposed to the rigid dogmatism of the Jacobins who sacrificed humanity to a principle and to the guillotine (*J*, 1:666). Michelet's essential purpose in writing about the Revolution will be to set this record straight in the midst of the passions of his own day. He had, after all, been captivated by them to the point of postponing his history of the Renaissance to write the account of the French Revolution, not just as an event, but as an act of faith.

CHAPTER 4

The Revolution

I *Faith and solidarity:* Histoire de la Révolution française,
volumes 1–2 (1847)

MICHELET was working at fever pitch. After *The People*, he taught his course and completed the first volume of the *Revolution* in about a year. Again his course began the day after publication, which this time was unusually late (11 February 1847), even for the Collège de France where much latitude was given. Concurrent with his lectures was work on volume 2, to appear in November 1847. We shall consider the course, then the two volumes, but first we must mention the death of his father, Jean-Furcy, in November 1846. Michelet honored him in eloquent pages as a witness of the great Revolution, one whose recollections would be included in his account, to supplement the documents which nourished it, one whose humanism (in the tradition of Voltaire and Rousseau) had inspired his life.[1] At home, Jean-Furcy would be replaced by Uncle Narcisse who was to live with his nephew until 1849, and then with Alfred until his death in 1867.

The first two lessons of the course, devoted to Mirabeau,[2] proved to be a critical experience for our historian. He presented the revolutionary leader fairly, he thought, as the aristocrat he was, basically a monarchist, a powerful orator, not a great thinker, an idealist out of touch with the masses whom he could not have guided for long; but to the man, Mirabeau, Michelet expressed his sympathy. This the radicals in his audience would not allow. As the *Lanterne du quartier* put it: "He forgives Mirabeau too much." There were disturbances and widespread protest. To calm his audience Michelet shifted his topic and discussed historical method, but he did not change his view of Mirabeau. In the second volume of the *Revolution* he returns to his defense and condemns the Jacobin opposition: "They seem to be the direct successors of the priests; they imitate their irritating intolerance" (*HR*, 1:537). Indeed, he will hold them responsible for the fact that the Revolution failed and died.

What then of his method? The search for guidance in the past is no easy task, for "the past contains only very little of the future." He asks his students to rid their minds of ready-made allegiances, since "the future stands to lose much from blind admiration." This is how he rejects the simplistic creeds of the right and of the left, of monarchists and Jacobins. He calls for critical perspective and the long task of educating the people, aware that his teaching and the popular books do not reach far enough. This is his concern and recurrent theme.

The second semester traces the Revolution to its classical inspiration, the Roman Republic. Here he separates himself from Quinet who saw 1789 as a return to primitive Christianity, in *Le Christianisme et la Révolution française* [Christianity and the French Revolution, 1845]. For Michelet, the Revolution is its own religion. It failed when it lost sight of its saints, the "great monks of modern times" described in the course of 1844, authors from Rabelais to Descartes and Voltaire, when it gave in to intolerance and the guillotine. The great task of the Revolution remained to be accomplished!

Now let us turn to the *Revolution*. The preface explains: "today I depict the era of unanimity, the sacred period when our entire nation, irrespective of party and still unaware of class distinctions, or nearly so, was forging ahead under the flag of brotherhood" (*HR*, 1:8). He is speaking of the years of solidarity, 1789–1790. The introduction adds: "I define the Revolution as the advent of law, the resurrection of civil rights, the reaction of justice . . . [for] without justice man cannot live" (*HR*, 1:21, 28). The Revolution is the new faith which replaces the old. To illustrate the contrast, Michelet compares the taking of the Bastille with the St. Bartholomew massacre which, he explains, was no accident but a dastardly act planned by the pope ten years before; royalist historians had obscured this fact.

The lengthy introduction is divided in two parts; they discuss the religion of the Middle ages and the monarchy, in other words, the "religion of grace" and the "rule by the grace of God," which means by the divine right of kings. Both deny the Revolution and its faith in man able to act and create his own universe. Here Michelet merges the principles of Vico and of 1789 (*HR*, 1:63). The alternatives are the regime of the Inquisition and of favoritism on the one hand, of justice on the other. No question then that the tyranny of church and kings must give way. In religious, even apocalyptic terms our historian adds: "For whom did I write all this if not for you, eternal justice . . . , for you are the true love, the identical equivalent of divine grace" (*HR*, 1:76).

It is a profession of faith inspired by the *philosophes* and illuminated by an unshakable confidence in the future (*HR*, 1:57). The Revolution is a word of eternal hope!

The historical account of the first two volumes of the *Revolution* includes some of the most memorable scenes in Michelet's entire work, especially the taking of the Bastille and the General Federation celebrated on its anniversary one year later. In the first there are gory details. When Hullin is separated by the crowd from De Launey, the commandant of the Bastille who had surrendered and whom he was trying to protect, De Launey is killed and his head affixed to a pike. Before Hullin knows what has happened, he sees the gruesome symbol above the human mass. However, as Gérard Walter points out in his masterful edition,[3] Michelet rather underplays the violence. His reticence strengthens the epic movement of his account which carried along so many readers (*JM*, 2:235).

The General Federation of 14 July 1790 was the high point of the Revolution for Michelet, the grand testimonial of harmony and good will which brought together the local Federations from all over France on the Champ de Mars. Almost surreptitiously, the king was also present (*HR*, 1:423). Two chapters entitled "the new principle" and "the new religion," describe this day of brotherhood. "Was it a miracle?" Michelet asks, and he replies: "Yes, indeed, the greatest and at once the simplest, the return to nature" (*HR*, 1:404). It was the victory of love over arbitrary power and abuses (such as the innumerable tolls on the Loire, *HR*, 1:405). Young and old were united, peasants and artisans, workers and the bourgeois. "I believe that at no other period the hearts of men were so wide open and the distinctions of class, wealth, and party more completely forgotten" (*HR*, 1:410). The leadership had been apprehensive but the vast celebration was held: "France wanted it and so it was done" (*HR*, 1:419).

One of the foreign delegations was led by Anacharsis Clootz, a wealthy German of Dutch origin who presented himself to the Constituent Assembly as the "orator of the human race." His claims may have been accepted too easily by Michelet (*HR*, 1:421; 2:1315), who presents Clootz as a prophet who foresees that: "Surrounded by the impotent desires of other peoples, [France] will soon be besieged by the hatred of foreign armies and kings" (*HR*, 1:421). This was of course the situation after the king's flight and capture at Varennes; was Clootz that clear-sighted?

Once again Michelet defends Mirabeau, but he admits his mistakes: Mirabeau stood behind Bouillé who had quelled a revolt in Nancy in a useless massacre (*HR*, 1:454, 509). Mirabeau was venal, at times corrupt, but not easily bought, always a patriot, never a traitor. He was a royalist, but so, at the time, were Marat and Robespierre. No one in these days spoke for a Republic; a debate on the subject held at the Jacobin club was stricken from the record.[4] Michelet grants that Mirabeau was fortunate to die as early as he did. He could not have held out for long, but France owes him a debt. He should again repose at the Panthéon where he was placed in 1791, but then removed on the initiative of Marat. When Mirabeau died, France lost "the spirit of peace in the midst of war, of goodness in a time of violence." The historian sees in him kindness and humanity, and concludes: "Let us savor his memory in our thankful hearts, in the very heart of France" (*HR*, 1:559–63).

After Mirabeau change was rapid. The king fled. This is rendered in detail—as is the indignation when the news was received. It fomented party divisions and a spirit of revolt. The stage was set for foreign intervention and war. In the face of these dangers Michelet returns to his vision of brotherhood. The French people, he tells us, are sociable; in association and solidarity they were able to save the country (*HR*, 1:591, 608–9).

II *The battles of 1848*

On 16 December 1847, Michelet began his new course (of "1848") but in a somber mood. The Guizot government and King Louis-Philippe were apprehensive and hostile to his revolutionary stance. Suspecting that his lectures might be suspended, he adopted the exceptional procedure of publishing them as he progressed. Eventually they appeared in book form as *L'Etudiant* [The Student].[5] His premonition proved correct. On 6 January his course was suspended. The Revolution of 22–24 February led to his reinstatement, in company of Quinet. Triumphantly they jointly returned to the podium on 6 March, with an empty chair reserved for Mickiewicz, and in his name Michelet issued a "fraternal salute" to Poland, "martyr of Europe" and symbol of universal aspirations (*ET*, 183).

All was not well even then. The first semester ended on 1 April, the second added six lessons to 11 June, but the activities of Louis Bonaparte were of grave concern. The violent repression of a workers' revolt on 23–26 June terminated all hopes (*J*, 1:690–93). The swell of enthusiasm which prompted Michelet to shift from the Renaissance to the *History of the French Revolution* was but a memory, and so were the proud moments of March when the liberals had gathered at the Madeleine to honor the dead of their Revolution. Furthermore, the revolutionary movements were foiled in Poland and throughout Europe.

Still, the course given before these disappointments had been a resounding success. It spoke of the need to lead the people. The task of reaching out was difficult. As the first lesson pointed out, of thirty-four million Frenchmen only four million could read, only one and a half million could be reached by the press, fewer yet by books (*ET*, 59). The problem was brought home when after the success of *The People* a fairly large edition of the *Revolution* was printed but remained unsold. Would even simpler books reach the people? Michelet still felt the need for them, though his friend, Béranger, advised him not to bother and let the people write their own (*ET*, 57, 163). Later, in *Our Sons* (1869), he points out once again that Béranger was wrong, for the books of the people remained unwritten.

If the course could motivate students to serve the people, the fatal separation between the elite and the uneducated could be overcome. They might help like Savast, who in 1812 left his post at the Collège de France to join Napoleon's Grand Army as a physician (*ET*, 72–73), or they might become political leaders like Kosciusko in Poland, or else communicate through painting as Géricault had done (*ET*, 100, 114). Above all they must act and not leave the people to the priests, for they will lead them only to the confessional and administer "the lie *in extremis*," i.e., capture their money and their souls on the death bed (*ET*, 120): "What is our role in all this, gentlemen? to stand up for Job and reaffirm our faith. . . . Whatever your wife or the world may tell you, yes, your intuition here is correct. Whatever priests or so-called friends may say, you are right when you remember [this duty]. Hero of our glorious times, be persistent and be yourself" (*ET*, 126)! This text is the conclusion to one of the untaught lessons. It reaffirms the Revolution and proclaims that one heroic peasant who fights his country's battles is more precious than ever so many words: may God grant us "as our crown and tomb" the courage to act which was his "cradle."

This appeal of January 1848 anticipates the February Revolution, but Michelet had no political ambitions. When, in March, a deputation from the Ardennes asked him to be their candidate, he declined and suggested Alfred Dumesnil in his stead. He considered his function as a moral historian more important, and the course retains the historical mold. Michelet admits that his preferred eighteenth-century authors may seem too aristocratic, like Voltaire, too literary or too abstract, like Rousseau in the *New Heloise* or the *Social Contract* (*ET*, 132), but their object was action; they can still serve as models. The historian hopes that his students will follow in their footsteps, and lead the people, for even conservative groups can be swayed: all that was needed in the Vendée was to convince the royalist partisans that the Revolution provided a better road to freedom (*ET*, 146).

Michelet wants to move his audience to action. This is also his essential purpose in writing the *History of the French Revolution*, in describing the taking of the Bastille, the Declaration of the Rights of Man (4 August 1789), and the General Federation. In his course he asks: Are we not still trying to realize the Revolution sixty years later (*ET*, 153–54)? To achieve solidarity he suggests the appropriation of wealth for the common good and public festivals, celebrations of national harmony, occasions of national significance like those the theater provided in Greece, in order to reach out and move those who could not read. Could the inspired legends of the Revolution not be acted out to inspire democracy (*ET*, 156–68)? Like a priest in his pulpit, Michelet preaches from his chair: "Let our hearts grow large!" Even after his reinstatement he warns against "political and religious Jesuitism" and the menace of intolerance. His "new priesthood" is dedicated to restoring justice to the world (*ET*, 174–75).

The second semester, not contained in *The Student*, is a preview of his *Bible of Humanity* (1864), an outline of a "People's Bible," predicated on the idea that cults die as others are born. His survey begins in the Orient, with India and Persia, proceeds to Judea and Greece, thence to Rome. Christianity is just another passing era. Inspired by Burnouf and recent scholarship, he gives much closer attention to the *Mahabharata* and the *Ramayana*. The last lessons describe the struggle of the new faith against the power of Rome, convinced that a God is needed, a new altar. The Christian gospel must adapt itself and give way, just as older faiths once did to make way for it.

The political problems raised by the ambitions of the future Napoleon III were also much on Michelet's mind; his notes show this, but it is uncertain whether a lecture on contemporary politics was ever delivered.

III Athénaïs and the course of 1849

On 23 October 1847 the young governess of the children of Princess Cantacuzène in Vienna took it upon herself to write the author of *The Priest*. She told him that the book had moved her to seek "a guide" who was not a priest. She would have consulted her father were he still alive, but since his book had virtually transformed her, would he draw on his experience and help?[6] Michelet answered immediately, touched by such confidence. He suggested that she find God in the admirable words of Joan of Arc as recorded in his *History of France* (J, 2:603). This is the way Michelet's correspondence began with Athénaïs Mialaret, born on 17 October 1826 and twenty-eight years younger than he. She came to Paris to meet him on 8 November 1848. Four months later, on 12 March 1849, they were married.

As she had given to understand in her first letter and was to repeat in her biography, *The Memoirs of a Child* (1867), composed under Michelet's watchful eyes, in him she rediscovered her father "whom I loved so much," but in so doing "it was already you I loved."[7] Her father had had a life of adventure. He had served Napoleon on the island of Elba. After Napoleon fell, he had fled to America. Then he had returned to France, married, and raised a family in Montauban. Finally he returned to the United States and died of typhus in Cincinnati in 1846. His memory was sacred to Athénaïs, along with that of her childhood and the pets that she commemorated in *The Cats*.[8]

With Michelet it had been love at first sight. Their passionate but also frustrating relationship is described in every detail in the *Journal*. A son, Yves-Jean-Lazare, was born on 2 July 1850 but died six weeks later, on 24 August. The real problem, lovingly accepted by our historian, was her hypochondria and frigidity. She calmed his apprehensions by saying how much she suffered. The pattern was set on the wedding day. He writes: "I hardly had this desired treasure in hand when I was refused everything. By her? No, her good little heart was burning to make me happy. She was afraid that my disappointed desire would make me sick" (*J*, 2:32). But how sick was she? The next morning she took her mother to the museum, still suffering. . . ? She reassured him also by explaining that her ill health made her age so rapidly that the age difference between them would soon disappear.

Michelet saw in her the ideal of feminine virtue, in spirit and in the flesh. She stimulated him to work and showed pride in his accomplishments. Whatever her failings, Athénaïs brought him an understanding that he had never known.[9] On 20 June 1849, when his intellectual passions were still new to her, he writes:

> My soul would have had a higher degree of unity and so more happiness, if history had not forced me to relinquish happiness so often, if my wife [amie] had enjoyed more constant health, if I had been able to associate her even more closely with the movement of my ideas. The obstacle was the infinite variety of subjects. I had no way of following with her a gradual program of education and initiation. Every day, I poured out my heart to her, telling her just how it felt, treating her as a comrade to whom one tells everything. (*J*, 2:55)

Love for Athénaïs was a progressive sharing of all concerns. In the course of 1849—one semester was taught before the marriage, the other after—their love became the symbol of universal harmony. It was an intellectual relationship he had never enjoyed with Pauline, and only briefly with Mme. Dumesnil.

The course developed the theme of unity, so sadly lacking in the modern world, in the struggles between classes and interest groups. The strains within families must be reconciled just like those on the national level, and so must conflicts between religions. As in the second semester of 1848, he sketched the development from India, Persia, Egypt, Judea, to Greece and Rome. The mother goddess, Isis, seemed to evoke Athénaïs.

In speaking of the interdependence of husband and wife, a new note is evident. Michelet insists that the wife needs complete freedom. This will permit her to adjust to her husband all the more easily, and to realize the ideal of motherhood, the essential symbol of life around which Michelet builds his new religion, in opposition to the sterile Christian concept of original sin. He calls for courage and sacrifice in love which is an "initiation."

Meanwhile the government grew more hostile. Michelet was reprimanded for canceling lectures on the occasion of his marriage. His response was a more combative tone in the second semester, where he returned to the ideal of justice, to the contributions of 1789, 1830, and 1848 in shaping the "cathedral" of modern times. From Galileo to Newton, from the *Encyclopédie* to Lavoisier (who was guillotined!), there had been progress. He sums it up as a battle between two schools, that of death (with Molinos, Hobbes, and Spinoza), and that of life (with Voltaire, Rousseau, and the Revolution). We may shrink at such oversimplifications, at the image of an outdated Spinoza facing Leibniz, the apostle of enlightenment, but we can appreciate Michelet's appeal for justice, presented as God's claim on man, as a mission and a duty.

At one point he exclaims: "Back with you, barbarians, strangers to our cult" *(arrière barbares, arrière profanes)*, with the connotation: "Get thee behind me, Satan."[10] Those opposed to justice represent Satan; they are "death" threatening "life." The two terms recur constantly to emphasize the need for personal renewal, for the resurrection of the past through history, but also and above all, for the faith in justice and the Revolution, for freeing the slaves, the victims of the system to be overcome.

IV   *Growing tensions:* History of the French Revolution,
volumes 3–5 (1849–1851)

In six months' time and with the encouragement of Athénaïs, Michelet completed the third volume of the *Revolution* (February 1849); the next two followed about a year apart (January 1850; March 1851). They are remarkable accounts, precious also because the archives of the city and the police on which they draw were destroyed by fire in 1871, and because they keep a critical distance from the *Moniteur* and the *Parliamentary History* of Buchez and Roux, the principle sources of previous volumes. Michelet accuses them of "lying" as he analyzes the different "sections" of Paris, e.g., their attitudes during the "massacre of September 2" when political prisoners were killed in the panic of fear of foreign invasion (*HR,* 1:1046). He is equally critical of Dumouriez's *Memoirs* and shows how this general, who betrayed the Revolution and joined the enemy, belittled his associates (e.g., Dampierre) in an effort to acquire personal glory (*HR,* 1:1237). Oral traditions are included: Michelet tells how the mayor of Rennes, Leperdit, is said to have calmed rioters.[11] Volumes 6 and 7 will show many of these same qualities, but they were written "in exile" at Nantes and could draw only on the archives of the Vendée.

Volume 3 begins with the capture of the king at Varennes (June 1791). Book 5 describes the end of the Constituent Assembly (14 September 1791). Book 6 tells of the ill-fated Legislative Assembly which lasted only ten months. The constitution which took four years to work out, served only to 10 August 1792, the day of the insurrection which, for all practical purposes, ended the monarchy.

The image of Athénaïs is never distant. We find her in the notable portraits of Mme. Condorcet and especially that of Mme. Roland and her older husband, an idyl compared to Julie and Saint-Preux in the *New Heloise* (*HR*, 1:650–58). The self-seeking Mme. Roland is completely transformed by Michelet's ideal of beauty and love.

As for the Constituent Assembly, our historian has little good to say. It is qualified as royalist and reactionary because it declared the king innocent—had he not tried to join the armies of his "cousins," i.e., the enemy?—and for being insensitive to the petitions of the people, their "collective writings" which demanded that a Republic be established (*HR*, 1:695). Troops sent by the Constituent Assembly to the Champ de Mars caused fifty deaths on 17 July, 1791 (*HR*, 1:702)! Barnave is seen far more antirepublican than he was. He might have harbored illusions that he could win over the queen to the revolutionary cause; Michelet sees him simply as a traitor in love with her (*HR*, 1:723–30; 2:1220), and adds that by his doing, the Constituent Assembly is caught red-handed in a reactionary plot (*en flagrant délit d'aristocratie et de royalisme, HR,* 1:730–32). Thus the Assembly lost much of its authority and the Revolution floundered. Priests and Jacobins, the radicals on the right and on the left, are blamed for its demise (*HR*, 1:742–45, 756). This left the Legislative Assembly an impossible task, the enforcement of the new constitution.

Danton's reply: "Action, action, and again action!" (*HR*, 1:906). On 20 June 1792 the Tuileries are invaded, and rightly so, for "Monsieur véto," the king, had abused his rights and gave only lip service to the constitution. Had his attempt to flee not rendered it inoperative? When the people entered his palace, he was hypocrite enough to wear the red bonnet of the Revolution; he even forgot to take it off when he escaped by a secret stairway (*HR*, 1:922). On 10 August the Tuileries will be seized again, and for good, while Louis seeks refuge in the Assembly.

. This dramatic event is described in volume 4. Was it planned? It may have been a spontaneous reaction to the demand of immediate surrender, issued by the commander of the invading armies, the duke of Braunschweig (*HR*, 1:945). France rose to the challenge. The enemy was stopped, in spite of internal dissension, at Valmy and at Jemmapes (20 September; 6 November). Michelet is convinced that the taking of the Tuileries was the essential condition of military success: "Let us repeat, it was a great act of France; she would have perished had she not taken" the Tuileries (*HR*, 1:967). Even so it was a close call. Our historian shows the disarray at Valmy. French troops stopped the invader almost in spite of themselves; it was the impressive achievement of "unity of passion and will" (*HR*, 1:1119), for it was France itself advancing with one terrifying, unanimous shout, men frantically fighting for the Republic (*HR*, 1:1128–32). Similarly Michelet finds that at Jemmapes "God was with France." It was a victory of faith, the reply to the gloomy predictions, freedom for the people of Belgium, a clarion call of the new age (*HR*, 1:1224–25, 1241).

Internal dissension continued. "The battle of the gods" pitted the Gironde (Vergniaud and Mme. Roland) against Danton and Robespierre. In the power struggle, Michelet favors the "generous" Danton. Vergniaud has his admiration as a powerful orator, but Vergniaud prevaricates: he attacks the court and the king without rejecting the monarchy (*HR*, 1:1001, 1290). Of course it was dangerous to condemn the king to death, for the execution could cause the "innocent Republic" to be hated, and the weak and undistinguished king to be "canonized by the guillotine" (*HR*, 1:1278). Vergniaud was right in predicting the reaction which the death of Louis was bound to produce abroad (*HF*, 2:114), but he was unable to draw the consequences and so he perished: Vergniaud was a tragic figure, infinitely more appealing than those who brought him to the guillotine. Once again Michelet finds that the extremes meet; he speaks of "the league of royalists and Jacobins" (*HR*, 1:1026).

There is no question in his mind that the king was guilty; only there were attenuating circumstances: the milieu, the traditions that made Louis feel he was innocent even as he stepped up on the platform of the guillotine. He hoped to the last that his appeal to the people might sway them. Still, the historian's sympathy is not forgiveness. He brings out the evidence of Louis's dealings abroad, documents which were unknown to those who tried him (*HR*, 2:8,

17). They had to judge by his escape and capture, and as a matter of principle.

Danger arises from the fact that judgments by principle are divisive. The polarization of France becomes ever more evident. Our historian is apprehensive lest intolerance, Robespierre and Saint-Just, who quote the *Social Contract* and rule by principle, pervert the generous objectives of the Revolution. The issue affects Michelet so much that his enthusiasm for Rousseau is affected. Around 1850 he begins to distinguish the sensitive and religious author he loved, the author of the *Confessions* and the *New Heloise*, from the abstract theoretician of the *Social Contract* whom he calls "Rousseau-Mably" and rejects along with Saint-Just and Robespierre.[12]

A surprising element in Michelet's interpretation is his sympathy for the royalist resistance in the Vendée. He insists here, as he had in *The Student*, that the leaders, Cathelineau and others, were men of the people, valiant and upright. If only they could have been converted, but this was not to be. "Drunk with discord," the Vendéens caused 5,000 deaths (*HR*, 2:264–66). A similar situation arose in Lyons where the delegate of the Convention was massacred and revolt was rampant. The treason of Dumouriez confused minds further and the king's trial divided loyalties. Michelet follows all this in great detail in volume 5.

Threatened from all sides, the Convention was faced with dissension everywhere. Before his act of treason, Dumouriez had wavered between Philippe Egalité and the Dauphin (*HR*, 2:299); even more serious were the battles between Girondins and Montagnards; finally, the Montagne took charge in a kind of coup d'état by gaining control of the Committee of Public Safety. Now the "pit of Curtius" was open, "the abyss into which the fatherland, in its danger, cast its best citizens for its own salvation" (*HR*, 2:313). Volume 5 ends with the arrest of the Girondins. "Personally innocent," they never intended to divide the country, but their policies were "impotent"; they could not save France. They did not know how to organize in the face of danger from abroad. Michelet points with pride to the heroic achievement of the Committee of Public Safety. It organized the defense; it planned the great schools of France, the Ecole Normale Supérieure and Polytechnique, established in 1794 but projected the year before (*HR*, 2:399–400). This was one last moment of unity and brotherly love, when Danton praised Vergniaud as well as Saint-Just. Remarkable to note, here Louis Blanc agrees with

Michelet. He appreciates the idealism of the Girondins in like manner, though he does not share other views.[13]

Michelet's images are often striking. At one point he describes
Lady Hamilton's extracting diplomatic secrets for England from her
willing victims in Naples, "a Venus, Bacchante, and Sibyl." England,
as well as Rome and the Vatican, were the centers of anti-French
agitation. This leads our historian once more to Piranesi and his
Prisons, hallucinations described in the course of 1840 and *The
Priest*, this time used to show that the Revolution brought light into
the dungeons of oppression (*HR*, 2:213–15).

V   *The last courses at the Collège de France (1850–1851)*

Michelet was still the apostle of the "new faith" (*J*, 2:668) whose
hope was the renaissance of the family. Only woman could bring
it about, for she is the "heart" in the face of material concerns and
a male dominated society.[14] Man's hope is woman! Michelet evokes
Dante's Beatrice, Petrarch's Laura, Imogen and Desdemona from
Shakespeare, Dorotea in *Don Quixote*. It is also an ode to Athénaïs,
to the historian's own happiness, to the interdependence of man
and woman. Ever since the course of 1842 he had been developing
his theory of "the two sexes of the mind," the female heart, the
male logic, which he will increasingly discover to be intermingled
in all human beings. The course of 1850 makes clear that man needs
woman to save him and the nation, that woman needs man's intellectual discipline to restrain her fantasy.[15]

The second semester emphasizes the religious mode. Woman
appears as the priestess of social action, "the living gospel of work,"
designed not for the dark recesses of the cathedral but for the light
of day. The young mother is idealized. The example is Maria Rosetti,
the English wife of a Rumanian patriot and poet who followed him
with her children through revolt into exile.[16] Michelet's "Virgin" is
married, fertile, brave, and an equal partner in private and public
life, like Athénaïs expecting Yves-Jean-Lazare[17] who was born and
died before the next course opened, in January 1851.

It began not only under the shadow of personal tragedy, but of
the threat of suspension which was to come in March. The historian
realized it might be his last opportunity to assert his leadership and
preach social action from his chair. Indeed, one section of the course
is devoted to predecessors at the Collège de France who suffered
the penalty of their forthrightness. Ramus was killed in the St.

Bartholomew massacre, Baluze was forced into exile in 1710, Tissot lost his chair under the Restoration, as did Quinet and Mickiewicz. Without illusions concerning his own future at the Collège, Michelet spoke out "in the high and absolute freedom of conscience" becoming his chair. He saw himself standing in judgment of France, speaking from a veritable pulpit *(une magistrature, un pontificat)*. He spoke of his "papacy of civil liberties," i.e., of his duty to oppose restraint, and confided: "I have never been more myself in my courses than right now" (*J*, 2:147).

As in the course of 1848, he pointed to the tragic gap between rich and poor, and more especially between "the two peoples" of France, the literate elite and those who cannot read (*J*, 2:146–48, 697): students should consider themselves missionaries and communicate the fraternity of 1789 to the nation at large. He was not inciting to revolt as the government believed; he was advocating social harmony, an active bond between the university and the common people. No question, though, that Michelet departed from the customary tone of erudition. Twelve hundred listeners applauded while conservatives were dismayed (*J*, 2:695–96). Colleagues who did not believe that democratic freedom could or should be taught at the Collège de France voted to suspend him. Julius Mohl, the orientalist, called his lessons "deplorable rhapsodies, mostly sheer nonsense, striving for originality and attaining a sort of fantastic madness,"[18] adding that he reluctantly approved "what they wished," the closing of Michelet's course as proposed by the government. It came on 13 March 1851, six days before publication of volume 5 of the *Revolution*. Losing his self-appointed priesthood *(sacerdoce)* left him so desperate that he did not continue his history for over a year. Instead, he wrote a number of pamphlets intended for the widest public, protests in the name of the defeated revolutions of 1848 against the repression which followed everywhere.

VI   Légendes démocratiques du Nord *(1851–1853)*

The account of the heroic freedom fighters of eastern Europe— then commonly called, "the North," even including Rumania—was first conceived as a vast *Golden Legend*, only part of which was written. Michelet did issue a number of separate pamphlets: *Kosciusko (Poland and Russia)* in 1851, *The Martyrs of Russia* in 1852, *Principalities along the Danube; Mrs. Rosetti* in 1853; they then appeared as a book under the title, *Democratic Legends from the*

North (1854). Under the inspiration of renewed revolts in Poland, the second edition was entitled *The Martyrdom of Poland* (1863).[19] The coup d'état of Napoleon III, who declared himself emperor on 2 December 1851, shows how timely these concerns were.

Michelet describes inhumanity and suffering with haunting realism and biting irony: Russian serfs are "obligingly" beaten to death by the police, anxious to please their masters (*LD*, 117). Officially the serfs had been freed in 1842 (*LD*, 198) and the death penalty had been abolished, but peasants could be starved to death, or condemned to 7,000 lashes when everyone knew that 3,000 were sufficient to end life. Others were sent to Siberia, frozen to death, or felled by disease (*LD*, 158). The Russian peasant lived in a world of misery and injustice. The descriptions, based on reports, often outstrip the fantasies of a Sade.

Since the only hope lay in solidarity, Michelet used the startling phrase: "The life of Russia is communism" (*LD*, 29). It called forth an *Open Letter* by Alexander Herzen who asked: "How is it, sir, that you are not frightened by your own words?" Herzen went on to say that one must not place the blame on the exploited Russian peasant, decimated by the emperor's conscription and without redress against landlords and nobility.[20] His state must not be confused with the barbarism to which he is subjected even though he cannot conform to bourgeois values and behavior. Some day he will rise against the czar! Herzen added that, fortunately, Bakunin had not been tortured to death as Michelet had thought.[21]

Herzen offered not only criticism, but his friendship. He sensed Michelet's noble idealism, and our historian was moved. He read Herzen's *Development of Revolutionary Ideas* and made use of it for the last part of his *Kosciusko*.[22] As to the phrase about communism, it is one of numerous texts where Michelet transcends his bourgeois attitudes. In *The People* he had insisted on his humble origins; in the *Journal* of 1850 he called himself "the son of work who has always worked and is going back for more work" since work is "sacred" (*J*, 2:125). Proudhon, a devoted listener in Michelet's courses in the early 1840s, was impressed and considered him a worthy candidate for conversion to his own radical views. George Sand, for similar reasons, maintained a long friendship with him; so did Alexander Herzen.

Most of the *Democratic Legends* concern Russia and Poland, but there is also the moving story of Rosetti and his wife fleeing from Rumania, never safe from the Russian, Turkish, or Austrian police.

The course of 1850 presented Mrs. Rosetti as the ideal of woman-hood; the *Democratic Legends* include a second glowing tribute.

Michelet fully intended to expand his series of portraits into "the golden legend dedicated to all freedom fighters, to the pure," as he puts it in a foreword to the *Soldiers of the Revolution*, conceived in 1851, but not published until after his death (1878).[23] The book contains biographies of generals of the Revolution, especially of Desaix and Hoche. Many passages duplicate others in the *Revolution* or the *History of the Nineteenth Century*. The favorite is Lazare Hoche—modest, dedicated, brave, at one time maligned and jailed by Saint-Just, later assigned the thankless task of pacifying the Vendée; he finally died of tuberculosis in Germany at the age of twenty-nine. A section appended to the *Soldiers* returns to 1848 with the remarkable portrait of Mameli who fought to unite Italy. Mameli distinguished himself in the battle of Rome where Garibaldi resisted the onslaught of the French under Oudinot, the son of the famous general of the Napoleonic Wars. Ironically called "the prudent Ulysses," Oudinot claimed that he came to free Rome, but actually did all he could to kill the independence movement, and with papal blessing. Mameli was wounded, returned to battle, and died two days after the French entered Rome.[24]

The military chronicles of the *Soldiers of the Revolution* form a transition between the historical and the popular work of Michelet, just like *Les Femmes de la Révolution* [Women of the Revolution, 1854] with portraits of Mme. Roland and others. *The Golden Legend* remains incomplete. What we have immortalizes the ongoing fight for freedom.

VII *Robespierre and the Reign of Terror:*
History of the French Revolution, *volumes 6–7 (1853)*

The sixth volume of the *Revolution* takes the story from the fall of the Girondins in March 1793 to the "papacy of Robespierre," i.e., to his position of absolute power (bks. 11–14); the seventh shows the Jacobins *(la Montagne)* gnashing their teeth (*HR*, 2:811) as the "trinity" of Robespierre, Saint-Just, and Couthon takes refuge in terror in the face of revolt at home (Vendée, Lyons) and pressure from abroad. Suspicion grew and everyone felt threatened, and so the downfall of 27–28 July 1794 became inevitable. The death of Robespierre closes the dramatic canvas of innumerable actions and individuals, sections, committees, and parties, in what Michelet calls the first democratic history of the Revolution.

His technique distinguishes him sharply from his principal precursors—Guizot, Thiers, and Mignet—from their abstract reasoning and philosophical conclusions. Even Thiers, whose account is the most detailed of the three, emphasizes principles: to him, Robespierre is the man of envy, the incarnation of demonic hate, and terror personified, as opposed to Marat, the man of system, and Danton, the man of passion.[25] Guizot, whose father perished on the guillotine and whose mother is said to have thanked God on her knees for Robespierre's death,[26] could be no more favorable in his judgment than he was: he saw Robespierre as the incorruptible leader, forced to eliminate one enemy after another. Guizot remains resolutely partisan and admires the king who so bravely faced the guillotine.[27]

Mignet's condensed account, a masterpiece of analysis, says that Robespierre was doomed to die on the scaffold just as a conqueror might die by the sword.[28] He shows him as a single-minded leader, moderately talented, vain, incorruptible, and opposed to bloodshed, but with the makings of a tyrant, propelled by circumstances and fanatical followers to rule by the guillotine. His faith, based on the *Social Contract,* in the sovereignty of the people was as absolute as his deism. Mignet also made the dubious assertion that Robespierre's religion derived from the *Profession of Faith of the Vicar from Savoy.*[29] His objectives were noble enough: the rule of the people, magistrates without pride, citizens without vice, fraternity, virtue, simplicity of manners, austerity of character. The summary admirably illustrates Mignet's capacity for capsule definitions and his attempt to be fair.

In Lamartine's lyrical account in eight volumes, with the misleading title, *History of the Girondins* (1847), there is more detail but nothing is solidly documented as he claims.[30] It is essentially a lyrical meditation. Robespierre is drawn with considerable sympathy, enough to cause Lamartine's wife to be deeply concerned,[31] but Lamartine does not class him among the "pure, shining, immortal faces."[32] Mignet's history, frequently reedited, is a one-volume condensation but more accurate than Lamartine, whose grand effusion remains a document of the enthusiasm preceding the Revolution of 1848.

By contrast, Michelet presents concrete detail, often based on the archives of Paris, or Nantes for the last two volumes, composed during his one year "exile" there. He concentrates on the tableau, on individual interaction, of innumerable participants in the drama of the past ever so vividly described. He is quite accurate, though there is ground for challenge throughout, as we can see by the comments of Louis Blanc or, for that matter, the numerous corrections by Gérard Walter.[33] However, the main trends are never lost, and Michelet's recreation of the ideas, hopes, and passions of the past is infinitely more moving than the work of his competitors.

What then was Michelet's view of Robespierre? He expresses his sympathy for this remarkable figure, "great in willpower, an untiring worker like myself, and as poor as I used to be" (*HR*, 2:181). He pictures him virtuous, never venal, idealistic though ever more distrustful. However, our historian disagrees with his principles and, at one point, thinks back to his "daily altercations" with Robespierre, in the process of coming to terms with this legalist who, in his last days, refused to save himself by leading an insurrection against the opposition, always anxious to preserve the republic (*HR*, 2:981). In the days of foreign invasion, Michelet admits, "I would myself have been a Montagnard" (*HR*, 2:347). He exonerates Robespierre in another way as well: he emphasizes that the most despicable of men were against him, and this is to his honor (*HR*, 2:737). Michelet pictures Robespierre's death in such moving terms that even Ernest Hamel, a strict partisan of the Jacobins and Louis Blanc, expressed his admiration (*HR*, 2:1164).

There are, however, a number of issues on which Michelet refuses to compromise. Repeatedly he contrasts "the moral Revolution" with the "brutal" one, which is that of Robespierre (*HR*, 2:376, 388). He also objects vigorously to the cult of the Supreme Being. Michelet sees it as a palliative to the church, a betrayal of the faith of the *philosophes*, which compromises the revolutionary vision.[34] Most important is the objection to the Reign of Terror. Those who killed Clootz, Chaumette, Danton, Desmoulin, and Philippeaux have earned the gratitude of kings, shouts Michelet (*HR*, 2:445, 794). Elsewhere he asks: "Who brought us the Revolution? Voltaire and Rousseau . . . , who began the Revolution? Mirabeau . . . , who spoiled the Revolution? Marat and Robespierre" (*HR*, 1:283). Our historian believes that the "classical" Revolution failed because of Robespierre (*HR*, 2:982). Ever more "catlike," he set up a tyranny which prepared the way for Napoleon, while the idealism of the *philosophes*, the true and permanent Revolution, lives on and continues to inspire us (*vivifie, HR*, 2:623).

When Michelet takes stock, he finds a number of outstanding contributions of the Revolution, none due to Robespierre: the Code of Law (code civil), land reform, standardization of weights and measures and of the calendar (while the Revolution lasted), the creation of museums—the Louvre and his beloved Museum of French Antiquities (A. Lenoir) which inspired his youth—and schools—from the elementary level to the Ecole Normale Supérieure and Polytechnique (HR, 2:402–3). The list excludes the Constitution of 1793 which, according to Michelet, created Robespierre's new aristocracy and enabled him to guillotine charity and decapitate France (HR, 1:302; 2:809).

Since Michelet saw France of revolutionary times as weak and poverty stricken—modern historians speak of a relative prosperity which enabled the people to know what they were lacking—he admires the almost miraculous accomplishment of the Revolution, the fact that it was able to stop the royalist coalition and create the unanimity of brotherhood, the "universal banquet" envisioned by Danton (HR, 2:807). This is Michelet's conclusion even though he realizes that internal dissensions took their toll. He outlines the difficulties of Kleber and Hoche in dealing with the government (HR, 2:580–83, 680–83) and is fully aware of Danton's shortcomings. He tells us how painful it was for him to describe the deals which justified Robespierre's charges against him. Still, Danton remains the man of compassion, the generous leader, as opposed to Robespierre, the cold-blooded legalist and authoritarian mind. The associates of Danton, Anacharsis Clootz and Fabre d'Eglantine, are idealized, as are a number of women, Mme. Roland and above all Lucile Desmoulins (HR, 2:802, 828), the purest of the victims of the guillotine.

The Revolution was sanctified by its martyrs, but Michelet did not honor every victim of the guillotine. He opposes extremists like Jacques Roux, Charles-Philippe Rousin, Jean-Baptiste Carrier, the "missionary of terror" known for his drownings in the Vendée, and above all Jacques-René Hébert, the editor of the periodical Père Duchesne. The vulgarity of this paper so shocked Michelet that he calls Hébert a vile dog, a Homer of the gutter (HR, 2:526–30). As a group, the extremists (enragés) and Hébertistes drew his ire for perverting the Revolution; this includes those who brought Robespierre to the guillotine, e.g., Billaud-Varenne, "terror personified," who first worked for Robespierre, then against him. On the other hand, a man like Chalier, the wealthy merchant of Lyons who believed in the Revolution and was put to death by the reaction, is honored as a hero; Michelet sees him as a visionary and a mystic, like so many men of Lyons (*HR*, 2:525), a surprising qualification (cf. that of Clootz, mystic spokesman for humanity). Here as elsewhere the critical comment of Gérard Walter is most helpful.

At times, incomplete documentation misleads our historian, at others it is his enthusiasm which seizes on certain details to the exclusion of others. There is, for example, reason to believe that Mme. Roland, pictured as an ideal of morality, preferred the guillotine to rejoining her husband, and that Charlotte Corday, whom Michelet describes as inspired by Rousseau—the historian's hatred of Marat makes her into a heroine—was too pious to have read him.[35] Both women are honored also in *The Women of the Revolution* (1854).

We find that Michelet was no infallible judge, but his sympathy, which at times leads him astray, also makes his account the most memorable of his century. Individual portraits are transfigured by his vision of the revolutionary ideal (Danton's "banquet"): "May this sublime vision that we had of [God] in this moment, in the solemn act of French fraternity, lift us all, author and readers, above the moral suffering of our time and restore in us a heroic spark of the fire which burned in the heart of our fathers" (*HR*, 1:609). He considers this process of resurrection so important because posterity all too easily forgets the past. A fragment, published by Athénais under the title "The Tombs of the Revolution" (*HR*, 2:992–96), describes how little remained of the heroes of those days. Their tombs were forgotten; a cabaret was erected on the cemetery grounds. Death is the haunting threat to the brotherhood of 1789, which must be preserved.

VIII   *The ideal society:* Le Banquet *(1854)*

Michelet was not given to utopian dreams. His situation in "exile"—he was now in Italy—hardly justified such hopes. Still, there remained the conviction that the Revolution, frustrated in 1794, in 1830, and again in 1848, could yet inspire the future. *The Banquet* was written at Nervi and Acqui (March to June, 1854) but published only posthumously and in adulterated form.[36] First Michelet examines the reality facing him, the small town of Nervi, just east of Genoa, poverty striken but administered by a mayor who dreams of redistributing communal lands. A law providing for this had been passed but remained inoperative, much like the ideals of 1789, which led to the guillotine and to Napoleon. Social harmony, we are told, can arise when we are willing to sacrifice, and so the local problem is transposed into the general sphere of economic reform. The mud baths he took at Acqui in June 1854 (*J*, 2:263–74) and to which Michelet attributes his recovery and spiritual renaissance, are not mentioned in the *Banquet,* but the idea of rebirth is everywhere implied.

This process of universalizing personal experience is applied also as he recalls his visits in Lyons. Again he speaks of the two elevations which represent opposing social views: Fourvières (with its cathedral) stands for the Christian tradition of submissiveness; Croix-Rousse (with its looms) for freedom and the need to progress beyond the poverty of the city's weavers. From such consideration of "material concerns" *(matérialité),* Michelet will derive "the joys of my soul." He is thinking of the apprentice slaving away at his task, but sustained by a dream: a new world will arise from present sufferings, just as the Roman Forum was built on the graves of the past, one containing an ever-bleeding head, a living symbol among so many of stone.[37]

Our historian rejects schemes of a "materialistic" reorganization of society, like those of Saint-Simon and Fourier, the regimentation of Fourier's phalansteries. He prefers to place his trust in his religion of social action which, it is surprising to learn, he claims to have adopted as early as 1831: "My starting point is indicated in my *Introduction to Universal History,* where I accuse the Middle Ages of having persecuted freedom and called it Satan. Our modern times gave it back its true name."[38] *The Banquet* calls for a faith that will change man's mind and spur him on in spite of the failures of the past and of present inadequacies. This doctrine is not unlike that of George Sand and Proudhon. Athénaïs believed that he had deferred publication because the book was too radical for the times. A more likely explanation is that Michelet was dissatisfied with his conclusion and preferred to return to writing history.

The answer to the question, How can we realize our new freedom and produce action, in the face of public apathy and widespread illiteracy? is at best vaguely suggested. Michelet calls for public festivals, patterned on the General Federation of 14 July 1790, and for books conceived for the widest possible audience, e.g., almanacs. He would like to develop a code of calls to action by the town bell. Once more we read of Roland, the giant bell of Ghent which called out in case of fire or attack (he had spoken of Roland in the course of 1839). He also considers that common action might be produced by songs like the *Chant du départ* [Song of Farewell]. All these are ways of creating solidarity, but we are surprised to find no mention of public education, no literacy campaigns. Does he assume that the masses will remain illiterate because his attempts to educate his maids (1843–1849) had remained fruitless? *The Banquet* is a lyrical book, inspired and hopeful, but it fails to develop a practical solution on a national scale. In that sense *The People* and the *Bible of Humanity* are equally open ended; they also envision reform only through the spirit.

In July 1854, after further travel in Italy, Michelet ended his exile. He established himself again in Paris, this time rue de l'Ouest,[39] to please Athénaïs, to resume the *History of France* where he had broken it off, and to write the story of the Renaissance. The return was a compromise with political realities which Edgar Quinet and Victor Hugo were unwilling to make, an accommodation for the sake of convenience perhaps, but also a means of writing more effectively. Let us recall Diderot who would not leave Paris, in spite of problems of censorship, feeling that he could not complete the *Encyclopédie* in any other location.

CHAPTER 5

From the Renaissance to Louis XIV

I *Renaissance and Reformation:* History of France, *volumes 7–8*

THREE days after settling in his Paris apartment, Michelet set out with unprecedented application to compose two new volumes of the *History of France*. He completed each in about five months. Volume 7, the Renaissance, appeared on 1 February, volume 8, the Reformation, on 16 July; this was two weeks before his daughter, Adèle, died of consumption, leaving Alfred with their two children, Jeanne (born 1851) and Camille (1854),[1] and with Uncle Narcisse. The worry and strain left the historian close to exhaustion, but as before, the answer to despair was work and "action."

The six volumes planned to take the account to 1789 became eleven. At that, there were thirty years to be covered by each, whereas the five years of the Revolution had been described in seven. This forced a considerable adjustment, especialy since half of the first volume was devoted to a restatement of method and principles. For this Michelet returned to the earliest Middle Ages, the simple but also heroic times when, as shown by the *Song of Roland*, there was no obstacle between the emperor and his people, and when Abelard's "logic and common sense," along with Bacon's "sensible chemistry," were on guard against superstition and "foolish alchemy" (*OC*, 7:52–58). There followed the triumph of "antinature," the "learned foolishness" of scholasticism, mocked by Rabelais (*OC*, 7:66). So convinced was Michelet of this regression that he cites the *Roman de la rose* [The Rose] only for its "platitudes" and Villon for his "sad gaieties" (*OC*, 7:55). Fortunately there were also indications of a new spirit, the welcome heresies which anticipate the Renaissance. They appear, sibyllike, among the Waldenses, in the "eternal gospel" of Joachim of Flores and in "the heroic gospel" of revolt against Rome: the slap administered by Nogaret to Pope

Boniface VIII, the doctrine of John Huss, the coming of Joan of Arc, still the Virgin but already Marianne *(la patrie)*.[2]

An essential event in this process of liberation was the invention of printing. The press, "that holy ark . . . , that sublime machine which consumes paper and puts out living thoughts" *(OC,* 7:203), was close to Michelet from his youth. He had celebrated its advent in the course of 1840 and again in *The People,* except that by 1846 Michelet was concerned that machines threaten the artisan. Now, in 1855, print appears as the great hope of universal education.[3] He admits that the printing press was to spread "theological absurdities," documents of superstition like Sprenger's *Hammer of Witches,* a guide for witch hunters,[4] but printing would above all serve freedom and discovery: men like Columbus, Copernicus, Luther.

The fundamental contrast—death in the Middle Ages, rebirth in the Renaissance—is applied to all branches of endeavor. Michelet has shed all remnants of sympathy for Gothic architecture, while Brunelleschi's neoclassicism seems "simple" and "natural." It is amusing to note that his masterpiece, the cathedral at Florence with its pointed arches, is considered Gothic. As often, Michelet's affections and judgments are all too categorical.

In the second part of volume 7 he studies the French discovery of the Italian Renaissance from Charles VIII to François I. It is a lively canvas in which French ambitions, e.g., the desire of Louis XII to retain Brittany by divorce and remarriage with Anne de Bretagne, mingle with papal politics. Cesare Borgia, son of Pope Alexander VI, brings Louis the much needed dispensation *(OC,* 7:159). There is the picture of Florence, friendly to France even though it loses control over Pisa, and the military leadership of Gaston de Foix, whose campaign seems to have the potential of Napoleon, only to be cut short by his death at Ravenna (1514). All along Michelet emphasizes culture: the humanism of Erasmus, "the Voltaire of that day" *(OC,* 7:178), a timid Lefèvre d'Etaples who bravely translates the New Testament *(OC,* 7:204), but above all Italian influence, and Michelangelo viewed as a prophet *(OC,* 7:205).

Michelet asks: Is there too much of Italy and of Europe in this history of France? and replies: No, for the interests of France are always at stake; his broad approach is European. He sees a vast conspiracy at work on the part of Austria, Spain, and even of England, in spite of the revolt of Henry VIII against Rome: it is a Catholic alliance against France and freedom. There is bitter irony in a brief sketch showing Louis XII, at fifty-two, marrying young

Henry's sister, age sixteen, already with a lover whom she rejoins the following year, when Louis dies (1514). Michelet does not even name this queen (Marie) and her lover (Suffolk); this heightens the satire; clearly such a marriage does not fit into the constellation of alliances.[5] Henceforth the protagonists will be François I and Emperor Charles V, and England will be hostile to France. Michelet's portrait of Charles was already singled out in the remarkable critique by H. Taine, just a few weeks after the volume appeared.[6]

A number of critics objected that Michelet was carried away by his imagination; even Taine was to speak of his "imagination of the heart," but by way of a tribute.[7] In order to meet such criticism, our historian emphasized, at the outset of volume 8, that he drew on important archives, such as the Granvelle papers, and that he showed the "material" reality of European politics, i.e., the power of gold at work, for he saw the Fuggers of Augsburg dominating the election of Charles V to be Holy Roman Emperor. Michelet is proud of distinguishing himself in this way from contemporary historians like Mignet (OC, 7:263) and, especially, from the "doctrinaire" school of Guizot; he proclaims its "collapse" in a startling passage which ends: "Step back, false scholars and false gods!" (OC, 7:468). The days of accommodation with Guizot are at an end; having lost his chair, our historian is free to speak out; but Guizot too had lost his influence and was in retirement in England. . . . For Michelet it was a matter of political commitment. His outcry must be understood as an enthusiastic endorsement of those he considered supporters of progress, i.e., those opposed to Hapsburg power and to its English associates. Against this power he welcomed not only Luther and the Reformation as allies, but even the Turks under Soliman. The attack on Vienna makes the sultan into "the savior of Europe," for he relieves the pressure on France. Those fostering links between France and the Turks were "damned" by the church, but they are Michelet's heroes (OC, 7:394, 451). He sees allies also in the Hungarians ruled by the emperor's brother, Ferdinand, for they appear to him as victims of Austrian power.

The lines are clearly drawn in black and white: Catholic Hapsburg policy threatens France. François I is captured at Pavia (1525), then forced to sign the ignominious treaties of Madrid (1526) and Cateau-Cambrésis (1559). Meanwhile Catholic Spain expels the Jews. There results the destruction of a whole people without parallel in history (OC, 7:271). Obscurantism rules, perpetrated by "batlike" minds whose wings, as Ulrich von Hutten put it, "threaten the light of day" (*OC*, 7:280).

On the side of freedom there is the Reformation. It is described at length, first in Germany, then in France. There are moving pages on Dürer's *Melancolia* and Luther's joy which encompasses Dürer's work (*OC*, 7:303–9). Michelet still struggles with what he considers Luther's paradox: his independence of action and his acceptance of divine grace as the only means of salvation. The historian repeats what he had said earlier, that Luther is part of the Augustinian tradition in Germany, beginning with Tauler, Suso, and Godescalc; nonetheless Luther appears as a moral force shielding the family from sellers of indulgences (*OC*, 7:313–14). Here Luther is welcome as an ally of the Renaissance humanists who battle antiquated practices in religion and politics, or aberrations in literature like the *Amadís* which has become the rage.[8]

Hapsburg mercenaries wreak destruction and sack Rome, while François I is a force for culture: he brings Leonardo da Vinci and Cellini to France (*OC*, 7:389, 436)! The triumph of the arts is fulfilled by Jean Goujon who produces the beautiful sculpture of Diane de Poitiers,[9] the impressive mistress of François's son, Henri II. Thus the French Renaissance incarnates progress, while Catholic power rests on Loyola's "machine of fanatic reaction," the Jesuits, opposed to creative thought, demanding only obedience, burrowing underground (*OC*, 7:442, 446, 467).

An interesting innovation is the importance Michelet attaches to health and medicine. In volume 7 he had commented on the spread of syphilis (*OC*, 7:142, 256); volume 8 shows the impact of the "terrible sickness" of François I on his politics (*OC*, 7:436). In his weakness he is no match for Hapsburg power and Fugger gold. The beginnings of the rule of Henri II were therefore ominous, even sinister (*OC*, 7:467). As we can see, there is no simple equation of France and progress, no constant advance of the forces of freedom, but a sustained, compassionate interest in its advance or failures. All this is expressed in original images which the reader cannot help but retain.

II *From Henri II to the wars of religion:*
History of France, *volumes 9–10 (1856)*

Another volume of the *History of France* and the first of Michelet's nature books were published in 1856; his production poured out at a frantic rate. Volume 9 of the *History* is dominated by the massacre of St. Bartholomew (1572). The rule of Henri II is its "sinister vestibule"; the rule of François II (1559–1560), controlled by the Guise family and "dead from Mary Stuart", his wife (*HF*, 3:403), a misguided interlude. Mary wore him down not only by her personality, but as the willing tool of her uncles, François, duc de Guise, and Charles, duc de Lorraine. They ruled François except during an initial spell when the queen mother, Catherine de Médicis, recalled the trusted advisor of Henri II, the Connétable de Montmorency, but soon the house of Guise gained control of Catherine as well; it became the center of power during her regency for Charles IX, who was ten years old when François II died (*HF*, 3:427). Later it was the turn of the "crazy" Charles IX himself; he staged the massacre, which is described in extensive detail (*HF*, 3:338–79).

It is merely the culmination of the violence Michelet finds throughout Europe. He sees the Protestants as martyrs, simple followers of primitive Christianity, helpless victims of evil forces like Emperor Charles V, an Attila, a Nebuchadnezzar (*HF*, 3:350, 363). By comparison Calvin is gentle; his burning Servetus does not erase the historian's sympathy (*HF*, 3:358–59, 496–97). In France, the Protestants were particularly vulnerable; they were misunderstood; their attitude toward the king seemed ambiguous (*HF*, 3:352). The Guises opposed them everywhere they could. They killed the king of Navarre whose wife, Jeanne, was a Protestant; at Vassy they massacred a large group. Allied to Philip II of Spain, they seem particularly hateful to our historian for "thus begins the Spanish role in France" (*HF*, 3:352, 387, 417–19). Eventually there remained only two Protestant leaders, Condé and Coligny, both related to the house of Bourbon of the future Henri IV, but Condé was killed in 1569, while Coligny perished three years later during the massacre.

Coligny is Michelet's hero. His loyalty to the king is noble and unquestioned (*HF*, 3:322, 331). The historian feels equal sympathy for Ramus, another victim of the night of St. Bartholomew, already extolled in the course of 1851. With grotesque irony we are told how the narrow-minded Charpentier bought a chair of mathematics at the Collège de France, for which he had "the solid preparation of knowing neither Greek nor mathematics." Charpentier then organized the persecution of his colleague, Ramus, who was stabbed, thrown from a window, and killed for having challenged Aristotle's authority: since Copernicus it was evident how dangerous such challenges could be "to the ancient darkness" (*HF*, 3:473–74). In 1572 man's inhumanity to man reached a climax.

Volume 10 traces the aftermath, the war of the League against Henri III, continued violence until the crowning of Henri IV. Michelet does his best to untangle the complex interplay of forces. He feels the tragedy of these struggles. In a futile attempt to control the League, Charles IX has Henri, duc de Guise, assassinated while Henri is his guest at Blois. Soon thereafter Charles dies. His successor and brother, Henri III, is killed by the mad monk, Jacques Clément. It takes two more years of war before Henri IV can enter Paris by accepting Catholicism, and conclude peace: the treaty of Vervins with Spain and the Edict of Nantes for religious tolerance are its monuments, but hardly satisfying ones for our historian. He sees Vervins as accomplishing nothing more than Cateau-Cambrésis had forty years earlier, and finds that the Edict of Nantes accorded Protestants fewer privileges than they held under Charles IX and Henri III. In fact, Michelet minimizes the Protestant aspect of Henri IV, especially when he shows the king getting rid of the Protestant leader, Philippe de Mornay, by letting him argue theology at Saumur (*HF*, 4:57, 68).

For good measure, Michelet includes the death of Mary Stuart (1587), showing her ambitions, her deceit. He feels that the widespread sympathy for her is due to the fact that she is a woman; it led Schiller to contradict his own ideals of justice and freedom as he presents her on the stage (*HF*, 3:540). Is there no respite in all this violence? There is a chapter which honors women; another is devoted to science, to the physician, Paracelsus,[10] the first to realize natural cures (*HF*, 3:495); but it is little consolation: "How heavy is this history! and why is it that the spirit of the sixteenth century, which so recently stirred me on to write my Renaissance, has suddenly abandoned me? . . . It is because I have faithfully followed this terrible century. . . . I sank too deep into its carnage. I was part of it and lived only from blood" (*HF*, 3:494). Michelet's exasperation with the turn of events is clear, but he will not succumb; he will not condone the *fait accompli* or injustice. He will oppose any "philosophy of history" which derives its ethics from the course of events, any accommodating fatalism:

I declare that this history is not impartial! It does not preserve a cautious and prudent balance between good and evil. On the contrary, it is frankly and vigorously partial; it favors man's right and the truth. . . .

So, no accommodation, no compromise, no willingness to bend right to the fact or to tame the fact and bring it into accord with the right. I do not deny that in the course of centuries and in the total view of humanity, fact and right tend to coincide, but those who introduce that fatal opium called "philosophy of history" into individual situations of the past, into the struggles of the world, and accept an unjust peace, place death into life, kill history and ethics, and cause the spirit, turned indifferent, to ask: What is evil, what is good?

I have stated the moral foundation of my work. (*HF*, 4:70–71)

This is the eloquent conclusion to so much violence. It could only perpetuate injustice and extend it into the Thirty Years' War. The people were its victims; the evil power of Spain plunged France into misery (*HF*, 4:66, 77).

Michelet appends explanatory notes which, he adds, could have made up an entire volume (*HF*, 4:77), again to counter critics who praise only his imagination. Of course he used documents; but what strikes the reader is the vibrant tone, the sympathy for suffering. He speaks for the Protestants, not because he espouses their theology, but to defend their freedom. Its cause is defeated many times but he will not despair. Here his pages on Montaigne are revealing. He finds undeniable greatness but also an excess of individualism, insufficient commitment. Montaigne did not act at the time of the massacre; when the plague hit Bordeaux, he withdrew. Besides, his broad spectrum of doubt, his fideism, i.e., the acceptance of established religion which appealed to Pascal, stand in stark contrast to Michelet's ideals (*HF*, 4:54–56). Our historian is a believer in reason, but also in society, and in the eternal gospel outside and beyond the church.

III   *From the Edict of Nantes to the siege of La Rochelle:* History of France, *volume 11 (1857)*

What better way to prove that his was not a traditional kind of history of kings than to break off the volumes at events more important than their succession or biographies. The tenth volume ends with the Edict of Nantes (1598), the eleventh with the reduction of La Rochelle, the base of Protestant power (1628). The decline of the Protestants clears the way for absolutism, a disheartening development after the great hopes of the Renaissance and Reformation.

Nonetheless the account emphasizes royal affairs. Michelet shows Henri IV first inspired by Gabrielle d'Estrée—she soon dies, probably poisoned—then by Henriette d'Entragues to whom he promises marriage; only considerations of money and influence force him to marry Marie de Médicis, daughter of a duke called "the maker of popes"; all this, our historian adds, "as if in punishment for Henri's ingratitude toward Italy" (*HF*, 4:103), for her first wish will be the return of the Jesuits to France. Jesuit power is described in all its unlikely detail. La Varenne gets the king to found their Collège at La Flèche. Possevino, whom we have found as the power behind St. François de Sales in *The Priest*, makes his presence felt (*HF*, 4:101–3, 119–22). The reader is left with the vivid impression of a decline of freedom. Henri is lucky only in uncovering the plot of Biron; with biting irony Michelet tells us that it would have restored "the great days of the League when dead rats sold for twenty-four pounds each and when mothers ate their children" (*HF*, 4:116).

The black humor continues as we find the royal confessor preparing his questions for witch trials, or when the sinister Ravaillac, the king's assassin, is compared to Rabelais's *Chicanous* or furry cats (*chats fourrés*, *HF*, 4:125, 143). The historian is convinced that Ravaillac was part of a conspiracy. He describes his last days in every detail, right to the quartering of his body, while the young Louis XIII dines in luxury and accepts the regency of his mother, Marie de Médicis (*HF*, 4:151–53).

Michelet's conclusion: Henri was a great king, but his last years were dominated by two gigantic plots, his plot to save Europe from Catholic Hapsburg power, and the plot of an important group of courtiers to kill him. As for the famous plan for European peace, it is found in Sully's *Memoirs* more than in Henri (*HF*, 4:133, 138), so all revolves around Catholic influence.

Decline follows decline. First the "double Spanish marriage"; characteristically we must wait for the details: Louis XIII is married to Anne of Austria, daughter of Philip III of Spain, while Elisabeth of France marries the future Philip IV (*HF*, 4:149, 166). By way of literary parallels, there is the "boring" *Astrée*, all too close to that Spanish aberration, the *Amadís* (*HF*, 4:137). The pedantic Ronsard still has some lyrical qualities, but soon his place is taken by a non-entity, Malherbe. Michelet asserts his lack of appreciation with belligerence and adds: Sainte-Beuve, Cousin, and Ranke misjudged these developments because they study only individual detail, i.e., they do not subordinate their appraisals to an evaluation of basic trends, in this case, to the realization of nefarious Spanish influence: "I like the microscope and I make use of it [but] in history it has its dangers. It makes the organic cultures and mold it observes seem like high forests; it suggests that a tiny insect . . . has the size of the Alps" (*HF*, 4:171). Michelet will not be distracted from the grand sweep of decadence. His literary comments make sense only in this context. Malherbe is but an example of tyrannical power taking hold. Had 1614 not seen the last convocation of the Estates General? No others were to occur before the French Revolution (*HF*, 4:159). At that, all the Estates accomplished was to frighten the nobility, for it was proposed to abolish the right to sell or inherit positions of privilege *(la vénalité des charges)*. This threat seemed so horrid that major struggles broke out. Concini was assassinated (1617) with the knowledge of Luynes, the king's favorite, and even of the king himself. After 1614 only the clergy was organized enough to make its power felt (*HF*, 4:165, 167).

Richelieu centralized France but this was all for the worse. He stands accused of duplicity: in Germany he supported the Protestants, at La Rochelle he laid siege.[11] Michelet makes the charge in spite of his sympathy for the Protestants in the Thirty Years' War: the volume ends with an invocation to Gustavus Adolphus without whom there would be no hope; he is seen as one of the two great men of the century; the other is Galileo (*HF*, 4:236, 274). So incensed is our historian at Richelieu, that he will not approve of any of his policies and turns to satire. French Protestants were accused of three great faults by the Catholic majority: they were not adulterers; they had public spirit; they realized that Spain ruled France. If you want to find out nothing about Richelieu's role in all this, read his *Memoirs* (*HF*, 4:198, 205)!

Everywhere morality seems to disintegrate except among the Protestants. Michelet sees no virtue among the nobles and the clergy, while the bourgeois describe themselves in *Reynard the Fox*. As to the lower classes, they remain without rights. Their hope, to assert themselves by "association" or in groups of kinship, is unrealized; they are given to witchcraft. Is it not natural to turn to Satan if one is excluded from society and God's church? Sprenger's recipe for identifying witches, his *Hammer of Witches,* is studied; so is perversion in convent life, the trial of Gauffridi, burned at the stake, on the testimony of nuns who saw Satan in him and then went on to accuse others (*HF*, 4:175–96). Much of this, often word for word, will reappear in *Satanism and Witchcraft*.

Among the contributing causes of such decadence, Michelet identifies the rule of money, tobacco, and alcohol (*HF*, 4:178–79), forces undermining society as much as "the libidinous tyranny" of priests who thrive on sorcery, on the Sabbath (*HF* 4:168–74). What hope was there for life and children when women were buried in convents and thus given to death? Michelet set out to prove the moral agony of France; he made it strikingly clear.

IV *The turn to absolutism:* History of France, *volume 12 (1858)*

Barbarous times like those of the Thirty Years' War must be told "barbarously." Unlike Schiller and Ranke, Michelet will not be impartial but proceeds to set the record straight. Germany was a "monstrous market of men" (*HF*, 4:243–45). A remarkable series of images points to the "hypocrisy" of Hapsburg troops; 40,000 died when Tilly sacked and burned Magdeburg (*HF*, 4:277)!

How could France lead Europe in the face of such chaos, directed as it was by "two invalids," Louis XIII, lost without Richelieu, and Richelieu who would not last two days without his king? (*HF*, 4:249–50) At home they were trying to establish their authority, abroad they aimed at a balance of power by supporting the opposition to the Hapsburgs, to Tilly and Wallenstein (*HF*, 4:288). The home front especially was complex. With sarcasm Michelet describes how the Catholic victory at La Rochelle was celebrated by a pagan triumph in Paris (*HF*, 4:247). The hardest part was to deal with Monsieur, the king's brother,[12] whom no one could trust, especially after he married Mlle. de Montpensier (*HF* 4:264). The queen, Anne of Austria, was scheming with Monsieur, but also with the duke of Lorraine and with her brother, the king of Spain (*HF*, 4:272, 310); and then there was the "court," constantly hostile to both the king and Richelieu.

When Gustavus Adolphus died, Richelieu shifted his support to Bernhard of Saxen Weimar, the new commander of the Protestant armies, but French money did not buy the desired control. Bernhard seized Breisach for himself rather than for France and became an enemy in Michelet's view,[13] but then all of Richelieu's enemies died in good time. With bemused fascination Michelet follows Richelieu's successes. The greatest of these, he tells us, was the birth of Louis XIV, for it insured that Monsieur would not rule, for Monsieur would have been a burden to France, another king as incapable as Henri III (*HF*, 4:314–17). Meanwhile the French people continued in misery and superstition: witness the "Spanish invasion" of the Carmelites and the sorcery trials at Loudun.[14]

After Louis XIII and Richelieu die, French troops win great victories at Rocroi, Nordlingen, and Lens. They pave the way for the Treaty of Westphalia (1648), but victory also leads to misfortune. Condé, the winner at Rocroi, develops an insatiable taste for glory and joins the Fronde, the insurrection of the nobility which puts the king's rule to its severest test (*HF*, 4:343, 349). The queen mother has to rely on Mazarin to defend the crown, and Mazarin is a rogue *(Mascarille)*, so "honest" *(désintéressé)* that he is soon wealthy enough to mount a private army (*HF*, 4:345). The historian waxes bitter in dealing with this "burlesque character" who first distinguishes himself by negotiating the Treaty of Casale, favorable to the enemy (*HF*, 4:266). He was justly ridiculed in the *Mazarinades*. In their "articulate rationalism" (i.e., satire) these appear as the ancestors of the modern press. Michelet even believes that they inspired Scarron's *Comic Novel*, the *Provincial Letters* by Pascal, Molière's *Tartuffe*, and Voltaire (*HF*, 4:393–94).

"The rule of Mazarin" created a centralized state but our historian remains unimpressed. All was accomplished by payoffs and bribes. Worse yet, Mazarin reversed the policy of Henri IV and Richelieu by integrating France into the Catholic alliance. He fought the Dutch and thus strengthened England (*HF*, 4:388–89)! What could be worse in the eyes of an anglophobe like Michelet? He cites memoirs and archives; he is widely read; but his account is notable above all for the vehemence of his opinions, especially his opposition to Hapsburg power. Readers could remain no more impartial than the historian; they followed him with enthusiasm or were offended in their intimate beliefs. This is evident from the critical reactions of this period.

CHAPTER 6

Of Love and Nature

I   *The principle of life:* L'Oiseau *(1856) and* L'Insecte *(1857)*

THE nature studies represent not only a return to the wider
public Michelet felt called upon to serve, but also an association
with Athénaïs who wanted to collaborate with him more closely. A
number of sections are indeed attributed to her,[1] though not as
many as she had hoped, and more carefully corrected by her husband than she wished. Even so their work in common was symbolic.
It is inspired by the dominant theme of love as a creative force in
the mystery of life and death.

It is precisely the search for "the source of all life" in the face of
the impending death of Mme. Dumesnil (1842), that had prompted
the historian to investigate the "unity" of nature as well as its "transformations" (i.e., evolution), and to seek out Isidore Geoffroy Saint-
Hilaire, a member of the Museum of Natural History (at the Jardin
des Plantes) since 1824, and in 1840 successor to the chair in zoology
of his famous father, Etienne. The friendship with Isidore, begun
in 1841, was to last to the scientist's death (1861). It was in discussions with him and his wife that Michelet first affirmed that he saw
nothing contrary to religion in the "transformations" of life, in scientific determinism.[2] His newfound interest in the lower forms of
life and their development led him to the *Encyclopédie nouvelle*
[New Encyclopedia] by Leroux and Reynaud, to articles such as
Animal and *Cetacean*, but also to the all important *Earth* and *Heaven*
(Terre et *Ciel)* which were to form the title of Reynaud's book on
the philosophy of religion and nature. It had much in common with
the views of Michelet.[3]

His bond with nature was reinforced by an almost mystical experience of renewal while taking mud baths at Acqui in June 1854
(*J*, 2:263–74). After the harrowing loss of his teaching position and
the frantic writing "in exile" at Nantes, then in Italy, the enforced

inactivity of the baths enabled him to recover his strength. "Perhaps for the first time in my life" I am completely immobilized, he explains to his son-in-law, Alfred (*J*, 2:746), and this, as much as his communion with mother earth (*terra mater, J*, 2:269) caused his regeneration. The exhausting baths stopped his "excessive application to work" (*J*, 2:272). He alludes to the experience only briefly in *L'Oiseau* [The Bird] (*OI*, xlviii), but confides more in *The Mountain*, where one chapter is devoted to La Bollante, the spring at Acqui, and to the "marriage between myself and nature" which, he says, is responsible not only for *The Bird* and *The Insect*, but for his view of the Renaissance (1855) as well (*MO*, 114–15). He conceived a grand parallel between his own renewal, metamorphosis in nature—the universal cycles of life and death—and the rebirth of humanism.

Michelet sees man ever present.[4] His view of nature is man-centered, and he feels that birds described by his friend, Alphonse Toussenel, are all alone; our historian studies animals in the company of man. This creates constant comparisons and parallels. The bird is seen rising like man's aspiring spirit, while "man wants to be . . . a winged god" (*OI*, 30). Michelet does his best to consider "sinister" birds of prey in the overall harmony of nature, but we sense his horror at their cruelty; he cannot help applying Lavater's physiognomy to them and sees criminal tendencies in their flattened foreheads (*OI*, 108–9). "Yes, ours is a barbarous world, dependent . . . on night, hunger, death, and fear" (*OI*, 105); but soon admiration recaptures his imagination as he describes the fly-catcher bird chasing eagles and hawks (*OI*, 112).

There is a good deal of accurate observation based on extensive reading and frequent visits to the Museum of Natural History.[5] Wings fascinate and inspire him. His favorite poem by Rückert, "Die Flügel, die Flügel"[6] ("wings, wings"), is his motto, and when he discusses the frigate bird, powerful in the air with his large wingspan, but awkward on land like Baudelaire's albatross, he evokes "the triumph of the wing" (*OI*, 45–49), even though the imbalance creates problems: the frigate bird may have to steal food for his young from the gannet, to seize it without landing on the ground (*OI*, 52). He wonders why penguins' wings do not support them (*OI*, 16); he admires the condor who puts the strongest quadruped to shame (*OI*, 29); he retraces the history of the heron from the augurs of antiquity to its medieval glory as a princely bird. He reads widely and quotes Alexander Wilson on the herons of America, Levaillant on tropical birds (*OI*, 71–74, 77).

The first part of *The Bird* studies the life span and habits of the birds; the second is more philosophical and contrasts such matters as the sublime freedom of flight with the servitude of the stomach or the need to sleep, which explain behavior (*OI*, 131). Michelet waxes lyrical when he contemplates bird instinct and migration. He presents them in a search for light and life. The most important comments are saved for the end: the function of birds in the economy of nature, the woodpecker eating worms (*OI*, 181), the starling protecting corn, the sparrow helpful to man by pursuing insects even when he pillages some seed (*OI*, 170). Finally Michelet studies his favorites, the lark, almost human as it watches the first attempts at flight of its young (*OI*, 238), and the nightingale. Its song says, as Romeo and Juliet might have: "It is not dawn as yet!" (*OI*, 264). He notes the emotions of his pet robin, the jealousy aroused when Toussenel brings him a nightingale (*OI*, 260). The poetry of *The Bird* inspired Walt Whitman![7]

Here as in the other nature books Michelet stresses Lamarck's transformational views as applied by Etienne Geoffroy Saint-Hilaire: the progression of the species. He opposes Cuvier's "fixed" classifications. Starting from the life cycle, he develops a theory of constant renewal and transformation—he calls it metamorphosis—a concept close to the modern term "evolution." Here lay the secret of eternal life.[8] The word "evolution" was not used by Michelet and his contemporaries because it was tied to Bonnet's "unfolding" of preexisting species, a concept developed to reconcile the single act of biblical creation with their gradual appearance. Only later, through geology and the work of Lyell,[9] did "evolution" come into general scientific use. Charles Darwin avoided it in the first five editions of *The Origin of Species*. Michelet read the book after it appeared in French translation (1862); he even corresponded briefly with Darwin.

The Bird was a tremendous success, with seven editions in four years. *The Insect* did just about as well.[10] It is even more dramatic in its presentation, not only because insects suddenly appear in swarms, but because their social organization lends itself to startling comparisons, e.g., with the warfare of man. Many of Michelet's observations were made firsthand, in the forest of Fontainebleau in June 1857 (*J*, 2:329–35). One day he approaches a tree trunk, dead to all appearances, but suddenly it swarms with thousands of woodworms (*IN*, xix)! Insects may be infinitely small, but they are capable of astounding tasks: they build coral reefs (*IN*, 34); one female termite reproduces at the rate of sixty a minute; termites are able to destroy a large table, or even the seaport of La Rochelle (*IN*, 237–40).

The transformations of insects are surprising. The larva (e.g., the caterpillar) becomes pupa (chrysalis) and eventually takes on the shape of the adult animal (the butterfly). How does the beauty of the butterfly arise from the unappealing chrysalis? Is the human embryo not a chrysalis?[11] Michelet speculates about the almost infinite number of species but adds that, should even one type of ant become extinct, it would be missed in the economy of nature (*IN*, 11). This is a strange statement since he generally accepts the creation or death of species. The "economy" implies a universal harmony and "useful" function of each creature; e.g., bees are needed to fertilize plants, "chaste, hard-working bees producing thousands of marriages" (*IN*, 248, 321). This example may seem more acceptable than one involving Chinese silk worms: Michelet hopes they will multiply to provide plentiful and inexpensive cloth for the masses (*IN*, 179).

He relates every creature to man, speaks of the soul of an insect, and perceives human qualities even in small beetles (*IN*, 124). One of the most extraordinary chapters involves the psychology of the spider, that great "loner" whose weaving is ruled by hunger and fear. It would not dare attack a fly outside of its net. The spider is an artisan by necessity, constantly intent on catching some prey, twice as hard at work when its net has been destroyed. Somehow, in spite of its habitual loneliness, the spider seems attracted to man. Michelet looks upon the spider that shares his room as a companion. He is sure it is attracted by music (*IN*, 223–24).

A final section is devoted to insects living in societies. This "human" characteristic seems to raise them in the scale of creation. Wasps are described as living in a warrior republic, forced as they are by their short life to be aggressive in seeking food; a kind of Sparta which Michelet distinguishes from the Athens of the bees, far more democratic, for the queen bee does not rule. She is a focus, an object of adoration; she can become a leader when the swarm founds a new republic—or should we say, a constitutional monarchy? She does not dominate the workers (*IN*, 129–31).

The society of ants poses a problem, for Michelet has observed an unexpected case of slavery. A species of large red ants have forced small black ones to work for them and feed them. They even enslave an additional three hundred black ants to add to their domain, until, one day of revenge, the tables are turned. Groups of six small black ants overcome one of their tyrants, while the other large reds run about senselessly. In spite of their strength, they show no sign of intelligence or organization (*IN*, 263–80). The account is a masterpiece, told with all the excitement of the battle of Agincourt, where light British archers vanquished French knights in armor, or of the light infantry of Gustavus Adolphus defeating their heavy opponents.

A first note, appended to the text, would define the meaning of the volume (*IN*, 357–74). It speaks of universal love and motherhood. Even the tiniest of creatures has a soul, it asserts. As always Michelet is open to scientific discovery. He celebrates Swammerdam, the Galileo of biology; he admires Mlle. Merian, a lady of German origin who studied and admirably drew the insects of Surinam. This ought to indicate that Michelet recognizes women's talent for science, but actually he remains unconvinced. In spite of Athénaïs, or perhaps because of her, he explains: "By its terrifying aspects, science seems more and more closed to women" (*IN*, 400). It offends the maternal instinct, love, and tenderness. How could women be ready to observe creatures that slaughter one another?

A final tribute goes to François Huber[12] who studied the bees, and to his son, Pierre, author of a *History of the Ants* (1810), worthy scientists who shared his own dual approach to nature, through matter and through the spirit. Michelet adds that his book begins and ends with the realization that insects have personality, that a keen observer would never consider them as mere objects; they live, they "will, work, and love" (*IN*, 481).

II   *Woman and the family:* L'Amour *(1858)* *and* La Femme *(1859)*

Michelet's two books on women are basically conservative; they aim to strengthen the moral fiber of the nation; but they also assess the social situation and radically break out of their staid and moral framework. The historian feels for society: "I have tears in my heart and for many a reason. I did not return unscathed when, ever so often in history, I crossed the Styx, the river of the dead. I am not insensitive to my times and feel their mortal wounds" (*AM*, 256).

He sees so many women suffer that there are moments when he is ashamed of being a man.

The point of departure is that of science. Many years of marriage and keen observation are supplemented by a long-standing interest in biology and related fields. The studies of Geoffroy Saint-Hilaire, father and son, the readings in preparation for the previous nature books, his particular concern for medicine and anatomy, provided a solid base, though the limitations of science in his day will, as we shall see, lead to some strange conclusions. Many doctors were among his close friends, from W. F. Edwards who influenced his early ideas of race, to the men consulted during Mme. Dumesnil's illness, including the famous homeopath, Samuel Hahnemann.[13] Charles Philippe Robin was the personal physician of Athénaïs, a friend, the author of a study of ovology.[14] The chemist, Marcellin Berthelot, had a close relationship with Michelet from his early days as an assistant at the Collège de France, and two anatomists, Antoine Serres and Louis Anzou, were his friends and often consulted. He attended their courses in 1845–1847 and in 1856.[15] Serres, in particular, was a trusted advisor. He made him aware of the tragedy of many marriages: "Alas, procreation so often takes place without love" (J, 1:401).

Michelet was fascinated with problems of reproduction, read widely in the field and, above all, observed the physical functions of Athénaïs with astounding assiduity. The *Journal* contains regular entries over many years. He even advises young husbands to keep just such a diary (*AM*, 159). It was his conclusion, inspired largely by Athénaïs's hypochondria, that woman is "wounded" one week out of four (*AM*, 49–51) and therefore unable to hold a regular job or pursue a profession. Consequently he defines the ideal couple as one where the husband is twelve years older than his wife because he will have to provide for both. Normally a man of thirty will marry a girl aged eighteen. He does cite Molière's *The School for Wives* to show that a great disparity of ages (like his own) rarely succeeds, but the twelve years in question are not considered a disparity.

Under these assumptions, the wife can contribute to society only in the home (*FE*, 34–37, 52), and even there her husband will be her guide. Being more mature, he will initiate her, "create" her, and finally "possess" her.[16] In *Woman* he adds that she will reciprocate and "create her creator" (*FE*, 330), even rule over him (*FE*, 278; cf. *AM*, 236), but the immediate task of enlightenment after marriage is the husband's. He must explain the risks of childbirth before she "dies for him" (*AM*, 161, 195–96). This could become the literal truth, for the odds at childbirth were not good and what constituted the possible sacrifice of her life had to be undertaken knowingly (*FE*, 548). Yves-Jean-Lazare died in his eighth week; in many similar cases the wife died as well.

Thus experience and psychology seemed to indicate that woman was infinitely vulnerable. To us this implies a double standard, even the physical inferiority of woman. Michelet did not realize this. He exclaimed: "Don't speak to me of the equality of the sexes; woman is superior" (*AM*, 174), but his idea of the "intellectual and moral fertilization" of woman by man does not allow her much initiative (*AM*, 166, 178). Furthermore, a number of "scientific" theories supported this double standard. The larger size of man's brain, proportionate to his overall size, was taken to indicate intellectual superiority. Examination of the brain during autopsy also produced strange conclusions. It was believed that a visual inspection could discover alienation and insanity; the brain could even resemble the person's face (*FE*, 56–57). A more amusing error of Michelet's physiology was his recommendation that, to avoid bleeding and immediate pregnancy, girls marry ten days after a period. Nineteenth-century science did not realize that this schedules the wedding night during the most fertile period, and such was hardly the intent in view of the dangers of childbirth.[17]

Telegony, the view that a pregnancy affects all future offspring, was another stumbling block. An Arabian mare that had mated with a donkey could no longer produce purebreds (*AM*, 326, 450–51) and a lover who has a child with a married woman will find that this child resembles her husband. Michelet applied this theory to a child of Louis XIV and Mme. de Montespan. The grotesque conclusion again leads to a double standard. In adultery both parties are guilty, but the act of the wife is infinitely more serious since she endangers all future offspring (*AM*, 318, 326). Michelet proposes a medical jury to determine her guilt; if she is convicted, emigration is the best way out (*AM*, 291–93; *FE*, 65). A radical solution is needed if woman becomes "mobile" as opposed to "fixed" in marriage. Of course this applies only to women! Telegony supports a fierce double standard.

We cannot hold Michelet responsible for the inadequacy of contemporary science; we must, on the contrary, recognize his progressive view of marriage. It must be a true partnership, for only in this way can love withstand the inevitable strains, e.g., when the husband feels that he is competing with the children for his wife's

affection, or later when love must overcome the problems of aging
(*AM*, 381). Widowhood is described in a special chapter. In the face
of death, love and faith in the immortal soul will be the consolation.
Here Michelet draws on Jean Reynaud, still cited with enthusiasm,
especially his articles *Earth* and *Heaven*.[18] The idea of immortality
is fundamental.

Michelet is most original when he considers the pleasures of love,
when he observes that the intimacy of the couple will transform
what shamed or scared woman into a source of happiness, when he
affirms that solace can be sought in love which is "the best narcotic,"
far stronger than tobacco or alcohol (*AM*, 348, 353). Is he not close
to admitting the unmentionable, sexual pleasure? Indeed, he protests against the Victorian environment which makes woman the
martyr of her shame (*AM*, 163). He realizes that there will be problems if man is violently attached to his desires and woman adamant
in her allegiance to her child (*AM*, 198), for "love is a thing of the
mind; every desire is first an idea" (*AM*, 431). Still, he is sure that
love can overcome such obstacles.

In *Love* he describes the ideal couple; in *Woman* he returns to
the sociological approach of *The People* and analyzes woman in society, especially the single woman in the hostile environment of
Paris. Machines have replaced her labor; in spinning and weaving
or as seamstresses they are so badly paid that many have been forced
into the streets, so much so that the number of registered prostitutes
has declined (*FE*, 30–33). If the single woman is educated, she can
become a governess, but she will be equally vulnerable, like the
heroine of a popular novel, *Une Position fausse* [An Awkward Situation, 1845], in which a young man abandons his sweetheart and
prefers the pickups in a dance hall (*FE*, 44–50). One young woman
called on Michelet for help in finding employment in Paris; he sent
her back to her home town, for there she could marry, be it in
limited circumstances, and did not have to face the hostility of the
big city (*FE*, 35–37). He paints a moving portrait of a working girl
in Paris, too sick to earn her way, who ends up in the grim coldness
of a hospital (*FE*, 60–63). Any home would be preferable to those
impersonal institutions (*AM*, 31).

An interesting section in *Woman* studies the child at two, five,
and ten, and brings out the essential sexuality even in the infant
(*FE*, 104). Here he points to Freud. Sex differences will lead to
misunderstandings while the seriousness of play can bring frustra-

tion, despair, and even death (*FE*, 111). Michelet recalls his own death wish; he will elaborate in *Our Sons*.

Many comments stem from Froebel and his disciple, Bertha von Marenholz, who won him over on her first visit in January 1859 (*J*, 2:459): the idea was that children learn through play; the kindergarten provides the freedom to learn without chaos (*FE*, 114, 214, 218). He welcomes Froebel's contribution, realizing that the education of girls had hardly progressed since Fénelon (*FE*, 99). In accord with Froebel, and Rousseau's *Emile*, he would stimulate the young by visits to the zoo of the Jardin des Plantes, by meaningful activities such as cooking or playing house, eventually by history (Plutarch) as a school for reason and the passions (*FE*, 160–75).

As for marriage, he shudders at the customary arrangement made by parents. He calls this "violation by contract" followed by thirty years of *ennui* so icy that it would freeze mercury (*FE*, 225). Instead, the mother must help her daughter find a suitable partner while letting her take the initiative. Even then will there be unpleasant surprises. Michelet smiles at a newlywed of seven days who is "already" in love with her husband (*FE*, 292). A strange extension of his practical advice into fantasy are comments on the beauty of exotic women: he recommends Haitians but hesitates before advising marriage with red Indians (*FE*, 213–15).

Finally there is a tribute to Carolina Jones who rehabilitated prostitutes in Australia and then campaigned for similar reforms in England (*FE*, 398–405). It is strange only to find, after all that has been said about immorality and prostitution, that Michelet objects to Balzac because he describes social decay (*FE*, 454–55). Michelet disapproves of such literature; he would not want to add to it, and yet he describes all the dangers (*AM*, 293); he even develops an explanation of *la papillonne* (flightiness), woman's need for a change,[19] and approves of *Indiana* by George Sand (*AM*, 275). The tragedy is that immorality seems to spread. In both his books Michelet quotes statistics to show that the number of marriages is declining (*AM*, 433; *FE*, 5–20), a trend which must be reversed if woman is to be creative and work for social harmony.

The present was grim. Ten thousand women were being committed to prisons each year in France alone (*FE*, 407). How was woman to reform and purify the nation? By being a model housewife. Michelet provides few answers beyond this. In a store she might associate herself with her husband; if he is an artist, she can inspire him. She might also develop her talents for medicine, an important theme in his book on witchcraft. Michelet emphasizes that both marriage and medicine begin with a confession; this makes woman adept at both. Or else she might devote herself to the young, orphans perhaps, whom she can guide (like Athénaïs later) and who will in turn console and inspire her. Even in old age she can derive joy from helping those who remain the hope of the future.

The most remarkable aspect of these two books is that love is presented in a physiological framework as part of the life cycle from birth to death. *Love* is structured to emphasize this; *Woman* adds: "One becomes a man by the firm manner of looking at life and death" (*FE*, 54). Difficulties must be sternly examined, problems accepted. Meanwhile the physical and the spiritual remain intertwined in the power of love; it provides the strength to face reality and hope for our immortal soul.

III   *Our evolving earth:* La Mer *(1861) and* La Montagne *(1868)*

Past success encouraged our historian to write two more nature books. The progress of evolutionary theory, most evident in *La Montagne* [The Mountain], added renewed interest. He prepared himself by travel as much as reading.[20] At St.-Georges, a small seaport near Royan (Charante), he witnessed the great storm of October 1859, a vivid memory also for Pierre Loti, then nine years old (*ME*, ix). *The Mountain* depicts man similarly pitted against danger in the Alps and in the Pyrenees. Michelet's admirable descriptions of the storm at St.-Georges, or of the glacier which swallows its victims and expels them at its base forty years later (*MO*, 34), set the tone. It is true that our historian never went to sea and, when he described the glacier "from close by," he was comfortably settled in a good hotel at Grindelwald (*MO*, 17). His poetic imagination makes up for it. As Pierre Loti said, it would be difficult to give a better account of the great storm.

He prepared his books with the greatest care, all the while sharing his studies with Athénaïs. To him they are important publications whatever their motivation: the satisfaction of pursuing his scientific interests, collaborating with his wife, or educating a wider public, in addition to obtaining the essential income these books provided. He composed them concurrently with the *History of France* and accorded them equal time. *The Mountain* was started as early as 1865 in the French Alps and Switzerland, and taken up there again in 1867.

He is attracted to nature also because it can be beneficial to us. He is enthusiastic about the new idea of bathing in the sea. Beach resorts were newly established. He speaks of their potential for restoring health, and mentions a doctor sending emaciated children from Florence to the Mediterranean.[21] Michelet advises the hardy to swim at Granville, the less strong at Arcachon and Royan. This is very much in line with his educational objectives, or what we might call the propagandistic nature of his popular books. In *The Mountain* (pt. 1, chaps. 8–9) he gratefully recalls how mother earth restored his own health with the waters of La Bollante, the mud baths he took at Acqui (1854). Like woman or the divine principle, nature is also an "initiation."

La Mer [The Sea] contains superb descriptions of the beauty and terror of the life-giving sea. Its salt is more fertile than the river Nile (*MO*, 19), but its force can be devastating to sailors bravely setting out to rescue others—and taking their casualties in stride— and when the waves howl like snouts of dogs (*ME*, 85–86). No wonder that legends arose of sea monsters, vastly exaggerated shapes of a shark or an octopus. The sea was the abyss for the Orient (*ME*, 3), Michelet tells us, as he recalls Odysseus, and Sinbad of the *Arabian Nights*.

The sea lives, not only because it threatens or restores to health, but as the habitat of an infinite variety of life, "the sea of milk,"[22] the viscous mass of microorganisms, most near the warmth of sunlight, many in the lower depths. Michelet is keenly aware that only the surface is well known, in the sea as on land (*ME*, 11; *MO*, 122). He tries to elucidate the progression from simple polyps and the medusa to crabs and shell fish protected by their armor (*ME*, 161–62, 207), and of mollusks, less protected but more agile, like the light infantry of Gustavus Adolphus (*ME*, 220). He illustrates the chain of being and implies the concept of evolution without using the term.[23] He assigns great importance to life in all its forms, but is most fascinated by the more complex inhabitants of the sea: fish with their shiny scales, seals, sea elephants, and above all the mammals, the whales and their customs; in their secluded mating grounds they join each other, but only by fighting since they lack sharks' hooks; they may rise above the water in their marriage dance like the two towers of Notre Dame (*ME*, 242). Michelet's account is startling, especially when he seems to accept sixteenth-century tales of sirens, of seamen and seawomen resembling humans who were destroyed as monsters by intolerant sailors (*ME*, 255–58). Man is often bent on destruction; this theme is illustrated also by the carnage perpetrated by harpooners in the mass killing of whales in recent times (*ME*, 328–29).

Michelet's nature is centered on man. The sea seems to serve his purposes as he discovers its channels and currents (*ME*, 31). There is progress in navigation and map making. Lighthouses are being established (*ME*, 50–52, 87). Above all, man is coming to grips with the sea itself. Speaking of Matthew Maury, the American sea captain and geographer, and his *Physical Geography of the Sea* (1855), he explains: "His book, so thoroughly honest and truthful, permits us easily to detect the internal struggle taking place between two states of mind: *biblical literalism* which represents the sea as a thing created by God at one moment, a machine revolving under his hand— and the modern sentiment, *sympathy with nature*, which looks upon the sea as a living, vital force, almost as a person, where the living soul of the world is engaged in a perpetual task of creation."[24] A religious philosophy of nature illuminates the discoveries of science and the "metamorphosis" (evolution) of nature.

The Mountain deals most directly with evolution. Michelet has read the *Systèmes des Montagnes* [Mountain Systems, 1852] by Elie de Beaumont and shares his opposition to the "fixed" categories of Cuvier. He has espoused the idea of gradual, constant change proposed in Lyell's *Principles of Geology*[25] and does his best to reconcile catastrophes, like the disappearance of Atlantis, with Lyell's gradualism. He speculates that volcanoes erupt "when they do not function well" and release excess pressure (*MO*, 166). He finds evidence also in the shape of mountains and rock layers, the result of violent convulsions and admits that " we must resort to many rationalizations before we can dismiss them and believe in slow, peaceful action," but he adds: "It is to be assumed that the *earth animal* has not undergone analogous cataclysms, and that its prolonged life has seen no abrupt and violent intervals."[26] His important conclusion is that nature's "revolutions" are a form of life, analogous to Vico's cycles in history (*MO*, 125). This makes Lyell's view of constant, gradual changes especially appealing to our historian. He joins further parallels:

These then are the two schools: the school of war, the school of peace. The latter is gaining ground. The principle of "peace at any price" which, through Cobden's exertions, prevails in the political relations of his country, seems to animate Lyell and Darwin. They suppress struggle in nature, and decree that the earth shall perform all her operations without violent excesses, that imperceptibly, through millions of centuries, she shall modify and transform herself.[27]

The radical English economist, Richard Cobden, devoted to free trade and disarmament, was largely responsible for the commercial treaty between England and France of 1860.[28] His role suggests analogies between evolution and commercial development which appeal to Michelet. At the same time he is able to reinterpret Darwin's survival of the fittest and reconcile it with the fundamental gradualism he postulates.[29]

In all this Michelet makes no claim to originality. In fact, he limits scientific data in his text and explains that additional citations of sources would confuse or distract the reader (*MO*, 367). What matters is not the detail, but the discovery of the sufficiency of nature, its beauty and peace. Such an appreciation can inspire a more judicious use of its resources. Michelet protests eloquently against deforestation—"valleys of death"—and the replacement of rare varieties of mountain forest with the common pine. Can we recoup such losses (*MO*, 355)? If we deplete rare and precious plants, we lose our rich fauna and sacrifice traditions and beauty.

The final salute to mother earth (*MO*, 363), to the regenerative forces in nature, adds a positive note. In *The Sea* he had called for international conventions to protect sea life; here he would replace the "enervating, sick literature of our time" by new hope (*MO*, 356).

CHAPTER 7

The Decline of the Ancien Régime

I   Louis XIV, the personal rule:
History of France, volume 13 (1860)

THE "grand epoch" of French classicism was close to Michelet's heart from his youth; he could not help but orient his account around its famous protagonists (*HF*, 4:396–97, 480). But what of the history of the people? of the cause of freedom? Michelet urges us to look behind the imposing machine of Marly, beyond the luster of the court, the king, and his "great machinist," Colbert. Without denying the period its greatness, Michelet finds the apogee of royal prerogative oriented toward the past. Louis buries a world (*HF*, 4:397–99, 480). This "pope of a king," looking for adulation, not free subjects (*HF*, 4:526), steeped the country in untold wars and perpetrated the "moral infamy" of revoking the Edict of Nantes (1685). This act, "toward which the entire century gravitates," is the very antithesis of the ideals of 1789, "a weighty reality, immense in material consequences, horrifying to ethics." This is why Michelet's preface calls for "dedicating our lives to truth" (*vitam impendere vero*)[1] and bravely standing up before such injustice as did those who emigrated after the Revocation (*HF*, 4:520). How is it, he asks, that other historians like Mignet cannot see this (*HF*, 4:468)? Louis made France the object of hate for all of Europe and allowed the torch of freedom to pass on from France to William of Orange who united Holland, then assumed power in England.

Michelet has pains admitting this even though his readings for the nature books (from Lyell, Darwin, etc.) have changed his attitude toward the British. He emphasizes how Parliament hesitated before recognizing William and adds in irony: they finally discovered that there ought to be a social contract between the prince and his people, for under that convert to Catholicism, James II, "tolerance" had meant only favoring Catholics and absolutism had prevailed

(*HF*, 4:536, 540). Besides, France did have a part in William's triumph: a valiant band of French Protestants fought for him from the landing at Torbay to the final victory at Boyne. How could Macauley fail to point this out? (*HF*, 4:539–47). The hope for freedom henceforth resided in the European alliance against Louis.

The king's wives and mistresses are a traditional subject Michelet could not resist. Not a word about the king's affection for the queen, Maria Theresa, but when her father, Philip IV of Spain came to die, she served Louis well: he could stake his claims to Hapsburg lands, to Flanders and the Franche Comté. Only the opening of the dikes saved Amsterdam and The Hague (*HF*, 4:462). For some time Louis is in love with Henriette of England, wife of Monsieur, his brother, who does not mind. Improving on Saint-Simon, Michelet describes the king's brother, as "that girl, all madeup, affected, flirty, called Monsieur" (*HF*, 4:414), and accepts the theory that one of Monsieur's male lovers poisoned Henriette when she triumphantly returned from England. She had concluded an alliance with her brother, Charles I, and her success was a threat (*HF*, 4:452). Louis also loved Mlle. de La Vallière. We are even to assume that at one point he stayed with the inaccessible Mme. de Montausier, "Julie" of the *Garland* (poems composed for her wedding after a long courtship) who was the governess of the royal children (*HF*, 4:437–38).

The king's "animal pleasure" (*HF*, 4:493) then turns to Mme. de Montespan. He pays her husband to leave her (*HF*, 4:447) and so she rules over him (*HF*, 4:475–76) until Mme. de Maintenon, the governess of their children, captures the king. Following the theory of telegony proposed in *Love*, the first child the king has with Mme. de Montespan resembles her husband![2] There follows Louis's "sinister" marriage to Mme. de Maintenon, inexorably tied to the Revocation of the Edict of Nantes in the mind of the historian; he is sure that, in violent reaction against her Protestant background, she confirms Louis in his resolve to abolish dissent (*HF*, 4:502).

The source of many of these intrigues is the remarkable letters of Elisabeth-Charlotte of the Palatinate, Monsieur's second wife, and the *Memoirs* of the Grande Mademoiselle, the duchesse de Montpensier (*HF*, 4:395), at odds with Louis ever since the Fronde, hostile because he rejected her marriage to Lauzun. Elisabeth-Charlotte, on the contrary, liked the king; he did not even mind her unusual forthrightness. The irony of events has it that after her brother died (1685), Louis claimed the succession of the Palatinate and invaded it ruthlessly (1688). It was the most inhuman act of destruction of his reign (*HF*, 4:542).

Intertwined with the account of the king's loves are comments on Molière; his plays are assumed to be inspired by them. Michelet recognizes Henriette in the *Princess of Elide* and in Eliane of the *Misanthrope;* in *Amphitryon* he sees the portrait of a liaison during the campaign in Flanders (*HF*, 4:429, 435). As the political situation deteriorates, the plays begin to show it: *The Miser* is grim, *Georges Dandin* painful, *Pourceaugnac* horrible (*HF*, 4:447). The historian forgets that these are comedies! He had done likewise for *The School for Wives*—"it mocks hell" (*HF*, 4:417)—and for *Don Juan*, saying that the play seals Fouquet in his tomb (*HF*, 4:422), for after the grand feast at Vaux, Louis, seized by jealousy, had Fouquet arrested and kept in prison until he died (*HF*, 4:407–9). Molière is made to play the role of a political satirist which he would never have dared assume. Michelet presents him much as he will Voltaire in the eighteenth century.[3] His commentary on Molière, who appears as a pensioner of the court and as its chronicler, is part of the critique of Louis XIV. The historian assumes that Molière knew the king intimately and adds that it would be senseless to compare Molière to Shakespeare, for Shakespeare did not live in Elizabeth's apartment (*HF*, 4:422)! Fortunately not all of Michelet's portrayals of literary figures are that politicized: Racine's *Phèdre* is "a heart that hates and wills her crime, filled with remorse and desire, the sensual regret of not being further in sin" (*HF*, 4:478).

Louis's principal assistant, Colbert, is judged like the king himself. Colbert may have contributed to order and law, built roads, and notably furthered colonial and naval policy, but all is vitiated by the methods of the regime: Colbert builds on the ruins of public ethics (*HF*, 4:443), he spreads the king's terror and ultimately adds to the misery of the people described by Boisguillebert (*HF*, 4:494, 496). Michelet includes a chapter on the depopulation of France and the declining marriage rates (*HF*, 4:444–45) described in *Woman*. There emerges an oddly negative portrait of Colbert: he began his career handling Mazarin's thefts, is the tool *(ouvrier)* of Louis's plans, and dies detested and damned (*HF*, 4:402, 440, 474).

Louvois appears in far more positive light because, if only for reasons of state, he opposed the *dragonnades* and only reluctantly agreed to the invasion of Ireland in support of James II to spite Mme. de Maintenon, who was so opposed to it. Indeed, our historian believes that she came to hate Louvois so much that she commissioned *Esther* to be performed by her pupils at St.-Cyr in the hope that the king would turn against his minister in the same way that Assuérus turned against Aman in Racine's play.[4] Two chapters entitled "the fall of Louvois" try to document the supposed hate of Mme. de Maintenon (*HF*, 4:555, 558). Mme. de Maintenon represents the dark side of Louis XIV, while Louvois supports Louis's better self. At all times Michelet takes his side. The historian tries to show that Louvois counseled against the cruelty and terror unleashed on the Protestants (the *dragonnades*) and on the Palatinate, and credits him with planning the glorious victories of the Maréchal de Luxembourg at Fleurus and at Mons (1690). Louvois worked for the good of France; he encouraged the bright side of Louis; and so, in spite of intrigues, Louvois was still in office when he died in 1691 (*HF*, 5:11–12).

Terror, cruelty, destruction, superstition, these are the themes that dominate this volume, to the point that it seems to be a preview of *The Witch* (1862). It is all the more frightening because the shadow of the king, sanctioning such crimes, falls on these scenes. Michelet illustrates the degeneration of Louis's reign in stark detail: the sick are exploited in the hospitals, e.g., under Guichard, alias Hérapine, whose patients were scandalously dying on him (*HF*, 4:510–11); there was virtual slavery on the king's galleys and the poor, driven from abyss to abyss, found drowning a kinder fate (*HF*, 4:511–15).

Such was the dark side of the "grand epoch" of Louis XIV. It began with the burning of Morin (*HF*, 4:415–17) and ended with the conviction of la Brinvilliers for poisoning her father and her brothers. When she confessed she was accorded treatment more humane than usual: she was not burned before being beheaded! Michelet adds to the black humor by explaining that the judges did not dare omit the torture of "the question" (*HF*, 4:484). Was it surprising that this was the period of hallucinations and somnambulism, of visionaries like Marie Alacoque and Mme. Guyon (*HF*, 4:477, 532–35)?

The worst fate befell the Huguenots. Persecution continued with increased vigor; often children were seized, an outrage to which the historian returns again and again.[5] Many died for their faith now that their spokesman, Jurieu, "the Mirabeau of that time," was proclaiming the right to dissent.[6] Some managed to emigrate to Holland or to Geneva—but conditions there were especially miserable and crowded (*HF*, 4:522–23). There followed the repression of the Protestants in the Cévennes and the persecution of the Waldenses, who were being pushed off cliffs just to see them die.[7] But then Louis's terror was not reserved for dissenters; he also ravaged the Palatinate! The Sun King had become a monster, a "new Theodosius" (*HF*, 4:490).

II   *The end of an era, 1689–1715:*
History of France, *volume 14 (1862)*

Michelet sees France in ruins! There is widespread poverty; "skeletons" are knocking on the golden gate of Versailles (*HF*, 5:35, 86)! He notes the decline *(amoindrissement)* of religious belief and of "our two great corpses," the nobility and the clergy (*HF*, 5:2, 99). Not even Fénelon's pupil, the talented duke of Burgundy, Louis's grandson, could have salvaged this world which was bound to die; it was incurably sick from old age! True, there are two plans for reform—Boisguillebert's *Awakening of France* and Vauban's *Royal Tithe;* they will concede nothing to privilege, but the authors must suffer for their courage; they fall into disgrace and Vauban is exiled (*HF*, 5:35–36, 83–84). It is a "dismal carnival" that Michelet feels compelled to depict (*HF*, 5:100).

As a patriot he found some solace in the continued victories at war: the Maréchal de Luxembourg wins at Steinkerk and Nerwinden; Trouville recovers from his debacle at La Hogue and defeats the British fleet at Lagos, but doubts arise when Jean Bart burns fifty-four ships and Dugay Trouin takes his toll, for "the king becomes a pirate" (*HF*, 5:20–31). Then fortunes change. Luxembourg dies. With bitter scorn Michelet introduces his successors: Villeroi at fifty is "still irresistible," but not on the field of battle; Marsin is a pious light weight *(dévot, léger);* Montrevel's greatest victory in the Cévennes is burning a mill in which 300 Protestants have come to celebrate Easter![8]

The problem was not only such incompetence; it was that Louis overreached himself. When his grandson, the duc d'Anjou, became Philip V of Spain (by the testament of Charles II in 1700), Louis's intransigence unleased the war of the Spanish succession. He would not guarantee that Spain and France would remain separate. So great a threat united his enemies. Michelet is horrified by the two brilliant generals France now had to face: Prince Eugene, "the dagger of Austria," and Marlborough, deputy of the British stock exchange, as he calls them, "sinister" leaders, masters at ruse and intrigue (*HF*, 5:51). It is with evident pain that he recounts their stunning victories which expelled the French from Germany, the Netherlands, and Italy.[9] He emphasizes the heroism of the French at Lille and Malplaquet. Was this a victory? Michelet thinks so because the battle inflicted unprecedented casualties as a result of which the Whig cabinet fell and Marlborough was dismissed, and "buried in gold."[10] Then comes Denain, "a defeat from which Eugene's fortunes will never recover." Michelet exaggerates success as much as Louis's willingness to conclude peace. Had the situation been that bright, would Louis have offered concessions which were "unlimited" (*HF*, 5:93, 108)? In truth, the peace of Utrecht (1713) simply kept Philip on the throne of Spain and confirmed the treaties of Nimwegen and Ryswick!

When Louis dies (1715), the historian finds new signs of hope. Philippe d'Orléans seizes power and the regency. This forestalls catastrophe, for the alternative was the rule of the duke of Maine, "that son of adultery" (of Louis XIV and Mme. de Montespan) who frolicks at the king's death and has only himself in mind. By contrast Philippe weeps! This proves the regent has a good heart! Michelet admits that he is weak and corrupt, but points out that he is also intelligent and of good will (*HF*, 5:118–23). Our historian never concedes defeat; he believes in France.

He places remarkable stress on women. Sarah, wife of Marlborough, holds Queen Anne in the palm of her hand (*HF*, 5:92), while Philip V, king of Spain, is ruled by his wives; first by "the little princess," Maria Luisa of Savoy and her confidente, Princess Des Ursins, then by Elisabeth Farnese who "leads him by the nose." Meanwhile Maria Luisa's sister, Adelaïde, marries another grandson of Louis XIV, the duke of Burgundy, Fénelon's pupil (*HF*, 5:52–55, 68–69), and there is worse in Versailles! The regent marries Mlle. de Blois, whom Michelet prefers to call Mme. Lucifer, the incarnation of "infernal pride." When his mother, Elisabeth-Charlotte of the Palatinate, hears that he chose this illegitimate daughter of Louis XIV and La Vallière, she slapped his face in public (*HF*, 5:105, 160). The fact that neither the two princesses of Savoy, nor Mlle. de Blois are ever mentioned by name, adds to our impression of the irresponsible and mad atmosphere of a carnival.

Mme. de Maintenon appears, as she had in the preceding volume, as an essential and unfortunate influence behind the throne. She turns St.-Cyr into a convent, and wants to make up for the ill-fated expedition to Ireland by having William III assassinated; two of these ill-advised attempts become public knowledge (*HF*, 5:13–14,

23, 27, 34). Her confessor, Godet, turns her into a belligerent anti-Jansenist, which to Michelet means pro-Jesuit (*HF*, 5:8, 40, 79). While historians do not generally ascribe that much power to her— she was admittedly but an average mind—Michelet traces her influence through ministers like Seignelay (*HF*, 5:1–2, 11) and especially the "occult power" of the duke of Chevreuse behind the ministry of Chamillart. Indeed, Michelet describes a "government of saints" (*HF*, 5:75, 83, 126), pious and irresponsible, fighting the Jansenists instead of Marlborough (*HF*, 5:90), not satisfied with the destruction of Port-Royal, pressing for papal action against the Jansenist propositions of Quesnel which will be condemned by the bull *Unigenitus* (1713). The historian conceives of a grand conspiracy in favor of this misbegotten *(avorton)* edict of Pope Clement XI which, as Quinet put it, stabs not only the church but also God (*HF*, 5:110).

The strangest interpretation of all is that of Fénelon. There remains a glimmer of sympathy, since Michelet liked *Télémaque* when he was young, but it is hard to find a more biased interpretation. He feels that Fénelon risked nothing when he criticized Louis XIV from his sheltered position. He condemns him as a religious director, a new Molinos who makes his disciples miserable by his abuse of passion to fight passion. Mme. de Maisonfort, the assistant of Mme. de Maintenon at St.-Cyr, is Michelet's prime example (*HF*, 5:8–9, 14–15). Another victim is Mme. de Montberon; startling erotic imagery is used to describe their relationship as an impotent analogy to intercourse: "The arid and desperate spectacle of two souls who wear each other down by sterile friction *(frottement à vide)* and continue these motions *(agitation)* beyond the death of their hearts, unable to satisfy each other or love each other, altogether unable to either live or die."[11] Mme. Guyon is a similar case, for in spite of her mistaken emphasis—in Michelet's view—on another world and on the "radical impotence" of the individual, she lives and acts freely until buried under the heavy hand of Fénelon, her director. Strangely, our historian sees no coincidence between their ideas (*HF*, 5:2–6, 39).

A friend of Mme. de Maintenon, an opponent of the Jansenists, Fénelon is seen as a pro-Jesuit, as "the man of the bull" *Unigenitus* (*HF*, 5:110). The remark of the king's confessor, Le Tellier, that "if Jansenism, which is a heresy and the avant-garde of free thought *(des libertins)*, is not suppressed, all is lost" (*HF*, 5:112), makes Fénelon, with his pro-Jesuit orientation, into an enemy of the *philosophes*—whereas the Jansenists are their unwitting allies, and "the last pure Christians" (*HF*, 5:39, 100). Michelet imagines strange battle lines and demands that we choose sides. He cannot forgive Saint-Simon for describing Jesuits and Jansenists with impartiality.[12]

The Jesuit victory through *Unigenitus* is a grim omen indeed, for they are hypocrites: they teach freedom, i.e., free will, only to besmudge it (*HF*, 5:100)! But once again the historian finds cause for hope: against their danger there arises the strident laughter of Voltaire, sufficient for an entire century (*HF*, 5:103, 109, 125). It heralds the future. Meanwhile the death of the king permits free thinkers like Fontenelle to live (*HF*, 5:113). Michelet seems unconcerned that Fontenelle had written his important work before Louis XIV died; he assigns Fontenelle's reign to the regency. After William III, England seems to revert to materialism, to its brokers and Jews,[13] while France, under the regency, will favor the *philosophes*. The torch of freedom returns to Paris; there was no hope for the future except in France!

III   *The Regency:* History of France, *volume 15 (1863)*

How much Michelet welcomed the policies of the regent, Philippe d'Orléans, and the great importance he attached to those eight years (1715–1723), is clear from the fact that he devoted an entire volume to them; the others in the series cover about thirty years each. To reveal the new spirit of the Enlightenment—Voltaire would be its bible, Rousseau its gospel—the historian will "lift the roofs" to show the true thoughts of the inhabitants, like Lesage in the *Diable boiteux* [Limping Devil, *HF*, 5:130–31].

Most important was Philippe's opposition to Catholic power, and this is the interpretation Michelet gives to his break with Spain. When Philip V seized Sicily in violation of the Treaty of Utrecht, the regent entered alliances with England, Holland, and finally Austria (1717–1718); he broke with the British pretender and attacked Spain. As a result, Philip V, ruled by his "Italians" (his wife, Elisabeth Farnese, and Alberoni, the ambitious prime minister), began a vast plot against the regent. It was fortunate that the "conspiracy of Cellamare" (the Spanish ambassador in Paris) was discovered. The duke of Maine, that "fanatic bigot" and "serf of Spain," was found implicated and imprisoned. Triumphant, the historian will not mention the regent's compromise with the duke of Maine who lived out his life at his "court" at Sceau. Michelet paints in stark colors! Spain is the Inquisition, while the regent and his government have "entrails" and "feel the hunger of the people."[14]

This is not to say that Michelet exonerates Philippe d'Orléans. He speaks of the excesses, the debauchery of the Parc aux Cerfs, and about the duchess of Berry, the regent's daughter, who died at the age of twenty, an example of perversion and excess. Michelet notes that nowhere is Saint-Simon as bitter as in his description of her death in childbirth. He speculates about her heritage: the grandfather, Monsieur (brother of Louis XIV) was "king of Sodom," i.e., a homosexual; the father, Philippe, was dissolute; and there were "Bavarian tendencies" in the family. Our historian repeats much of the striking detail in Saint-Simon,[15] and adds that the duchess of Berry was mad, as evidenced by the cracked (fêlé) appearance of her brain. While the autopsy is a matter of record, this observation—the only sentence in quotation marks even though it stems from Michelet's imagination—simply expresses his belief, stated in *Woman*, that the physical aspect of the brain can indicate mental aberration.[16] It is his way of applying science to history, of taking account of the "material" forces which shape it. In the face of so much immorality and abuse of nature, he welcomes coffee, first imported at that time, that "anti-erotic" and "cerebral" beverage, stimulating to the mind, an antidote to the influence of alcohol and tobacco (*HF*, 5:189).

The evil of the age and the weakness of the regent are clearly brought out, but the noble intent of his regime is emphasized. In this context the scheme of John Law—his sale of notes for the development of Louisiana—which today is viewed as a fiscal innovation, appears as an economic revolution (*HF*, 5:131). It failed because there were only two years' time where a century was needed—so that values created by developing Louisiana could back up Law's certificates—and Michelet correctly points out how the collapse enriched those "cheats," Prince Conti and the duke of Bourbon, while the poor suffered. Conti arrived with three large wagons to load with gold in exchange for his certificates, gold the people were forced to surrender when sixty percent of all coins (and half the bills) were called in; it was a belated effort to stem the tide.[17] Other beneficiaries were Pâris-Duverney and British banks when all shares had to be recertified, in the "affaire des visas," while John Law was expelled and had nothing left but his honor. Michelet's account is tendentious and not always accurate—he claims that the value of gold declined—but it is also striking and perceptive. He shows how the hope for quick gain brought out the worst in men, e.g., in the Dutch nobleman, Horn, who was executed, or in the stampede on Law's office, rue Quincampoix. He tells how ruin was followed by despair as the plague breaks out in Marseilles. Thousands die, and even Paris is affected when a shipment of silk spreads the germ of death (*HF*, 5:222–34). Michelet and his contemporaries knew nothing about the cause of the plague. He speculates that good food protects one; this may be true if people who eat well have fewer rats in their cellars.

The commentary on literature is extensive. The *Memoirs* of Lahontan, a virulent attack on abuses under Louis XIV, are rightly seen as the work of one wounded by abuses. Michelet interprets Lahontan's Indian sage, Adagio, as a symbol of humanity in a non-Christian world (*HF*, 5:190). In 1705 the book had to be published abroad: by contrast, Voltaire's *Oedipus* appeared under the freedom of the regency. The historian brings out the irony that this story of incest was dedicated to the regent, the father of the duchess of Berry! This shows Voltaire's lightheartedness, discovered also in his early verse and in his acting the role of a priest in his tragedy (*HF*, 5:163, 189). In revision of earlier judgments, Montesquieu's *Persian Letters* (1821) are praised for their new ideas and as a fantasy recalling the *Arabian Nights*. Had Watteau lived to read the book, it would have renewed his spirit (*HF*, 5:243). *Manon Lescaut* (1731), Michelet insists, must have been written earlier, for its show of sentiment and imagination seem characteristic of the regency. He adds imaginative comparisons with the *New Heloise* and *Paul and Virginia*. With his usual emphasis on women dominating the action of men, Michelet considers Manon, rather than Des Grieux, to be the protagonist, and somehow feels that *she* has the noble soul.

IV An attempt at a novel: Sylvine *(1861–1863)*

If the literary imagination is so important, why not attempt a novel? It might be the way to translate the problem of woman threatened by a corrupt society into terms a wider audience could understand. This is why Michelet developed themes from *Woman* and from his account of the regency in *Sylvine*, "the memoirs of a servant girl." The Présidente, who finds Sylvine destitute, begging on a roadside, adopts and educates her. A relationship develops which is not merely Platonic and arouses bitter jealousy. The Présidente is falsely accused of participating in the Cellamare conspiracy while Sylvine is emprisoned. Finally, to save her, the Présidente must give her up—and find her a husband. The melo-drama in its eighteenth-century setting delves into the sin and evil Michelet had condemned Balzac for portraying. His call for public morality, and his fascination for cruelty and perversion were at odds with each other. Is this why the novel remained incomplete in manuscript? Its editor in 1940, Alcanter de Brahm, feels the his-torian was afraid to shock the bourgeois (p. 12). *Sylvine* completed might well have been regarded as a successor to *Madame Bovary*.

V   La Sorcière *(1862)*

Michelet did not forget his readers. If *Sylvine* was abandoned, another "popular" book, *La Sorcière* [The Witch], was to be his greatest success in the long run: the English translation by Allinson (1904) is still in print! It is Michelet's most poetic book, with its lyrical inspiration and numerous instances of blank verse.[18] Let us add that the previous year Michelet had republished the *History of France* with corrections as significant as those of the 1852 edition, but this time carried out for all the volumes and notes,[19] often with the deletion of statements that no longer expressed his religious views. *The Witch,* and *The Bible of Humanity* two years later, would be their forceful restatement.

The witch is studied as a sibyl, a mythic force, a mediator between the equally unacceptable positions of Christian orthodoxy and ma-terialism.[20] Her progress appears as a social phenomenon and psychic necessity. Her first incarnation is the fearful wife of the serf in feudal times, seeking protection at a time (beginning in the thir-teenth century) when the castle, the shelter provided by the feudal lord, had become a prison *(SO,* 1:37), partly because the feudal bond of friendship and mutual aid had become impersonal, a mere exchange of money for services, partly because the lord began to consider the serf as his slave; he perpetrated "the most blatant outrage to the heart," the right to deflower brides-to-be, leaving peasant girls insecure and even with child *(SO,* 1:56, 59). Is it surprising that she withdrew to her room, put on her wedding dress, and dreamed about an ideal lover? Tempted by Satan, she would awake and swear that a miracle had occurred *(SO,* 1:93). Alienated, born of discrimination, the witch sought not faith or even reason, but human warmth to fill her need. "Today you laugh at them. For a thousand years people did not laugh. They wept bitter tears, and even today one cannot write about such blasphemy without a swelling of the heart and the indignant grating of paper and pen" (*SO*, 1:88). Michelet's method is to report her magic as a social fact, not as an illusion or a preposterous aberration.

While Christianity "crystallized" into "monotonous prisms, Spitzbergen-like," and while the church-centered world view of St. Thomas and Dante seem to relegate Christians to an immense *in pace*, the life in death of the convent, the witch, in her second incarnation, turns to the freedom of nature, to its magic and charms, to soothe pain, fulfill desires, and tranquilize men, somewhat like a modern homeopath (*SO*, 1:105–7, 111). The Christian dogma is confined to a vaulted cathedral which houses the faithful, while those aspiring to see the sky (nature) become Satan's disciples. The church and its ally, the university, keep the people inside, teach them to bear their fate and suffer, to be resigned and hope for death. The witch, born of despair, seeks an escape (*SO*, 1:8, 13–14)! She discovers helpful poisons, belladonna as a remedy for St. Vitus's dance. She establishes herself as a healer; even the lady of the castle would turn to her (*SO*, 1:111–12, 121). She was often insulted, called "dirty, indecent, forward, immoral," but she was consulted and this was her "triumph."[21] Leprosy in the thirteenth century, epilepsy in the fourteenth, syphilis in the fifteenth were her concern. Of the Renaissance physicians, only Paracelsus followed the same natural path. Charms and filters, the orgies of the Sabbath, were her domain, or rather, that of Satan; but was Satan not the part of God left out of the church? His rituals were the inversion of the divine service (*SO*, 1:130–46).

As medicine develops and priests become directors of conscience in the seventeenth century, the witch enters her third incarnation; she becomes a professional, the lady-in-waiting ready to organize black masses, residing no longer outdoors, in nature, but in the alcove of her mistress's apartment. Michelet is less concerned with this stage, but depicts its effects, erotic fantasies being realized in the "frenetic black orgy" of Charles VI, in the burial chapel at St.-Denis (*SO*, 2:4), and in the circumstances leading to four witch trials, told in great detail: Gauffridi (1610), Grandier at Loudun (1633–1634), Madeleine Bavant at Louviers (1640–1647), and the seduction of la Cadière by the Jesuit, Girard (1730). These accounts are developed from parallel passages in the preceding volumes of the *Histoire de France* or, in the last case, parallel a chapter of the next, where the judgment of la Cadière appears as a flagrant injustice (*HF*, 5:309). *La Sorcière* is more explicit. The girl who innocently sought the help of Girard and became pregnant accused him in court but was sentenced to be hanged! The judgment was not executed but she disappeared into the *in pace* of some convent. The historian concludes: "The prodigious creation of science and modern institutions," though "excommunicated stone by stone" by the church, will yet triumph and right the injustices inflicted on the witch (*SO*, 2:200).Frail, vulnerable (like Athénaïs), but also a strong voice for freedom and the rights of women, a sibyl steeped in magic and mysticism, but also a solace to man in his alienation, is presented as an archetypal figure whose biography, or rather, successive incarnations, appear strikingly modern. *The Witch* established Michelet as a myth-maker and has attracted an ever growing audience.

About the time the book was put on sale, Michelet noted in his *Journal:* "I have assumed a new position which my best friends have not as yet clearly adopted, that of proclaiming the (provisional) death of Christianity, one which our fathers, Diderot, Voltaire, Goethe, espoused to such good purpose" (*J*, 3:152–53). He was quite correct in the appraisal of his contemporaries. The silence of critics when the book appeared was startling. Besides, to make publication possible, two passages had to be removed and a new publisher found.[22] The first of these texts qualified dogma, especially that of the Trinity, as boring, the saints' lives as insipid (*SO*, 1:11–12); the second described in detail how father Girard had la Cadière undress and assaulted her in "criminal debauchery! He placed shameful kisses on this poor body he would have liked to see dead" (*SO*, 2:143–44).

Michelet's attack was fierce, intended to rouse the public from its lethargy and found a new faith. He was convinced that Christianity had to die before even what was good and valid in it could be reborn (*J*, 3:153).

VI   *Faith and the torch of freedom:*
La Bible de l'humanité *(1864)*

La Bible de l'humanité [The Bible of Humanity] takes up this attack, but the book is notable above all for its enthusiastic evocation of "the peoples of light," India, Persia, and Greece, in a new framework for history, for much has changed since the *Introduction to Universal History* of 1831, when India appeared steeped in the fatalistic dream of pantheism, and Greece was barely considered.

The basic conception of both books goes back to Michelet's visit in Heidelberg in 1828, for there he met Creuzer and, more important yet, discussed the ideas with his friend, Quinet, who that very year, in his *Origins of the Gods*, proposed that "the dream of immortality has been animating humanity ever since its cradle," since the early pantheism on the Ganges, and that the "filiation" of successive faiths, all absorbed into the beliefs of classical antiquity and of Christianity, mirror the rise of civilization. In his *Genius of Religions* of 1842, Michelet's essential source even in 1864, Quinet further developed his concept, which may be an inversion of history, that religions create civilizations, and studied the dual movement of the ancient fertilization of the West by the East (because the earliest religions are those of the Orient), and the recent rediscovery of the East by the West. Quinet called this "la renaissance orientale," the Oriental renaissance, and Raymond Schwab adopted the term as the title for his remarkable study.[23] In the *Genius of Religions,* Quinet pictured Greek polytheism and Christianity as the heirs to the world's religions. A second edition (1850) carried the idea to Rome and its gods, while a new book, *Christianity and the French Revolution* (1845), pictured 1789 as the result of a Christian renewal. While Michelet did not accept this interpretation of the French Revolution any more than Quinet's attack on the *philosophes* who did not understand religions his way, Michelet, like his friend, saw a grand movement of civilization and faith from East to West, accompanied by a gradual change in emphasis: the forces of nature, dominant in Indian religion, eventually gave way to those of the human spirit and of freedom, most perfectly realized in the history of France, and in 1789. The *Bible* does not, however, extend its account this far. It ends, as we shall see, in debates of Christian dogma, especially the cult of Mary in the early church.

If Quinet was the essential source, many others, part of the "Oriental renaissance," stimulated Michelet's interest. He had met Creuzer in Heidelberg in 1828, but did not use his *Symbolik* extensively until 1837 when Guigniaut's adaptation began to appear; it now furnished him material on Bacchus and Greece.[24] Then came the contributions of Pierre Leroux and Jean Reynaud: *Humanity*[25] by the first, the *Encyclopédie nouvelle* by both men, a work frequently used by our historian.[26]

More important yet for his study of India were the commented texts of the *Rig Veda* (Langlois, 1841–1842), the *Râmayana* and *Mahâbhârata* (Fauche, 1854, 1863), and for Persia the Zoroastrian

Yasna, part of the *Avesta* (Eugène Burnouf), and a new rendition of the *Shah Nameh*, "Persia's Homer." Michelet had come to know this work in the Goerres edition, but now used the translation by Julius Mohl (1838–1855), his colleague at the Collège de France. Disagreements with Mohl and Barthélémy Saint-Hilaire (editor of the *Vedas*, 1854) did not prevent our historian from benefiting from their work. For Greece, his principal guide was Louis Ménard.[27] My list is far from complete. He also knew the contributions of others like William Jones and H. H. Wilson, and read about scholarship abroad in current periodicals (*BH*, 77).

What appeals to the reader is Michelet's compassion, his sensitive portrayal of individual myths. Admittedly he is not composing a history of religions but a moral essay on how man creates his gods (*BH*, 33, 56). He loves India for its humanistic monotheism within the very multiplicity of its gods, and provides a moving portrayal of Râma who loses his beloved Sitâ as she pursues a magic gazelle, the all too alluring incarnation of the evil spirit, Râvana (*BH*, 66–67). We read of the victory of Râma with the aid of the comic but appealing monkey, Hanouman (*BH*, 74–75). The helpful giant dog and elephant (*BH*, 22–23) are characteristic of the solidarity of living creatures in Indian lore.

In Persia Michelet finds a more active, work-oriented, and casteless society. The *Zend-Avesta* spells out an ethic of individual effort and justice (*BH*, 77–80). He admires Hôma, the tree of life (*BH*, 83), the interplay of good and evil, Ormuzd and Ahriman, and the Fravashis, guardian angels, the feminine principle he seeks out everywhere (*BH*, 87–89, 121). The *Shah Nameh*, a late epic from Mohammedan times, seems nevertheless to grow out of the ancient traditions. Here Firdousy dedicates his life to building a canal, but is prevented from doing so by his ruler, Mahmoud, who sends the necessary money the day the hero is being buried. Firdousy's noble purpose, his respect for his wife, his opposition to an Arab ruler, explain Michelet's enthusiasm, for he sees Mohammedan rule in Persia, like the Brahman hierarchy in India, as a phenomenon of decline.

His account of Greek myths is more extensive. The cycle of life and death begins with Demeter and Persephone, her daughter, who is taken to Hades and can return only upon a direct appeal to Zeus. Since Zeus had loved Persephone, he sends Hermes to bring her back to earth, but she will have to descend again, a story of love and separation, death and rebirth (*BH*, 150-52). Michelet is happy to find no priesthood in Greece, no tyrannical hierarchy (*BH*, 159), and singles out the moral tone in Homer: the *Iliad* punishes adultery—in contrast to medieval literature which "glorifies" it—by the destruction of Troy; the *Odyssey* sings of the "heroic" homecoming of a husband (*BH*, 170–71). True, the *aristoi* of Sparta reduced the Ilotes to slavery (*BH*, 182), but the heroic battles of Athens against the invaders from Asia, the defeat of Xerxes at Marathon, the victory of Themistocles over the Persians at Salamis, saved Greece and freedom, and even Sparta (*BH*, 132, 187).

Greece died young, but saved Europe and worshiped woman. The oracle at Delphi was a woman. Athene taught Hercules (Heracles) and he, in turn, labored for his fellowmen, like Prometheus, the most compassionate and noblest hero of Greece (*BH*, 189–244). Michelet admires Aeschylus's great play, *Prometheus Bound*, and mentions that the author fought at Marathon. Actually our historian is still tied to Rome; he uses the Latin equivalents for the gods, Minerva, Jupiter, Ceres, Proserpina, Pluto, but he is convinced that Greece, and Apollo, brought light, ascension, education, and brotherhood to the world (*BH*, 201–13).

After "the peoples of light," he discusses Egypt, the Oriental Bacchus, and the Judaeo-Christian tradition under the title "the peoples of twilight and night." Among these, Egypt, land of pyramids and death, is treated with the most sympathy, for the trinity of life—Isis, Osiris, and their son, Horus—are fertility idealized.[28] Michelet finds the eternal principle of love in Isis and Osiris, and in the cult of woman—in Egypt she could rule—for "voluntary monogamy" was common even while polygamy was permitted. He finds all the heroic qualities in Egypt; they set the country apart from the decadent spirit of Asia. Michelet cites Champollion and asserts that "Egypt is all African, not Asiatic" (*BH*, 285–89).

Then on to the realm of dusk and decline: Syria is identified with Moloch, Astarte, and Priapus, with the rule of Bacchus and sensuality; it is the disintegration of man and disregard for woman (*BH*, 318–20). Solomon's Shulamite, Michelet insists, must be Syrian, voluptuous as she is (*BH*, 389), and Baal, like the vengeful, jealous God of Israel, reduces man to a slave. Alexander steeped Greece in impotence by his "military orgy" (*BH*, 345–54), Bacchus is his equivalent on another level, but worst of all is the influence of Syria's Moloch and the dangerous Astarte.[29] The "enervating" effect of such divinities brought a long pause to the flowering of freedom. Its progress is not in a straight line, but revolves like Vico's cycles.

One of the obstacles is the Christian ideology, especially in its later medieval manifestations: Dante's universe seems to condemn man to impotence, and "a word from Rousseau," i.e., the emphasis on Christian faith by the vicar of Savoy, launched a century of reaction (*BH*, 482). This is the harshest rejection of Rousseau in Michelet's work, a bitter attack against Christian aspirations in the name of the great church of justice which the historian hoped to substitute for it (*BH*, 486). He realized that this polemic could be damaging to the *Bible of Humanity* as a whole: "I would have liked for this book to contain nothing of myself . . . , but in my last chapters the spirit of criticism took hold of me" (*BH*, 481). He means: I would have wanted to present the great faiths of the past for their own sake, but my critique of Christianity interfered, and this is true not only in the last chapters. We read, for example, that India's Râma is humble; he does not refer to himself as the son of God— which he is—and never accuses his father of having forsaken him.[30] Râvana was the spirit of evil, but only while his soul was bound by a spell; he is glad to see it broken by Râma's victory! Râvana was not evil through and through like the medieval Satan (*BH*, 76). In a similar way, Persia's Ahriman, the evil one, was being constantly reduced, but Christianity's Satan grew ever more powerful. The Faith of Zarathustra forgives but the Christian God becomes an executioner (*BH*, 95–97). The Greek Pandora is innocent, but Eve is sinful when she unleashes evil. Hercules and Prometheus help man and feel for him, while the God of the Old Testament banishes man from Paradise; he is a vengeful God who makes man his slave (*BH*, 193–96, 370).

Michelet admits that some stories of the Old Testament are beautiful: Ruth seeking a child from Boaz to create the seed of David is "irreproachably wanton" (*BH*, 404), but there are few such concessions to the New Testament. Our historian criticizes Jesus; he finds Renan's *Life of Jesus* (1863) far too favorable. Indeed, Renan's book and the extensive polemics it provoked was the immediate incentive for Michelet to write a substitute Bible. Pierre Leroux had spoken of "1800 years of lies" uttered in Jesus's name and Renan had exonorated Christ in the same manner, referring to "1800 years of lies committed in his name."[31] Michelet was unwilling to condone such indulgence, such sentimental attachment to the Christ figure. He called for a clear break with the Christian tradition and equal standing for all the great religions. Indeed he holds Jesus responsible for founding a cult of slaves. He sees hope only in the rival cult of Mary.

This is one of the most radical of his interpretations. He derived it from another critic of Renan, from his friend Alphonse Peyrat, whose *Elementary and Critical History of Jesus* (1864) he praises for its "impartial logic" (*BH*, 439). This appraisal is grotesque, for Peyrat's book, a storehouse of information, is presented with a strong satirical verve. Peyrat compares the Virgin to a cow that does and does not calve: she gave birth because she was with child; she did not give birth because she is the Virgin (85). Michelet preferred Peyrat to Renan for this bluntness, and especially because of Peyrat's exposition of the apocryphal *Book of James*, or *Protevangilium* of the second century, for this is the source of the cult of Mary and of her immaculate conception by Anne.[32] As our historian put it: "Christianity begins with Mary" (*BH*, 431, 493), and from Mariology there arose the cult of woman, and the important role of women in the early church.

All this becomes clearer when we examine Michelet's comments on the *Letter to the Romans*, that "Marseillaise of divine grace" (*BH*, 440). He criticizes Paul for saying that there is no sin without the Law,[33] i.e., that the Christian religion reveals evil in man and thus negates Michelet's faith in life and in the family.[34] On the other hand, our historian is glad to find that in Paul's church women played an essential role. He concentrates on Phoebe, the "deacon" who carried Paul's letter to Rome. She illustrates the "triumph of woman," the title of this chapter.[35] Of course, the otherworldliness of the early church must be overcome, just as the cult of Mary will have to be transformed—by the image of Joan of Arc—before it can become part of the "great church" of the future. Still, the rise of woman in early Christianity is a positive aspect; but this view of woman was rejected when the medieval world view took hold around 1300, introduced the cult of Satan, produced the great terror which destroyed the Albigensians, and led to the unified world view of a Dante (*BH*, 482). After 1300 there followed "immense evils, indefinitely prolonged," symbolized by the Spielberg, the horrid Hapsburg prison, and by "moral Siberias," sterility, a progressive deep freeze (*BH*, 483).

Of course Michelet will not end on so negative a note. He turns to his faith in the future, to purification and fraternity, to the new altar of the world soul, a family home (*foyer*) which will shine in peace, "the profound peace of enlightenment" (*BH*, 486). In this moment of exaltation, Michelet sees himself again as the prophet of a new faith. His entire world view is explained in the *Bible of Humanity*. It situates Michelet equally distant from Renan's nostalgic *Life of Jesus* (1863) and Marx's *Capital* (1867).

VII *Enlightenment and Revolution:*
History of France, *volumes 16–17 (1866–1867)*

It was only in 1794, with the enactment of the new Code of Law *(Code civil)* that the term "family" took on its modern meaning, Michelet would have us believe, for he finds that the decline and fall of the *Ancien Régime* was the result of the "family conspiracy." Here "family" designates the king, his relatives and cousins abroad, that world of court intrigue, privilege, and unfair taxation, unresponsive to the needs of the people.[36] Meanwhile the people were steeped in poverty and superstition, as witness the convulsion at St. Médard cemetery and the naiveté of la Cadière, seduced by father Girard but nonetheless condemned by a clerical court.[37]

Meanwhile the king thinks only of himself and his mistresses. He is overjoyed when la Nesle bears him a son, and weeps when she dies *(HF,* 5:332). On a visit to his troops at Metz, he eats and drinks so much that he falls desperately ill and endangers his country, for unlike the United States, able to weather Lincoln's assassination, France is tied to one man *(HF,* 5:47). Michelet's newfound sympathy for America is frequently expressed![38]

Some ministers honestly tried to improve conditions: Pâris-Duverney and Machault under Louis XV, Turgot under Louis XVI, but they fell victim to the system. D'Argenson, an appealing figure in his own right, sold out to the tax collectors, and as lover of Mme. de Prie, seems a *philosophe* worshiping Satan.[39] Michelet's portraits are striking. Fleury is simply "the priest"; Maurepas is "the tricky songster"; Choiseul, a convert to the "family religion" who is pro-Austrian and pro-English, opposes all innovations, and ties the hands of Turgot.[40] Thus the vested interests can triumph even though Louis XVI admires Turgot.

There was of course a difference between the two kings. Under Louis XV there was no hope, especially once Mme. Du Barry and her friends descended on Versailles like a "devouring swarm of vicious flies that thrive on fetid ground" *(HF,* 5:368), while Louis XVI meant well. He was not disreputable *(crapuleux)* like his predecessor, but how could he resist? He himself admitted: "They taught me nothing!" He was utterly unprepared *(HF,* 5:413, 471).

Under both regimes women are once again shown to be the power behind the throne. Mme. de Pompadour began to rule Versailles at the time of the battle of Fontenoy (1745). When her charms no longer sufficed, she procured mistresses, like Mlle. de Romans, a "Julie," to purify Louis XV from his orgies by the illusion of love (*HF*, 5:354, 437). The king's daughters were also important, first Mme. Henriette who died in 1752, then Mme. Adelaïde, so favored that M. de Narbonne may have been her son by Louis. The historian doubts such reports but features Mme. Adelaïde in the title of two chapters.[41]

Although not dissolute, Louis XVI is no more self-reliant. He is the lackey *(nègre)* and trembling slave of Marie-Antoinette who remains "enthroned" right to the end (*HF*, 5:492, 523, 534). Most extraordinary are Michelet's calculations to show that exactly nine months before the birth of each child, her "Austrian" influence reached a climax, for Marie Antoinette always accepted the advice of her mother, Emperess Maria Theresa. On 18 March 1778, negotiations with Prussia are broken off; on December 18, the duchesse d'Angoulême is born. On 22 January 1781, Marie Antoinette's protégé, Ségur, becomes minister of war; on 22 October, Louis-Joseph (1881–1889) is born. In June 1784, Vergenne's peace offensive is defeated by the Queen; in March 1785 the future Louis XVII is born, the ill-fated prince who will die in prison (1795).[42] The precise chronology is grotesque, and the pro-Austrian policies were less dominant than Michelet would have them.

Volume 16 closes with the year 1757 which heralds the revolutionary future: Damiens tries to assassinate Louis XV and Frederick the Great defeats the Austrian coalition (of which France was a part) at Rossbach. Austria, that stronghold of Catholicism, appears as the enemy of progess, while Frederick stands for free thought and common sense; he defends the freedom of the *philosophes* and the *Encyclopédie*.[43] Our historian feels that France simply chose sides against her better interests. As a result, she lost her colonies to England at the end of the Seven Years' War (1763), but this loss is minimized (*HF*, 5:451). Frederick's victory over that Minotaur, Maria Theresa, seems far more important. Only the partitions of Poland cast a shadow on Frederick's career. It will take the war of 1870 to change Michelet's view of Prussia.

Frederick is appealing also as the friend of Voltaire. They made up their differences after the crisis in Berlin (*HF*, 5:423) and share the concern for progress. Indeed, Voltaire dominates the last two volumes of the *History of France*, where almost half the chapters feature some aspect of his work. The early poems and *Oedipus* had been discussed before. Now Michelet welcomes the historian of Henry IV *(La Henriade)* and especially of Charles XII of Sweden; he prefers the narrative of the *History of Charles XII* even to the *Century of Louis XIV*, but above all he admires Voltaire as the opponent of Pascal, the enemy of "fatalism," the believer in "action," the defender of Calas and Sirven,[44] who seems to share Vico's faith in the future: man is his own Prometheus!

There are some aspects of Voltaire Michelet dislikes. He criticizes his praise for Maurepas and Choiseul; he believes that Choiseul and Mme. de Pompadour established him at Ferney; they needed Voltaire on French soil! The historian is proud of balancing praise and blame in his "impartial" judgment *(HF,* 5:412). There is no question, however, that his praise carries the day. The historian found an ally who believed in France and the future. He pictures Voltaire weeping when Turgot and Malesherbes were dismissed by the king *(HF,* 5:480).

Michelet's explanation of why Voltaire moved to Ferney is most dubious. He never mentions that Geneva prohibited theatrical performances in its realm and thus prompted Voltaire to leave Les Délices. Besides the sponsorship of Choiseul and Mme. de Pompadour, he gives as a reason the search for a more favorable climate for his niece, Mme. Denis, for Voltaire always was "somewhat of a satyr in spirit" *(HF,* 5:424–26). The idea of a difference in climate between two estates so close to each other is bizarre, but the intuition that Voltaire lived with Mme. Denis is remarkable. The facts were not known in his day. Michelet's enthusiasm was constantly rekindled. The satirical but inspiring rationalist became the herald of democracy, the defender of the persecuted. The "Voltairian faith" of his father sustained the historian in his enthusiasm.

Diderot's work was becoming more widely known. Michelet discovered another ally in "Pantophile" and his principle, "Expand God!" found in his *Philosophical Thoughts*. Besides, the *Encyclopédie* "erases so many outdated ideas" *(vieilleries),* that it appears as the rallying point for those preparing 1789.[45] Diderot gained stature in Michelet's view just as his admiration for Rousseau declined (after 1850); the association of the *Contrat social* with Robespierre produced his quandary.[46] Michelet tried to resolve his problem by distinguishing between the intimate and direct style of the *Confessions*, and the "entangled style" *(style noué)* of "Rousseau-

Mably," the advocate of rigid social theories in the *Contrat* (*HF*, 5:410, 427). Rousseau seems to advertise his poverty (*HF*, 5:430) and, worse than that, surrender to Christianity, not only in the *Profession of Faith of the Vicar from Savoy (Emile)*, but in the *New Heloise* where Julie now appears as the mouthpiece of the gospels: Did she not end up with the kind of drivel *(radotage)* which Voltaire had "pulverized" years before? Did her husband, Wolmar, who sacrificed Julie to his egoism, not end up as a convert to her faith, instead of committing suicide, as he should?[47] a controversial, if striking interpretation, to say the least, for who can prove that Wolmar was converted. Even so Michelet admits that the novel moved him beyond all others and that it was written in the informal style *(dénoué)* inspired by women from Mme. de Warens to Mme. d'Houdetot, stirring to the reader, dreamlike, suggestive (*HF*, 5:431). It is most encouraging to find that Michelet's anti-Christian attitude and his hostility toward Robespierre yield to empathy, to his sincere enthusiasm for Rousseau's prose. He even comes to apologize for his attack (*HF*, 5:414). Ultimately Rousseau remains his friend, though Voltaire and Diderot have priority in the manifesto of Enlightenment faith, the last chapter of volume 16 entitled "The Creed of the Eighteenth Century."

As Michelet's account nears 1789, his view of the monarchy becomes increasingly grim. He finds an "immense rate of mortality" (*HF*, 5:548), poverty among the people, corruption and incompetence in the government: Calonne is helpless, Loménie de Brienne, that "little senile priest," is unable to obtain credits from the Paris Parliament. He sends it into "exile" at Troyes, then recalls it to arrest its recalcitrant leaders, and thus precipatates riots in Paris and a "revolution" of provincial parliaments. They feared that the "coup d'état" of Brienne and the king, trying to set up more amenable bodies to authorize taxes, abridged their rights (*HF*, 5:537–40). Michelet notes with pride that he used the archives of the parliament of Grenoble (*HF*, 5:414) but his visit there lasted only two days (28–29 April 1867, cf. *J*, 3:457–58) and, at that, Grenoble was the exception, for the last two volumes of the *History of France*, rapidly composed, were based for the most part on published sources.

The decadence of the regime is dramatically evoked as he recounts the famous affair of the necklace (*HF*, 5:496–513). Rohan ordered it for the queen, but Countess La Motte—Michelet calls her La Vallière—sold the jewels, was seized, tortured, then jailed at la Salpétrière along with "7,000 other wretches" *(créatures immondes)*.

Finally she escaped to London but was subjected to blackmail and hanged herself. Her torture is described in detail and so is her stay in prison, "the workshop of sadists" (HF, 5:509, 516). Such was the case also for Damiens who had assaulted Louis XV (HF, 5:393). As in The Witch, the historian's fascination with gory scenes is evident.

There remained no solution for the bankrupt government but to convoke the Estates General. The Third Estate was to be assured as many representatives as the other two combined; the king believed that this proved his concern for the people (HF, 5:543, 549). Necker, urgently recalled, temporarily saved the situation by using personal funds—even his enemies are forced to admire him (HF, 5:545)—but all to no avail, for privilege would yield nothing. The complaints (cahiers) sent in by the estates, the clergy in particular, go to prove it; that "huge leech," the church, wanted its benefits increased (HF, 5:557)! As the spirit of resistance grew, Mirabeau's gigantic efforts were needed to contain it. In all this, the king remains the pathetic but human figure he was in the History of the French Revolution.

VIII   *Method and principle: The* Preface
to the History of France *(1869)*

The majestic *Preface* had been long in the making. An early version, largely of 1854, appears in the Viallaneix edition of the *Oeuvres complètes* under Vico's title, "the heroism of the spirit" (OC, 4:31–47). In its final form, it is even more critical of the historians of 1820–1830. Michelet sets himself apart and emphasizes his originality. Sismondi wrote "annals," not history; Hallam and Guizot composed "dissertations"; Thierry, whose genius is recognized, is all too concerned with theories of race. Michelet proudly asserts that—unlike his predecessors—he considered geography, climate, food (OC, 4:13). Much of the text analyzes the problem of the Middle Ages which were becoming his "enemy" but permitted him to discover his method as he turned to archives and original documents in his all-important third volume of 1837.[48]

The idea of the resurrection of the past is most forcefully restated (OC, 4:18, 22): Man's heroic dedication to shaping his fate and his world must be recreated by the historian, not in the way of a romantic portrayal in the colors of the past, but as a tribute to man's aspirations, so that, as Michelet once put it, the historian might rekindle in the men of his day, especially the youth, "the heroic spark which burned the hearts of our fathers."[49] Was this not the task of a life time? Michelet looks back on forty years of arduous effort:

I have walked past the [active] world and taken history as my life. It is spent. I regret nothing. I ask for nothing. Oh my dear France, could I ask with whom I lived? for I leave you with such regret. . . . How many passionate, noble, and austere hours did we not spend together, often even in winter, before dawn. How many days of labor and study buried in the Archives. . . .

Well, my great France, if a man had to give his life to rediscover yours and had to cross and recross so many times the river of the dead, he finds consolation in this and thanks you once again. His greatest sorrow is that he must leave you now. (*OC*, 4:26–27)

It is not unexpected that we should find him evoking the religious battles, not just as a way of tribute to Joan of Arc, heroine of action and incarnation of France (*OC*, 4:23), but to draw attention to his efforts to build the new faith so urgently needed to recapture "the soul of the nation." In 1829, he recalls, the churches were empty and Jouffroy proclaimed the death of Christian dogma. "No man of a free mind would then have doubted Montesquieu's prophesy that Catholicism was about to die" (*OC*, 4:15). For the first time Michelet admits that the new faith, propounded with such enthusiasm, the ideal of 1789, has not conquered France. This is a melancholy moment and not the last, but he will not surrender!

CHAPTER 8

Gleanings and Rededication

I *Recollections from the Collège de France: Paris Guide (1867)*

EVEN a nine-page notice concerning the Collège de France can become an eloquent restatement of principles under Michelet's magic pen. Like many famous contemporaries, he contributed to the two-volume guide issued on the occasion of the Paris World's Fair of 1867. Victor Hugo wrote the preface of welcome, Théophile Gautier described art at the Louvre, Michelet provided an historical sketch of the Collège de France. He goes back to the day when Abelard taught on the hill where the Collège was established by François I in 1529, to offer instruction in disciplines rejected by the conservative Sorbonne: Greek, Hebrew, and an expanding curriculum in the sciences. Of course we find echoes of the battles of 1843, a tribute to Quinet and the "messianic" Mickiewicz, and of the struggles of 1848 and 1851. Generalizing from his own experience, Michelet accuses the government of destroying the tradition of free speech.

The important conclusion is twofold. The first part reflects the ideas of the great *Preface* of 1869 and tells how the native son of Paris, "feeling the pavement under my feet," became the historian of the people, of its collective conscience. He quotes Berthelot who said, as Vico had, "We know only what we have done," and calls this his own method. That is why, he explains, "I called my history *resurrection.*" He likes the scientific analogy and calls his courses "a social physiology" examining the tree of life, the masses.

The second thought arises from a paean of praise for modern science. From its "ocean" of "creation" there follow not only inventions which rapidly transform the world (the steam engine, fertilizer), but the constant generation of new species (plants, animals) which is accompanied by a new understanding of life. What used to be considered inorganic matter evolves and lives like everything around us. Claude Bernard's studies in nutrition and discoveries in medicine and hygiene convince Michelet that "the barrier of death is being broken." In his enthusiasm for science the historian remains an idealist. He proclaims that nature is spirit and spirit is life; then the triumphant shout: "Oh death, where is thy sting?"[1] Death and resurrection have haunted our "poet of the Père Lachaise" since early youth; he rejoices in the creative effort of his colleagues, protests against the regime of Napoleon III, and looks to the future. He could speak out since *Paris Guide* was published in Brussels.[2]

II *The meaning of the French Revolution: rejoinders of 1868*

Once the *History of France* was complete, there finally was time to read and reflect, to compare his method and purposes with those of contemporaries, and so the year 1868 was spent perusing, among others, the twelve volumes of Louis Blanc's *History of the French Revolution* (1847–1861), the three-volume biography of Robespierre by Ernest Hamel (1865–1867), and Quinet's two-volume *Revolution* (1865) which he had already briefly examined in 1866. There was a gulf between the apologists for Robespierre—Louis Blanc and Ernest Hamel—and the resolutely anti-Jacobin Edgar Quinet who condemned every aspect of the Regime of Terror; but they stood equally far from Michelet's Dantonist point of view. There was so much criticism in the first two authors that Michelet thought it might take him ten years to refute them (*HR*, 2:1016); the rejection by Quinet was implied for he mentioned Michelet only in one final notice, as our historian had sadly noted (*J*, 3:378). Strange to say, the only favorable comment our historian could find was an appreciation by Ernest Hamel: "The pages Michelet devotes to the end of Robespierre are truly beautiful and moving" (*HR*, 2:1164).

The case of Edgar Quinet had special relevance because of their long and lasting friendship, still echoed in *Guide France* and now affected by their fundamental disagreement: Quinet's assumption that the Revolution had failed because it had not led to a religious, Christian renewal. Already in 1866 Michelet had noted: "Quinet believes that the Revolution could have been saved by some other form of Christianity" (*J*, 3:370). All that remained, according to Quinet, was the slogan "liberty, equality, fraternity." He completely discounts what mattered most to Michelet: the faith of the Revolution, i.e., its belief in enlightenment and in the democratic ideal as a substitute for Christianity, such as Michelet had presented it

in his conclusion to volume 16, entitled "The Creed of the Eighteenth Century." Michelet's reaction was a firm letter and public
silence. Nowhere in the three prefaces which he adds to the *History
of the French Revolution* is Quinet even mentioned.[3]

The first of these prefaces for the Lacroix edition of 1868–1869
calls for unity in the face of the threat to civil liberties by Napoleon
III and his ill-advised intervention in Mexico and Italy.[4] The second
(for volume 3) recalls the unanimity of the Federations of 1790 and
adds two letters, one from Béranger (1847), the other from Proudhon
(1851), to show that a constructive dialogue with liberals and radicals
was possible (*HR*, 2:999–1004). The third, entitled, "The Tyrant"
(for volume 5), attacks "the dictatorship" of Robespierre. It is his
answer to Louis Blanc (*HR*, 2:1004–22). Unity is the motto of all
three texts, a joining of hands of partisans of Mirabaud, Vergniaud
and the Gironde, Danton, and Robespierre, in the name of that
great communion, or *agape*, the General Federation of 14 July 1790.
By his unrestrained attacks, Louis Blanc was guilty of "breaking the
unity of the great church" which is the Revolution (*HR*, 1:20).

Louis Blanc had admitted that "Michelet's account breathes profound sympathy" for the "illustrious leaders," Danton and Desmoulins, who were put to death on 5 April 1794, and that he himself
"would be ashamed not to share such feeling," then he continues:
"But how easy it is for generous hearts to go too far and side with
the victims. What requires a painful effort is to be just, even toward
those who struck them down."[5] He agrees with Michelet that there
was good in Danton, even touching devotion to the Republic, but
justifies his death because he accepted bribes from the court. Michelet realizes Danton's corrupt practices but will not sacrifice the
great leader to principle. Louis Blanc becomes more intransigent;
he calls Michelet deluded: "A man who spent thirty or forty years
of his life believing that what is false is true, looking upon a great
man [Robespierre] as a monster, cannot easily recognize that he has
been wrong over so long a period."[6] Let us compare Michelet's
reply. He disputes that Robespierre was a great leader. He tells us:
"[His was] a prodigious life [but he is] a pitiful figure, lacking bril-
liance who, one morning, finds himself exalted . . . ; nothing like
it in the *Arabian Nights!* In no time does he rise higher than the
throne . . . ; what a triumph of virtue!" Michelet grants him hon-
esty, even "a certain amount of talent," willpower and sustained
effort, but concludes: "If this suffices to make him a great man, we
owe him that title" (*HR*, 2:1005).

Louis Blanc shared Michelet's republican ideals but as a socialist he conceives of Robespierre as the pure leader—compared to the tainted Danton. Michelet prefers Danton's humanity to Robespierre's inhuman principle. There are moments when Louis Blanc admits that Robespierre was unfair: he continued to pursue the defeated Vergniaud and prevented members of the Convention from testifying on Vergniaud's behalf;[7] but generally Robespierre emerges as a saint betrayed by those dedicated to the Regime of Terror. Louis Blanc minimizes Robespierre's association with the guillotine and is furthermore convinced that the revolutionary tribunals did not condemn blindly: they even acquitted frequently, far more often than the white terror of reaction[8]—he discusses this reaction at length while Michelet's account ends with the death of Robespierre.

There might have been the possibility of a reconciliation in spite of such divergences—similar to the understanding with Proudhon— had Louis Blanc not added extensive appendixes to a number of chapters listing Michelet's innumerable inaccuracies.[9] Our historian retaliated by claiming that Louis Blanc could not have composed an adequate account in London where he had written all but his first two volumes. It is almost comical to find each of them proving the other wrong in historical detail in order to invalidate his basic interpretation. As Gérard Walter has shown, most of the corrections by Louis Blanc are indeed accurate, and Michelet's defense, that he omitted footnotes in order not to drown his text in them, hardly excuses the omission of references or mistakes, but it is equally clear that Michelet's references can be reconstituted—as G. Walter did. Still, the issue lay not there. It was a matter of ideology and commitment!

III   *An education for the people:* Nos Fils *(1869)*

The long line of books for the people continues. After the *Bible of Humanity* there came *The Mountain;* and now, a year later, *Nos Fils* [Our Sons] takes up themes from *The People, The Student,* and *Woman*. It translates Michelet's humanism into a broad theory of education from early childhood to the university. Michelet's personal experience provides the most moving pages.

The point of departure is all too traditional: the cornerstone of the nation is the family, its focus the mother. She is the principal educator of the nation. Here our historian adds refreshing new perspectives, for he sees the mother communicating her attitudes

to the child even while she bears and nurses him, and this, he
assumes, she will do for two years (*NF*, 48–60). Her song will transmit her joy even to the unborn, just as her feelings of guilt
or sinfulness will bequeath frustration. (*NF*, 42–43, 66). This is
the greatest danger! She must overcome "1,000 years of antinatural
education" (*NF*, 150) and develop the bond of happiness which is
essential to the child and to the family (*NF*, 63, 93–101). The child
must feel loved, unfettered, encouraged, and independent (*NF*, 78),
if he is not to become discouraged and experience the death wish
at an early age (*NF*, 86–88). The intensity of the warning indicates
a personal experience. *Our Sons* posits a positive education, one
based on the faith in life and action found in Rabelais, Rousseau,
and Voltaire (bk. 3, chaps. 2–5) as well as in the recent principles
of Pestalozzi and Froebel (chaps. 6–7). These Michelet had learned
from Mrs. Marenholz in 1859 and already incorporated in *Woman*.

Vico's concept, "man is his own Prometheus," Voltaire's idea of
"action," Rousseau's program of instruction for Emile, are translated
into a proposal for active play as a way of learning applicable throughout, from the first step the child takes to the mastery of moral
principles like duty and justice (*NF*, 131–36). There must be a
creative alternation of activities, of study and experimentation, of
outdoor exploration and crafts learned in a shop, and this even at
the most advanced levels. Students of antiquity should visualize the
subject by constructing relief maps and by viewing Virgil and Ca-
tullus as "a homeopathy of the passions" (*NF*, 275, 281). Industry
and agriculture should be taught as actively as the arts and letters
(bk. 4, chaps. 3–4). Medical students should learn from dissection
rather than from memorization; students of law should relate the
cases they plead to moral principles and beliefs (chaps. 5–6). Active
participation is essential; lectures should be cut in length. Michelet
bemoans how few of his colleagues realize that they become utterly
ineffective after speaking for two hours (*NF*, 263).

Yes, the university needs reform, but with all of its faults it remains the guardian of freedom; teaching is the priesthood of modern
times (*NF*, 269, 393)! Michelet seems to relive his years at the
Collège de France as he insists that instruction reflect the needs of
the times, for men have learned more since Leibniz and Newton
than in the previous 2,000 years (*NF*, 191). As a trancendental idealist he sees progress not just in scientific terms, but as a remarkable
"augmentation of the human spirit" (*NF*, 420); he insists on the
dualism of material and spiritual values, as he had in *Guide France*.

The problem remains how to communicate with the masses, or even the less gifted like his own son Charles, whom Michelet could never reach and who spent his final years in small employment in Strasbourg (he died in 1862). The historian recalls how Béranger had suggested, around 1848, that he not bother composing books for the people; they would create their own literature; but where are these books?[10] Michelet continues to feel that it is incumbent on him to write books accessible to the common people, but as in *The People*, in *The Student*, and in his courses at the Collège de France, he is also searching for other ways of reaching out, for ways of creating community action and solidarity. This is why he speaks, as he had in 1839, of the town bell of Ghent, Roland, calling the citizens to communal action: "March on, go, don't be afraid! To-morrow you may be smashed by a stone but the world stands behind you and will support you! You will triumph, I swear! Don't you hear my voice? Roland! Roland! Roland! . . . The trumpet sound of the last judgment would have sounded less terrifying" (*NF*, 36). Where books and the press cannot reach, other means must be found to communicate the message and stir the people to action.

What modern equivalents might there be? Michelet recalls nostalgically the manifestations to honor the dead of the Revolution, held at the Madeleine in March 1848.[11] What could be done now? Vote "no" in the impending plebiscite, he advises, "no" to the emperor and his coup d'état. When *Our Sons* appeared in November 1869 it seemed that such a vote would assure peace and democracy. The plebiscite was held on 8 May 1870. Napoleon III obtained an overwhelming majority. On 19 July he declared war on Prussia.

Michelet clearly transcends his basically conservative orientation, the moralism that made him reject modern novels, especially those of Balzac,[12] as a threat to the family and a picture of degeneration (*NF*, 101). The historian calls for practical, vital instruction, concerned "monitors" for the young, an open mind to scientific progress. Of course he cannot be ahead of his time in every concern. Athletics make no sense to him. The rational French, he tells us, will refuse to participate, for they always ask: "Why?" (*HF*, 288). Even so, *Nos Fils* remains an exciting proposal for breaking out of the educational mold. It is the *summa* of his professional and personal experience, and a reaffirmation of faith.

IV *War!:* La France devant l'Europe *(1871)*

The rapid sequence of events reflects the growing crisis. The day Napoleon III declares war on Prussia (19 July 1870), the Michelets seek refuge at Pierrefonds but the situation deteriorates. On 16 August they return to Paris to escape to Switzerland. They arrive at Montreux when Napoleon surrenders at Sedan (2 September). To witness a third occupation of Paris would be too much for the historian![13] In October they move to Florence and there, in forty frenzied days, he writes his apology for France in the face of defeat by the German armies. By the time the book appears (1 February), Paris has capitulated and a second edition of *La France devant l'Europe* [France before the Eyes of Europe] and a new preface are in order!

The impact on the health of our historian was terrifying; Athénaïs hid newspapers to no avail. On 9 February he is stricken by fever, on 30 April by partial paralysis, on 22 May he loses the use of his right hand and of speech—but he remains lucid. Soon he recovers and composes the first volume of the *History of the Nineteenth Century*. A preface of 1 January 1872 recounts the aftermath, the conclusion to his agonizing reappraisal. It was completed on the night of 3–4 May 1871, when he dreamed of an alliance between France and Russia (*J*, 4:265). In March, the son of his Russian friend, Alexander Herzen, had brought him the last letters from his father who died in Paris. Posthumously Herzen had completed the reorientation of Michelet begun in 1851, when Herzen's *Open Letter* aroused the historian's sympathy for the people of Russia. In *France before the Eyes of the Europe* he had still conjured up the danger of barbarous Russian hordes and tried to convince Germany to ally herself to France, the land of culture, instead of fighting her;[14] only in 1871 did the pattern of his allegiances change.

As early as 1831 Edgar Quinet had warned that German nationalism was turning against France,[15] but Michelet had had difficulty accepting this, in spite of evident contradictions. What had happened to the Germany of philosophers, of heroes like Luther, scholars like Grimm, to the country of Froebel and Beethoven? to *Gemüt* and *Gemütlichkeit*, to the kindly South Germans from Baden and Bavaria who were now accused of atrocities?[16] To reconcile his prejudices, Michelet invented the fragile myth of Prussia as a Slavic state holding Germany in chains; he expressed his hope that she would wake and free herself from this slavery. This is all the more striking since Frederick the Great had only recently appeared to him as the soldier of freedom![17] These were not days for logical argument but for marshaling sympathy and identifying the threat to European civilization. Michelet appealed to all nations to join with France, for "the judges shall be judged" (*FR*, 5).

It was a matter of soliciting aid and, especially, of counteracting Bismarck's idea that German unity required fire and sword.[18] The shock of seeing his country dismembered is evident; incorporating Alsace and Lorraine into Germany was tearing France limb from limb, for Strasbourg, though speaking a Germanic dialect, was tied to France by deep affection (*FR*, 106). Michelet did not consider French conquests of the past, but only the present onslaught of a new and unsuspected military power, uncultured and exploiting its own people.

The German victory came as a complete surprise since, before that time, the historian had failed to appreciate German nationalism and even the effect of the new artillery. A German cannon exhibited by Krupp at the Paris fair of 1867 provoked only his amusement because it seemed immobile, cumbersome, close to useless, and the American Civil War had been too far away to provide a lesson, even though Michelet mentions the presence of powerful, mobile artillery (*FR*, 68–70). When Prussia defeated Austria at Sadowa (Königgrätz, 1866), he had applauded, for was Austria not Catholic repression personified? Was the "good Franz," Emperor Franz Joseph I (1848–1916), not inextricably identified with his political prison, the Spielberg (*FR*, 31, 57)?

The French defeat convinced Michelet that war had changed. Light infantrymen, like those of Gustavus Adolphus in the Thirty Years' War, were no longer the heroes of the day when heavy artillery was destroying cities, firing not at fortifications but at civilians, when open cities were no longer respected! Man was abusing the machine. Michelet had always welcomed it as a tool of progress, but he had changed![19] Man can corrupt his genius, his inventions; this is the first significant conclusion.

The second involves the terrifying power of government. Many French had voted "no" for peace but Napoleon declared war. The Russians found serfdom abolished but were more dependent than ever, with increased taxes. The Germans were used by Bismarck who played with their hate and fears. Governments were misguiding the people![20]

What could an individual do in the defense of freedom? Our historian could be proud that his book circulated so widely. It was translated into English and many other languages; it was serialized in Austria and Hungary; its proceeds went to war relief (*HD*, 1:5–6); his effort had not been in vain.

Shortly after the volume was published, Michelet collaborated with his wife on the writing of *Nature* (1871). He contributed a remarkable chapter on the marshes of Tuscany, on the constant threat of death from malaria, the causes of which were then unknown. The wind seemed to sweep the disease into the homes of the fatalistic inhabitants, in the form of imperceptible spores. "This dead life can only gain in the peaceful immobility of the tomb; rest is quite assured; no shiver of life can return."[21] The constant danger of death has turned into a death wish!

V   *Beyond the Revolution, Napoleon:* Histoire du dix-neuvième siècle *(1872–1874)*

Michelet's testament as an historian, his history of the Napoleonic era, is a personal memoir with vivid recollections and oral testimony from contemporaries. The first volume of the *Histoire du dix-neuvième siécle* [History of the Nineteenth Century] covers the years 1793–1795 and continues to exploit the records of the Paris Commune *(registres des sections)* which he had copied before they burned with City Hall, in 1871. This explains the short time span covered compared to the second volume that takes us to 1800, and the third to 1815.

The work constitutes a spirited attack against Napoleon, a reply to apologists like Las Cases whose *Record (Mémorial) of St. Helena* built the Napoleonic myth. Here Michelet was not alone. Philippe de Ségur and P. Lanfrey[22] before him, the *Memoirs* of Mme. Rémusat (1879–1880) and the work of Colonel Jung (1880) later— Athénaïs cites them in footnotes, in confirmation of Michelet's hostile judgments—make up a movement that Taine (1887) was also to join.

Bonaparte appears as a despot (*HD*, 3:244–49), a charlatan, miracle worker, and magician (*HD*, 3:353–54), a charismatic leader who convinces his followers that he has answers to all problems (*HD*, 1:334), who believes he can save France even after his final defeat at Waterloo. Michelet's animosity goes so far as to make some of Napoleon's victories incomprehensible; those at Lodi Bridge and

Marengo are told as if they were not his doing. He is shown apt to delay and hesitate, or jealous of a general, Masséna.[23]

Napoleon's accommodation with the pope make him particularly hateful to our historian. When, by the treaty of Tolentino (1797), Napoleon allows the pope's domains to subsist, and even though he seized them later, Michelet calls him a traitor to the Revolution; since Tolentino left Venice in the hands of the Austrians, Napoleon is also their dupe (*HD*, 2:105–25). Even the treaties of Leoben and Campo Formio do not satisfy Michelet because Austria still remains powerful. We might ask: why this animosity? Is Austria not fighting the tyrant? The historian admits this much but feels that Austria is doing so as a Tartuffe; if he must choose between his antipathies, the cause of France will still be the lesser evil.

In dealing with his wives, the emperor plays the role of a villain, like Cromwell in the novels of the Abbé Prévost. While married to Josephine, he covets her daughter, Hortense de Beauharnais, one more temptation of incest. When he divorces Josephine to marry Marie Louise of Austria, "she is delivered to him ash white as to the Minotaur."[24]

Michelet is closer to the truth when he finds that Bonaparte is unable to understand the peoples who might have supported him had he espoused their independence—the Portuguese and especially the Poles—and so the Russian campaign is off to a bad start; but soon he exaggerates again. Following Ségur, he accuses Bonaparte of choosing the worst road back from Moscow, one bound to lead to destruction.[25]

On only two occasions does the historian show sympathy for the emperor: in Egypt, where he finds him organizing a representative assembly more democratic than anything the Egyptians had ever known, and again after Moscow when "the lone lion" (according to Géricault and Delacroix) is subject to the atrocities of royalist propaganda, for Michelet hates the sanctimonious (*béat*) Comte d'Artois, the future Charles X, as much as the fat, gout ridden (*ventru, podagre*) Louis XVIII whose incompetence seems evident.[26] The French Bourbons are no better than the Spanish branch—than Ferdinand, who kills representative government and restores the Inquisition. Here Michelet echoes Benjamin Constant and Sismondi, who wondered where to stand when Napoleon returned from Elba.[27]

The accumulation of negative judgments is almost overwhelming, but there are samples of Michelet's great art, e.g., his account of royalist landings and the battle of Quiberon. There is also his portrait of Hoche: first the pacifier of the Vendée, a thankless task, then the imaginative leader of an invasion of Ireland which failed, finally the promising general in the west who died too young.[28] Another remarkable element is the historian's sympathy for egalitarian idealists: Goujon and five others who tried to reform the Assembly and commited suicide when they failed; also Babeuf whose tribulations are followed in detail.[29] At first a moderate—Michelet insists on this—he turned radical through his contacts in prison, by reading Sylvain Maréchal who wanted to redistribute property. Babeuf stands out against the "depopulation" of France by the guillotine, a victim of his fight for justice and the Constitution of 1793 at the very time it was being forgotten. In his youth, Michelet had helped his father print one of Babeuf's forbidden tracts; now he sees only one crime in Babeuf: like Fourier and Saint-Simon, he frightened conservatives into supporting Bonaparte (*HD*, 1:11).

Two instances of bias are particularly revealing. Czar Paul I and his advisor, Rostopchine, appear as allies of France opposed to Catherine, Paul's mother, and Alexander, his son who ruled after Paul was assassinated. Actually Paul was no more a friend of the French Revolution than the rest of the family; his freeing Kosciusko must be balanced against his authoritarianism about which we hear nothing. Influenced by Rostopchine who resided in Paris, and by Ségur, Rostopchine's relative, Michelet transforms Paul into a hero of Franco-Russian friendship.[30] An equally slanted image is that of Queen Louise of Prussia, said to be hostile to France, whereas her husband, Frederick William III, is a friend (*HD*, 3:231). Michelet's ambivalence toward Prussia and his desire to show the power of women, make him read discord into a united couple. At times he is too generous, at others too severe.

It would be unfair to expect Michelet, paralyzed in 1871, beset by age, with time sliding by him ever faster (*HD*, 3:1, 9), to equal the achievement of his *Revolution*. On his travels to Switzerland, Italy, and southern France, he had difficulty documenting himself, although he speaks of seizing every opportunity (*HD*, 1:18–19). Furthermore, he had become less resilient. The great faith of the eighteenth century and its culmination in the General Federation of 1790 seem compromised: the "rule of death" by the guillotine left France seeking refuge in sentimentality and in a cult of pleasure,[31] and then again in the militarism of Napoleon. The Restoration was no better. The events of 1830 and 1848 led to defeats which paved the way for the empty heads *(petits-crevés)* around Napoleon

III (*HD*, 3;12). Each progressive development seemed worse than the last!

It is ironic that, for an explanation of Michelet's term, we had to turn to Littré's outstanding dictionary (article: *crevé*), for Littré is attacked as a "fatalist" along with two famous researchers in medicine, the French histologist Charles Robin, and the German pathologist Rudolf Virchow (*HD*, 1:11). Their positivist determinism considered man's moral sense as an acquired characteristic, while Michelet was convinced that it was an instinct inborn. He felt that their positivism threatened his ideals of freedom and justice, but this shows the distortion of his ideology and polemic style, for he respected Robin as Athénaïs' physician (since 1856) and as a scientist (*J*, 2:771), while he knew Littré as a neighbor and even a political ally (*J*, 4:118, 422); the spirited liberalism of Littré and Virchow did not erase Michelet's objection to their philosophical principles!

He does keep up with his times and never rejects science. He celebrates Watt's steam engine—though he adds that it was misused in war—he supports the discoveries of Lyell and Darwin; he stands with Geoffroy Saint-Hilaire against Cuvier (whose orthodoxy led him to abide by the date of 4004 B.C. for the earth's creation) and for Lamarck—though a political note enters this debate. He rejects Cuvier in part because Cuvier aimed to please Napoleon, while he praises Lamarck for his opposition to him.[32]

In any event, Michelet does his best to reconcile his fundamental idealism with modern science. He tells us:

At the risk of an apparent inconsistency, I advanced just as the world advances, in this two-fold direction, on both wings. Our master, Voltaire, gave us the example: while attaching great importance to things material, he saw matter mobile and live in the spirit, so that, appearing and claiming to be a materialist, he introduced into materialism so vivid a movement, such flexible elasticity, that the rigid qualities of matter melted away; it seems as if all were spirit.[33]

Michelet accepts determinism even while he proclaims the triumph of the spirit. He defines "matter" and "spirit" to suit this purpose.

He did not intend to write a tract against Napoleon, but rather a history of militarism. His object was the broader issue, even while he remained the guardian and executor of the dead.[34] In the way of broadening his scope, he included perspectives on Egypt, its institutions and religion, and on colonial policy in India under Cornwallis, Wellesley, and Wellington, along with religious questions not previously included in his histories, though considered in the *Bible of Humanity,* a long passage from which is quoted.[35] Michelet continued to the end to look forward and outward. He was preparing the fourth volume of the *History of the Nineteenth Century* when he died.

CHAPTER 9

Conclusion

I The uses of history

THE historian's principal task is to organize the multitude of data from the past into historical knowledge, to organize the facts into meaningful trends to be conveyed to an audience. This ability was one of Michelet's great accomplishments. By observing his mind and sensibility at work, we can derive the following model for his process of interpretation.

From omnivorous reading and the study of original documents, he has the genius to reconstruct the past, identifying each country or period with an idea which lends its logic to the chain of events. With often uncanny insight he will marshall actions and movements into a meaningful order, described in striking images which the reader can understand and retain. This task for the historian was complex, for he would distinguish himself from his predecessors by writing a "democratic" history, a record of the people and not one of battles and kings. The *History of the French Revolution* may be the best illustration of such an enterprise, picturing, as it does, innumerable simultaneous actions, drawing a multiple canvas which the individual actors of history enter in turn. It will include not merely political and diplomatic events, but literature and the arts, philosophy and religious concerns, all viewed through the essential perspective, constantly kept in mind and used to illuminate every aspect.

Michelet puts mind and soul into this task; in other words, he manifests sympathy and compassion for the aspirations of those he describes, with distinct appraisals of victors and victims in the ongoing struggle of men and issues. At times he will approve and come close to sanctifying forces of progress, like Joan of Arc; at other times he will apply bitter irony and black humor to the proponents of intolerance, or despotism, such as those who set out to rid France

163

of its Protestant minority. He will, however, not simply praise or condemn, as his predecessors had done, but visualize what each was trying to accomplish, with unending human concern and empathy. In the Revolution, even Louis XVI and Robespierre have his ear. None shall be judged without a full hearing, an attempt to portray their background, the circumstances which dictated their action. Still, the historian is increasingly aware of the moral dimension of the past and asserts that there must be no weak compromise with the facts, with victories and power, for the forces which triumph are not necessarily those of progress.

This partiality shapes his understanding of forces and events. It implies an invincible faith in the future which will not capitulate before defeats, and these are many, not only in the past but in the present; the constant disappointments of successive governments and regimes, from the Restoration to Napoleon III and defeat in the Franco-Prussian war. There are moments when Michelet is tempted to give in. The last volume of his history contains, in an appendix, his comment on Grainville and his poem, *The Last Man,* a vision of despair, but in the face of such gloom he will resist and return to his task; he would have carried on even then, had life given him time. A final act of faith remains his essential conclusion to every issue and every contest he portrays.

In many ways, Michelet's popular books on science and society follow a similar pattern. He is open to scientific discovery; he depicts the life force, the "soul," even in microorganisms; but he will reconcile it with the forces of determinism, just as he will at times describe the actors of the past as men caught in the inevitable mesh of fate, but still view them as human beings worthy of their hopes. His picture of woman in modern society shows many parallels with this view. Ultimately and in spite of all obstacles, he will add his word of encouragement and reaffirm his hope in life, and in the future.

Here we touch on the haunting theme of his entire work, best expressed in terms of death and resurrection. *The Mountain,* which contains some of his most intimate confessions, speaks of the death wish of the child. Material distress, awkward unpreparedness at the Collège Charlemagne which called forth the mocking ridicule of his classmates and sent the boy hurrying to the cemetery of Père Lachaise, to seek consolation in his studies and the classics he was reading with passion; all this sets the stage for a lasting orientation, reinforced by the death of Paul Poinsot (1821) and of his wife, Pauline

(1839), then of Mme. Dumesnil (1842), not to mention the less traumatic experiences. The historian comes to feel that men and women of the past are claiming his attention, asking him to speak for them, to translate their actions in a perspective they did not possess. History becomes a living, personal experience, the interpretation of the past so as to inspire present and future generations. In *The People* (1846), Michelet finds his definition, resurrection, on which he will elaborate in the great *Preface* to the *History of France* (1869).

Death must lead to life. From the start, the eschatology of the Christian church, fears in anticipation of the end of the world, first illustrated in his picture of the year 1000, but repeated in all of his accounts of Christian unworldliness, are not to his liking. Michelet prefers the rationalism of an Abelard, or else the mysticism of heretics like Joachim of Flores who seems to announce a revolutionary end of the world, an "eternal gospel" transcending the established church, for such independence of thought is preferable to an acceptance of what seemed to be thought-control and superstition perpetrated by a powerful hierarchy. From the start, in 1833, but increasingly so, Michelet's attacks may sound sacrilegious; and I hope to have avoided offending my readers in restating his forceful attacks on orthodoxy. His assault, first on scholasticism, later on the Jesuits and priests who are directors of conscience, is indeed an ever more strident call for action, the kind of action and advocacy of reform in which he tries to drown his personal sorrow, as he comes to consider himself, more and more, a "modern monk," a priest of the new faith, using his chair at the Collège de France to convert as much as to inform. This explains why his academic life, resolutely apart from the political scene, seems ever more offensive to successive conservative governments which will suspend his teaching, first in 1848, and definitively in 1851.

Surely then, his form of "resurrection of the past" is no colorful literary attempt to recreate scenes from history, the way Chateaubriand practiced it, but a reawakening of the revolutionary fervor, of the spirit of 1789–1790 which united France from the taking of the Bastille to the feast of the General Federation on the Champ de Mars. In a way, the spirit of the Renaissance, defined in the introduction to volume 7 of the *History of France*, and the "Creed of the Eighteenth Century," evoked in volume 16, are transpositions of the same spirit. The "uses of the past" are to be understood essentially in terms of the inspiration Michelet could pass on to his contemporaries. Of course this implies a commitment to principles which arouse enthusiasm in readers just as they sustain his own sensitivities. Such are the themes of his inspiration *(les principes inspirateurs)* which I have tried to define in my book of 1954. They involve ideals to be shared with his public, but they do not constitute a "philosophical system," for he consistently opposes systems which, like straitjackets, might fetter the free mind.

His passion for biology, especially in the field of reproduction, his books on natural science and on women, lead much to the same conclusion. Here the analogy to the resurrection of the past is found in the regeneration of the family and in constant rebirth, in the life cycle of birds and insects or sea life, even in the geological transformations viewed in *The Mountain*. Ultimately there is a great unity in Michelet's world view, called forth by the experience of death, and in response to it. His image of revolutions which failed have led critics (e.g., Hayden White) to speak of his "cataclysmic" view of history, but while failure and death seem omnipresent, the life force appears always new. Science supports our hope for a better future, as does history! There are moments when Michelet hesitates, as when he views the unparalleled devastation of modern war, the abuse of the machine and man's creativity, but soon he conceives a ray of hope. Even *France before the Eyes of Europe* has a positive conclusion.

II   *Of style and method*

We have found our historian resisting the appelation "romantic," because he was far more concerned with his message than with descriptive technique. Still he remains the romantic historian par excellence. Without the dramatic detail and his empathy, for the battles of history as for those of ants and spiders, he would not be the great author he is. Besides, there are other qualities which have fascinated his readers. He appears as a voyeur not only in the *Journal*, when he observes Athénaïs, but in picturing the cruelty of man to man, the intolerance of the Inquisition, witch trials, the quartering of a regicide, or the atrocities of the Russian police in repressing the serfs. He often seeks out the abnormal, the satanic, the destruction of the individual by thought control. His realistic illustrations from the past outstrip literary fantasy, and so it is amusing to find his objection to novelists like Balzac who depict decadence: his own scenes of exploitation and injustice break through the conservative, bourgeois framework of a moral society which he wants to uphold. We have made it a point to cite some of the scenes which bear the distinction of great literature. His style is never wordy, but nervous, appropriate to the variety of subjects described, the very opposite of the swell of sentimental platitude in which Athénaïs buried his prose when she began "editing" some of his manuscripts after he died. True, she inspired him; she transformed his image of woman and marriage. We can be thankful that he let her collaborate in the nature books, but also that he reserved his right to modify and revise.

Even more remarkable is the framework he imposes on what he observes. He seeks out the "silences of history." He subordinates man's battles to his long struggle with nature, to the conquest of matter by the spirit, of fate by freedom. This is how we are to understand the progress of religion and civilization from the earliest days of India to the manifestation of brotherhood on 14 July 1790. Michelet conceives of it as a long voyage from *terra mater* ("mother earth") to the victory of the spirit, such as he finds it in history or in his own life, magically restored at Acqui. It is not an easy road as we are so often reminded, for instance in *The Witch:* the chthonic forces of the underworld must be tamed if culture is to triumph over nature, and if man with his science is to be "his own Prometheus," to create a better world for his fellowmen out of compassion. These concepts are never far from his mind: they provide the "structure" and the myths of his "text," as Lionel Gossman put it in his masterful summary of fundamental themes.[1]

Implied here is a commitment to progress—Michelet's idealistic transfiguration of the past; but fortunately, for all his insistence on the triumphant spirit, on his faith in the future, he never hides the truth: he describes the ugly reality, the dangers of the single girl in Paris, the inadequacies of well-intentioned ministers and kings at Versailles, and the brutality of the masses, a topic particularly painful to the historian who set out to write *their* story, even though, from Hannibal and Caesar to Napoleon and his generals, he all too often concentrates on individuals. Still, the noble intent is there, the desire to place the people squarely in the center of the historical action as a testimony to his own humble origins and to his democratic ideology.

As Michelet advances in his career, he becomes ever more aware of the distance which separates him from "the people" among whom he was born, with whom he wants to communicate, who must be reached if France as a whole is to be propelled to action. His courses, his appeals to students to become missionaries among the people, are attempts to reach out, as are the "popular" books addressed to as wide an audience as possible, whether they deal with political action in the past or present (like the *Democratic Legends of the North*), with scientific or social observation.

His commitment to popular education became part of his "method," as he understood the term. Moral and religious themes permeate his work. The progress of civilization, the movement of the torch of freedom he follows in the *Introduction to Universal History* and again in the *Bible of Humanity*, is after all the progress of the people. He would never have attacked the inadequate (i.e., unworldly) faith of the early church, or of the Middle Ages, if the affirmation of a new religious faith and solidarity had not been so essential. His call on Christianity to be reborn is the echo of a profound concern, a way of reaching out to the people. Here Vico's message, summed up in the formula, "man is his own Prometheus," becomes part of his "method" and fundamental purpose, and is not unrelated to the belief that the divine voice of conscience (proposed in Rousseau's *Emile* and basic in spite of Michelet's late rebuttal that Rousseau capitulated to the Christian church) enables us to create a moral and humane society. The historian perceives a call to act, a categorical imperative, which is the essence of his message, of what Michelet calls his "method."

Of course, we can also define his "method" in more habitual terms and refer to his subordinating historical detail to dominant themes—though in discursive style—and so distinguish him as much from chroniclers like Barante or even Sismondi, as from philosophical analysts like Guizot, Mignet, and Thiers, but less so than Michelet thought from the admittedly more limited scope of an Augustin Thierry. Michelet was proud of having combined the emphasis on the spirit and meaning of history, with "material" considerations, such as race, geography, and economics; he dwelled on this for many pages in his *Preface* of 1869. Even so, his is an epic view compared to the factual, "scientific" history of other contemporaries or successors, of Ranke and Renan in particular. Michelet subordinates facts to a vision of the past which Ranke's ideal of writing history "just as it was" cannot recapture with its emphasis on objectivity. Michelet might well have listed other "material" factors which distinguish his "method," the introduction of scientific theories—some, like telegony, seem fanciful since they have long been discarded—to explain actions and influences of the past, such as the power of women behind the throne. This is especially noticeable after his marriage to Athénaïs. We read of seduction at Versailles, of the "Austrian" pressure (through Marie-Antoinette) on Louis XVI. We may wonder why the *Preface* of 1869 analyzes only the "methods" of the early volumes; possibly it is because Michelet hesitates to reveal his later self in such a public statement.

I have found the "method" of his later years so fascinating that I have devoted more space to it than is usual. His later works may not be monuments of historiography like his *History of the Middle Ages* and the *Revolution*, but they are remarkable applications of his method. If the reader becomes interested in the way Michelet's mind works, in his use of "material" factors to explain the spiritual unity of France and its eternal mission, he will find as much of interest after 1853 as before that year, when the historian completed his *Revolution*.

Michelet's resurrection of the past expresses his commitment to the democratic ideal. Michelet may be biased, but he will always be biased in a noble, selfless way. That is why even today readers are moved by his work. As Gabriel Monod put it in his essential biography, *The Life and Thought of Jules Michelet*, we cannot reread him without being affected and carried away. New facets of the past have been discovered; nineteenth-century interpretations are dated; but Michelet remains the greatest French historian of his day, one still worth reading. He is the historian he wanted to be, the artist who confers immortality "with his power over men's dreams."[2]

Notes and References

Chapter One

1. For a list of the abbreviations used, see the selected bibliography, pp. 185, 187 (Monod) 188 (Viallaneix).

2. In *Oeuvres* (éd. Pléiade), 1:515, Rousseau rejects literature including his *New Heloise*. Michelet writes under the spell of Rousseau, and asserts that Rousseau is not the only man to have revealed himself to humanity (*EJ*, 182). He even composes a "letter of Jules to Michelet" (*EJ*, 24) which recalls *Rousseau, Judge of Jean-Jacques*.

3. The Michelets did not know that the book was by Fabre d'Olivet, a masonic mystic whose anonymous publication brought him no royalties; see L. Cellier, *Fabre d'Olivet* (Paris, 1953), pp. 7, 421.

4. In J. Michelet, *Lettres inédites*, ed. Sirven (Paris, 1924).

5. See A. Govindane in *Romantisme* 10 (1975):197–202 and *J*, 3:739; for the explanation to Poinsot, cf. Monod in *JM*, 1:38.

6. The only rival for Michelet's affection in *JM* had been his work; his letters to Pauline are always tender and affectionate, cf. *J*, 1:706–19. On Pauline cf. *EJ*, 341; see also chap. 3, sec. 1 below.

7. His mother's death, in 1815, had come as a relief after her quarrels with Jean-Furcy; Jules regrets that he became involved; cf. *EJ*, 215. Death remains a haunting theme as Pauline dies in 1839; Mme. Dumesnil in 1842; Jean-Furcy in 1846; Michelet's daughter, Adèle, in 1855; his son, Charles, in 1862; his son from the second marriage, Yves-Jean-Lazare, in 1850, soon after birth. Death viewed as the fundamental theme of history is even more important.

8. Paul Viallaneix (*EJ*, 20) lists parallel passages in the *Mémorial* and *The People* (*PE*, 67–70). The comparison is interesting.

9. Locke's *Essay on Human Understanding*, bk. 2, sec. 17 is analyzed in V. Cousin, *Cours de philosophie sensualiste*, pectures of 1 and 16 December 1818, and in the *Cours de l'histoire de la philosophie* (Paris, 1829), 2:209.

10. Plutarch was born in 46 or 50 A.D. and eventually lived in Rome. Trajanus, the first emperor of non-Italian origin, was born in Spain in 53 A.D. Their relationship is unclear.

11. Cf. Augustin Thierry, "Vue des révolutions d'Angleterre" in *Le Censeur européen* (1817), and Guizot, *Histoire de la révolution d'Angleterre* (1826–1827).

12. Michelet read the *Handbuch . . . des europäischen Staatensystems* (1809, translated in 1821), and other works; cf. *EJ*, 321.

13. The *Discours* was printed. Sismondi and Benjamin Constant sent enthusiastic responses. The latter presented Michelet with a copy of *De la Religion*.

14. "De l'Allemagne et de la Révolution," *Revue des deux mondes*, 1 January 1832. This and subsequent articles were gathered by P. Gautier in *Un Prophète, Edgar Quinet* (Paris, 1917). Michelet found them "violent and terrifying" (*JM*, 1:249–50; cf. *OC*, 2:685), but their friendship was unaffected. Michelet intervened to have Quinet paid for his limited contribution to an archeological expedition to the Peleponnesos and upheld Quinet's claim that there were great French medieval epics (*OC*, 2:683, 687). In *Ahasvérus* (1833) Quinet pictures himself as the wandering Jew, since he traveled throughout Europe while he was unable to marry Minna Moré.

15. See S. Bernard-Griffiths in *Romantisme* 10 (1975):145–65. Only one brief note in Quinet's *Révolution* mentions Michelet.

16. The *Autobiography* and *New Science*, trans. T. G. Bergin and M. H. Fisch (Ithaca, N.Y.: Cornell University Press, 1948) and abridgment 1970; *La Science nouvelle*, trans. A. Doubine (Paris, 1953).

17. A. Pons, "Vico and French Thought," in *G. Vico, An International Symposium*, ed. Giorgio Tagliacozzo and Hayden White (Baltimore, 1969), pp. 165–85; O. A. Haac, "Michelet and Vico," *Forum Italicum* 2 (1968):483–93; see also *VR*, 214–38. *Verum, certum: OC*, 1:432–36, axioms 10–11 (secs. 138–41 in the Bergin and Fisch abridgment, p. 21); on freedom: axiom 11 (sec. 141); cf. the Doubine translation, p. 65.

18. *VR*, 228 cites the course of 1828 according to Chéruel.

19. *VR*, 229–30, text continued in Pons, p. 182.

20. The motto recurs in 1869 (*OC*, 4:13) and in the preface to *Nos Fils* (near the beginning).

Chapter Two

1. The notes of Michelet's students, preserved at the Ecole Normale Supérieure, have been transcribed at Clermont-Ferrand by M. F. Berriot; for a listing see *VR*, 500.

2. "Tableau de l'Italie," *OC*, 2:347–54; "Tableau de la France," *OC*, 4:331–87; cf. *JM*, 1:123–36.

3. *J*, 1:53; cf. 51–55; *JM*, 1:145–69. The list of scholars is far longer and includes: Zachariae (Germanic law), and at Bonn, Welcker (Greek history), Gieseler (church history), Lassen (Sanscrit).

4. *OC*, 2:242; cf. *J*, 1:60, 65, 67.

5. Michelet is complimentary to Thierry in 1831 (*OC*, 2:343); in 1833 he quotes him on the Capet monarchy and acknowledges his debt (*OC*, 4:321–27, 625). In 1834 he writes Thierry a glowing letter (in A. Augustin-Thierry, *Augustin Thierry* [Paris, 1922], p. 144). It was only in 1837, in writing to Sainte-Beuve, Peyrat, and Nettement, that Michelet asserted his

superior view of race as one of many factors, and pictured Thierry as a slave of the race theory (*JM*, 1:273). Thierry, in turn, criticized Michelet in his *Considérations sur l'histoire de France* (1840) for being too much of a symbolist, for seeing the history of Rome as the pattern for all others (C. Jullian, *Extraits des historiens* [Paris, 1896], p. 99). Finally in 1866, Michelet identified Thierry with the "fatalism of race" (*OC*, 2:335), even though Thierry realized that race was no longer a uniform force in the modern world. The real argument between the two historians was political: Thierry held to the July monarchy, Michelet adopted a more republican stance. Thierry also laid more stress on detail, Michelet on the grand sweep; Thierry's *History of the Tiers-Etat* is limited in scope. Both favor the cause of the people. Cf. *J*, 1:358, 573, 876 of 1840–1844. Thierry died in 1856.

6. Humboldt's *Researches on the Original Inhabitants of Spain Viewed Through the Basque Language* (1821) identifies the Basques as "Iberians," pre-Celtic, and pre-Germanic. Michelet's essential sources include Amédée Thierry (Augustin's brother), *Histoire de la Gaule sous l'administration romaine* (1828), and the brochure of his friend, Dr. Edwards, entitled *Des Caractères psychologiques des races humaines dans leurs rapports avec l'histoire* (1828), where race is associated with long-lasting psychological characteristics. Edwards, whose essay takes the form of a letter to Amédée Thierry, relates the original populations to the pre-Hellenic Pelasgians. Cf. *JM*, 1:171–72.

7. See note 5 above.

8. This image of Germany recurs very often: *OC*, 4:171, 309–10, 499.

9. Joachim: *OC*, 4:588–89; stone to bread: Luke 4:3; passion in stone: *OC*, 4:668–69; these views of 1833 appear in variants, pp. 120, 149; for a later text see p. 600. Cf. also Jean Guéhenno's remarkable essay, *L'Evangile éternel*, p. 76, and Haac, *Les Principes inspirateurs*, pp. 194–95.

10. *OC*, 4:499. This includes the cathedral at Cologne, described according to Boisserée, *History of the Cathedral of Cologne* (1823); see *OC*, 4:603. Alsace is not discussed in the *Tableau* which limits France to the French–speaking provinces. In 1870, Michelet will take a different view.

11. *J*, 1:104–7 (1832); 226–32 (1837).

12. Compliment: *JM*, 1:314–15; objection: letter quoted by A. Augustin-Thierry, p. 142. For his own good, Michelet refrained from criticizing Guizot, *JM*, 1:259–60.

13. *J*, 1:147–52; *JM*, 327–30. On the poor laws, see Elie Halévy, *England in 1815* (New York, 1961), pp. 241–43, 377–81; on the exploitation of labor, the famous passage from Adam Smith, *Wealth of Nations*, quoted by Marx, *Capital*, chap. 14. Conditions had not changed much since 1776!

14. Irène Tieder, *Michelet et Luther* (Paris, 1976), p. 52. Michelet employed a number of "secretaries" including Rosenwald and Théodore Toussenel, the Germanist and brother of Alphonse whom we shall meet when we discuss *L'Oiseau*. Alphonse Müntz became a Protestant minister. (The Toussenel brothers are confused in *J*, 1:818; cf. Paul Bénichou, "Les origines

françaises de l'antisémitisme," *Commentaire* 1 [1978]:67–79; on Toussenel, pp. 70–73; Michelet, pp. 74–78.)

15. Tieder, pp. 66–67; on Luther also *JM*, 1:336–56; 2:227–36.

16. *Histoire de France*, vol. 7 in *OC*, 7:308–10.

17. Tieder, pp. 80–81, stresses the compassionate Luther who loves nature, animals, like Michelet.

18. Ibid., pp. 106–13.

19. Ibid., p. 132. Two further editions in 1838 and 1854 are a measure of fair success.

20. Trip to Aquitaine, *J*, 1:165–217; the report on the libraries appears in *OC*, 3:539–64.

21. Published by Vauthier, *Feuilles d'histoire*, 2 (1914):52–56, and *Revue des bibliothèques*, year 32 (1912):247–52. The *Journal* is more interested in art: *J*, 1:221–50.

22. These sources appear in *OC*, 3:635–57, a typical sample.

23. Nettement had said: "Guizot is the prose, Michelet the poetry of history" (*OC*, 5:595–600). Michelet's reply is found in E. Biré, "Un Chapitre de la presse royaliste," *Le Correspondant* 194 (1899):161–62.

24. Michelet makes the traditional distinction between *le droit réel* governing real property, and *le droit personnel* for personal property.

25. Manuscript course to appear in *OC*, vol. 12. Michelet began teaching at the Collège de France in 1838.

26. Better manuscripts existed at the Bibliothèque nationale; cf. G. Rudler, *Michelet historien de Jeanne d'Arc* (Paris, 1926) and the edition of Michelet's *Jeanne d'Arc* by Paul Viallaneix (Paris, 1974). Text: *OC*, 6:39–122. Ultimately, Michelet sees the reality of Joan's voices better than Rudler, a modern historian of the scientific school.

27. *OC*, 6:121; cf. the *Course of 1839*, edited according to A. Dumesnil by O. A. Haac in *Revue d'histoire littéraire* (1954), monograph supplement, p. 31.

28. *OC*, 6:212–16; cf. *J*, 1:104–7, 147, 226–32 with comments on art, architecture; also *Course of 1839*.

29. *J*, 1:256–57 (1838), 522, 529, 533 (1843).

30. Viallaneix commentary in *OC*, 6:24–25, 28.

31. *OC*, 6:285–86, 381; *Course of 1839*, p. 110.

Chapter Three

1. Cf. *JM*, 1:361–63; *OC*, 6:23–24.

2. His colleagues in the sciences were more reluctant than he to derive general principles from their discoveries (*JM*, 2:5).

3. That is, to April 1843. The "course of 1843" begins in December 1842.

4. These articles and related manuscript comments appear in *Moi Paris* (Paris, 1975), pp. 69–97, along with other notes on Paris, 1830–1834. Cf. *JM*, 2:17–21.

5. *JM*, 2:18; the text in *Moi Paris*, p. 80, is different.

6. *Moi Paris*, p. 95.

7. *Course of 1839* (chap. 2, n. 27): *clarté:* p. 118; renaissance: p. 129. The material cited and this edition concern the second semester, April to July 1839. Cf. also *JM*, 2:33–34.

8. *Course of 1839*, p. 129.

9. Ibid., p. 136.

10. Manuscript to appear in *OC*, vol. 12; cf. chap. 2, n. 25.

11. Monod says that Michelet was going to defend Napoleon as the unifier of France in the brochure he planned (*JM*, 2:50–51, 95) and Viallaneix concurs (*J*, 1:811, n. to p. 364). Napoleon does appear cherished by a poor weaver (*J*, 1:302), fallen in an act of faith (*J*, 1:313). His genius is recognized in the course of 1829 and especially in that of 1840 where he is called one of the three great generals of all times (with Alexander and Caesar) and the greatest of these. When Michelet revised his ideas, he destroyed all early notes. The praise of Napoleon is found in student notes: M. F. Berriot: *Les Petites Leçons, 1829–1832*, a typescript at Clermont-Ferrand, and the Dumesnil notes of 1840 in Paris (papers, 1494).

12. In manuscript, cf. *JM*, 2:65–80.

13. The instruction continued until July 1843 and the appointment was not terminated until 1845; relations remained cordial. Michelet was even invited to dine by the duc de Montpensier, the king's brother (*JM*, 2:118, 125, 153).

14. *J*, 1:412–67, also O. A. Haac, "A Spiritual Journey," *Proceedings of the American Philosophical Society*, 94 (1950):502–9, based on the parallel diaries of Alfred Dumesnil and Adèle Michelet. Cf. articles by Crouzet and Seznec in the bibliography.

15. Michelet cites Hegel's *Esthétique*, translated by Bénard (1840), and Schelling, *Système de l'idéalisme transcendental*, translated by Grimblot (1842).

16. Actually only Oken had political problems in Munich.

17. Haac, "A Spiritual Journey," p. 506. On Rückert cf. *J*, 1:433–34, 450. His verse, "Die Flügel, die Flügel," will be the motto of *L'Oiseau*.

18. As the outstanding goldsmith of his day and the trusted aide of King Dagobert, Eloi was much more than the lowly artisan Michelet suggests.

19. It was located on the present site of the Ecole des Beaux Arts, cf. *PE*, 67.

20. Jointly published in 1843. Other publications by Michelet in these years include: the Latin text of the trial of the Knights Templar, vol. 1 (1841), and reeditions of the *Introduction à l'histoire universelle*, *Histoire romaine* (1843), and *Histoire de France*, vol. 6 (December 1943, dated 1844).

21. See the introduction by Paul Vaillaneix to *JS;* cf. *JM*, 2:198.

22. Desgarets, pp. 10–12.

23. *JS*, 55, 78, 91, 97, 105, etc.

24. New ed. by L. Mickiewicz under the title, *Les Slaves*, published by the Musée A. Mickiewicz (Paris, 1914).

25. Ibid., and *J.*, 1:592 where Michelet modifies the thought: "Many men are needed," not one as Mickiewicz said.

26. Ibid., p. 100.

27. In *Le Christianisme et la Révolution française* (1845) dedicated to Michelet.

28. *PR*, 75. One lesson of the course was devoted to the bad taste of Jesuit art, manifest in the restorations at St.-Germain-des-Prés and Notre Dame.

29. Hobbes's pessimism seeing man in need of restraint might be "fatalistic," but Michelet's misunderstanding of Spinoza is startling.

30. *PR*, 216–17; cf. Paul Pelckmans, "Le Prêtre, la femme et la famille, notes sur l'anticléricalisme de Michelet," *Romantisme* 23 (1979):17–30; for a Catholic view see José Cabanis, *Michelet, le prêtre et la femme* (Paris, 1978), pp. 151–79.

31. Saisset's article appeared on 15 February 1845 in the *Revue des deux mondes;* he had studied with Michelet at the Ecole Normale.

32. See *OC*, 6:27 on Marie; *VR*, 54, *PE*, 21, and *AM*, 69–70 on Victoire who had learned to read; see also refs. in *J*, vol. 4. The Ecoles centrales had been a short-lived (1795–1808) project for higher education in all fields; they are discussed in the last lesson, second semester.

33. Paul Viallaneix, "Michelet, machine, machinisme," *Romantisme* 23 (1979):3–16.

34. *Prophets and Peoples, Studies in Nineteenth Century Nationalism* (New York, 1946).

35. Michelet's terms, "imitation" and "influence," have nothing in common with our critical vocabulary. It is hard to imagine *René* without *Werther*, but what he means is that Chateaubriand resisted foreign ideologies. Lamennais's *Livre du peuple* and *Paroles d'un croyant* bring him close to Michelet's point of view. Michelet sympathizes with the four authors he mentions and resists Balzac.

36. Letter to Eugène Noël in *J*, 1:902.

37. Michelet favors the rebellion by Tynowski in Krakow; it was crushed by Prussia, Austria, and Russia; cf. *JM*, 2:217–19.

Chapter Four

1. *J*, 1:656–59; cf. *JM*, 2:212. On Furcy and Voltaire, see chap. 1, sec. 1.

2. Michelet followed an eight-volume compilation connecting letters and other documents by a running text, *Mémoires biographiques, littéraires*

et politiques de Mirabeau, 2d ed. (Paris, 1841). His notes show how attached he was to Mirabeau.

3. Walter not only indicates Michelet's sources but compares his interpretation with modern scholarship, especially in the biographical appendix; cf. *HR,* 1:160, 1333.

4. *HR,* 542, 561–62; cf. p. 104. Mirabeau favored the king in order to prevent the formation of a new revolutionary aristocracy.

5. Cf. G. Picon, "Michelet et la parole historienne," in *ET.*

6. *Lettres inédites,* in *Oeuvres complètes de J. Michelet* (Paris, 1899), 40:15; cf *J,* 2:602; see also pp. 567–643.

7. *Les Mémoires d'une enfant,* p. i (dedication to her husband).

8. *Les Chats* (1868–1873), ed. G. Monod (Paris, 1905). Many chapters are corrected by Michelet.

9. Jeanne Calo, *La Création de la femme chez Michelet* (Paris, 1975), pp. 193, 195, 445–48. On Yves-Jean-Lazare see n. 17 below. Athénaïs so antagonized Adèle and Alfred that they did not attend the wedding. Tensions remained so that the family manuscripts were not reunited until the 1950s. After Michelet's death, she edited his manuscripts in adulterated form.

10. Matthew 16:23; Mark 8:33; these "barbarians" are unlike those of the course of 1843, first semester; cf. also *J,* 2:34–39.

11. *HR,* 1:1143; cf. 2:54–55, 62, 155, 161.

12. O. A. Haac, "Faith in the Enlightenment: Voltaire and Rousseau Seen by Michelet," *Studies on Eighteenth Century Culture* 7 (1978):475–90, esp. p. 481.

13. L. Blanc, *Histoire de la Révolution française* (Paris, 1857–1861), 8:452–54; cf. *HR,* 2:1073, note to p. 400.

14. The special function of woman is a response to man's irreversible trend toward specialization (the division of labor), as Rousseau had seen it in his *Essay on Inequality* and *Social Contract* (cf. *Ecrits politiques* [Paris, 1964], pp. 171, 360, 382), leading man to scientific and "material" concerns, as opposed to the immense need for spiritual unity fulfilled by woman (*J,* 2:55).

15. Cf. Edward Kaplan, *Michelet's Poetic Vision* (Amherst, 1977), "The Two Sexes of the Mind," pp. 115–30.

16. Michelet entered into correspondence with her in January 1850 and met her in April (*J,* 2:99 and note); cf. sec. 6 below.

17. He was named Lazare after general Hoche (cf. sec. 6 below) "in the religious hope of an awakening of nations. . . . Oh vanity of our hopes" (*IN,* 306); cf. Kaplan, p. 87.

18. Mary C. Simpson, *Letters and Recollections of Julius and Mary Mohl* (London, 1887), p. 66; cf. Haac, *Principes inspirateurs,* p. 129.

19. *Kosciusko (Pologne et Russie)* (1851), *Les Martyrs de la Russie* (1852), *Principautés danubiennes, Mme Rosetti* (1853) all in *LD, Légendes démocratiques de Nord* (1854), entitled *La Pologne martyre* in its 2d ed. of 1863.

20. The *Open Letter* appears in A. Herzen, *From the Other Shore; the Russian People,* ed. I Berlin (New York, 1956), pp. 177–192, and sq.

21. Ibid., p. 200, 208.

22. See Michel Cadot in *LD,* xv–xvi. Herzen's influence grew constantly; it is notable especially after 1855.

23. *Les Soldats de la Révolution* (1878) in *Oeuvres complètes* (Paris, 1893–1899), pp. 287–88.

24. Ibid., pp. 200, 208.

25. A. Thiers, *Histoire de la Révolution française,* 10 vols., (1823–1827), chaps. 10, 31.

26. Douglas Johnson, *Guizot* (London, 1963), p. 20.

27. Guizot, *The History of France from the Earliest Times to 1848,* ed. Mrs. Guizot de Witt, trans. R. Black (New York, 1878), 6:143, 206–13.

28. Mignet, *Histoire de la Révolution française* (1824), chap. 9.

29. Robespierre probably read only the *Social Contract.* Jacques Godechot, "L'historiographie française de Robespierre," *Actes du colloque Robespierre, XIIe Congrès international des sciences historiques* (Paris, 1967), pp. 170–71 (also on Mignet).

30. *Histoire des Girondins* (Paris, 1848), 1:1–2, 6.

31. Godechot, p. 176.

32. *Histoire des Girondins,* 8:2–8.

33. Louis Blanc, *Histoire de la Révolution française,* 12 vols. (Paris, 1847–1861); all but the first two volumes were written in London; Michelet refers to this fact to discredit its accuracy, in his preface of 1868, entitled "Le Tyran" (*HR,* 2:1004–22), see chap. 8, sec. 2 below; see also the numerous corrections Louis Blanc included in bibliographical appendixes to many chapters. The real contention is between interpretations: Louis Blanc is for Robespierre, Michelet for Danton. On Gérard Walter, see n. 3 above.

34. *HR,* 2:426–29, 860–72; cf. 1:4–5, 24–25, 30.

35. Roland, *HR,* 1:661–72, 1269–72; 2:619–22; also idealized in Lamartine, *Histoire des Girondins,* 7:223–46. Corday: *HR,* 2:497–511, 1333; Lamartine also sees her influenced by Rousseau: *Girondins,* 6:203.

36. The text Athénaïs published in 1879 is incomplete and "improved" in her abusive manner. We base our comments on the edition by E. Fauquet to appear in *OC;* cf. also *OC,* 7:25.

37. The bleeding head is described in the course of 1840 as that "of a man who was banished, a friend of Servius," sixth king of Rome.

38. Cf. however some of the variants of the *History of France* of 1833 in *OC,* 4:617–727, and chap. 2, sec. 5 above. The courses of 1839–1843 continue the transformation, but the view expressed belongs to 1843, not to 1831.

39. On 10 August 1854 he moved into the building which today is no. 76, rue d'Assas; he was not to move again; cf. *OC,* 7:26.

Chapter Five

1. Jeanne, later Mme. Paul Baudoüin, will maintain the family estate at Vascoeuil, between Rouen and Beauvais, and live there with her unmarried sister. Jeanne died in 1944. Her daughter-in-law turned over the family manuscripts (the "fonds Dumesnil-Baudoüin") to the Bibliothèque historique de la Ville de Paris; thus the papers joined those left by Athénaïs and deeded by Gabriel Monod.

2. *OC*, 7:72–75. Joachim: cf. chap. 2, sec. 5 and n. 9; Joan of Arc: cf. chap. 2, sec. 7 and *Course of 1839*, ed. Haac, p. 31.

3. Cf. chap. 3, no. 33.

4. Cf. *La Sorcière*, cf. chap. 7, sec. 5 below.

5. *OC*, 7:184, 192–93. Marie d'Angleterre is the sister, not the daughter of Henry VIII (Michelet's error on p. 193).

6. Taine's articles of 1855 and 1856, in *OC*, 7:643–47, 679–85, are most perceptive. On Charles V, p. 646.

7. Ibid., p. 680.

8. *OC*, 8:384; cf. *Histoire de France* (Hetzel ed.) 3:343; references to the *Histoire de France*, vols. 9–17 are given in vols. 3–5 of this edition (*HF*, vols. 3–5).

9. *OC*, 7:436, 452; the sculpture of Diane as huntress by Goujon: *HF*, 3:335.

10. In this tribute to his hope in science, Michelet groups Paracelsus (1493–1541), Vesalius (1514–1564), Servetus (1509–1553) who is credited with discovering the circulation of the blood and hiding his results in a treatise on theology, and Bernard Palissy (1510–1590), the great naturalist (*HF*, 4:495–97).

11. Buckingham's fleet stood off shore but failed to intervene, another discredit to the English (*HF*, 4:226).

12. As usual Michelet assumes that his reader is familiar with names, titles, and family relationships. Monsieur is Gaston d'Orléans, brother of Louis XIII. From his marriage to Mlle. de Montpensier there was born "La Grande Mademoiselle," the wealthiest heiress of the kingdom who had ambitions to become queen of France even though she was nine years older than Louis XIV. In 1652 she intervened in the Fronde, causing the cannons of the Bastille to fire on the royal troops under Turenne. All this is referred to but never explained (*HF*, 4:373).

13. *HF*, 4:279–80, 318. Bernhard took charge and won the battle of Lützen where Gustavus Adolphus was killed (1732). He was in French employ after 1735, and died soon after taking Breisach (1739).

14. *HF*, 4:298–305, retold in *La Sorcière* (1862), *SO*, 2:76–83.

Chapter Six

1. *OI*, xi–xxv; *IN*, 1–8.
2. *J*, 1:398, 405–6. Cf. Edward Kaplan, "Michelet évolutionniste," *Romantisme* 10 (1975): 111–28; and *Michelet's Poetic Vision*, chap. 2, 4, Kaplan's ed. of *L'Insecte* in *OC* will include the correspondence with Isidore Geoffroy Saint-Hilaire; on him, ibid., pp. 17, 174. Michelet read from E. Geoffroy Saint-Hilaire to Mme. Dumesnil two days before her death (*J*, 1:405).
3. Jean Reynaud, *Terre et Ciel*, appeared in 1854 but the *Encyclopédie nouvelle* of 1838–1841 (8 vols.) contained the essential ideas; cf. Kaplan, *Michelet's Poetic Vision*, pp. 9, 182. Reynaud believed that the Christian religion was outdated and had to be replaced by a modern faith. A church council at Périgueux (1857) condemned *Terre et Ciel*, but Reynaud maintained (5th ed., 1866) that he had not offended dogma, which shows that his views did not always coincide with those of Michelet.
4. Linda Orr, *Jules Michelet* (Ithaca, 1976), esp. chap. 11; Kaplan, *Michelet's Poetic Vision*, chap. 5, Alphonse Toussenel wrote *Le Monde des oiseaux, ornithologie passionnelle*, 3 vols. (1852–1855); on his brother, Théodore, cf. chap. 14, n. 2.
5. *OI*, 40, 108, 113. Michelet had friends at the Museum; cf. above on I. Geoffroy Saint-Hilaire.
6. *J*, 1:416, 432. The poem was read in 1842, in Germany.
7. G. W. Allen in *Etudes anglaises* 1 (1937):230–37; *American Literature* 45 (1973):428–32; A. Geffen, ibid., pp. 107–14.
8. Michelet learned much from his friend, Isidore Geoffroy Saint-Hilaire, and his *Histoire naturelle des règnes organiques* (1854), but his main source is Etienne. Cf. Kaplan, *Michelet's Poetic Vision*, pp. 10, 17–19.
9. Darwin credited Charles Lyell's *Principles of Geology* as the book without which the *Origin of the Species* could not have been written; Kaplan, p. 46 and p. 24 on Charles Bonnet, the author of *La Palingénésie philosophique* (1769).
10. It was an outstanding success even among the popular books: Hachette sold 33,000 copies of *L'Oiseau* and 28,000 of *L'Insecte* in eleven years according to Michelet's correspondence with the publisher; Bibliothéque historique de la Ville de Paris, fonds Dumesnil-Baudoüin, Cote 5716; cited by Stephen Kippur, *Jules Michelet*.
11. *IN* 76; cf. FE, 434.
12. François Huber, son of Michel (the translator of German romantic literature) is a Swiss naturalist, "the great historian of the bees" (*IN*, 260). The book by Pierre Huber (son of François) first outraged Michelet by speaking of "immoral" ants, but observation seemed to confirm his view (*IN*, 260, 264); the reference to the personality of animals may be to François Huber (*IN*, 401; cf. *J*, . 2:335).

13. Edwards: cf. chap. 2, n. 6; *JM*, 1:193, 218; the last reference gives a summary list of authors who influenced the nature studies; Hahnemann: *J*, 1:375, 377, 379.

14. *J*, 2:328, 330, 771.

15. Berthelot: *J*, 2:327, 770; Serres: *J*, 1:631, etc.; Michelet mentions their contact over twenty years; Anzou: *J*, 2:297, 299, 397.

16. *AM*, 47, 67, 84, 167; cf. J. Calo, *La Création de la femme chez Michelet*.

17. *AM*, 159; *FE*, 275; cf. *J*, 2:328–29, assuming woman is in heat *(rut)* at the time of her periods.

18. Cf. n. 3 above. Michelet and Jean Reynaud met repeatedly (*J*, 2:439).

19. *AM*, 252; the term comes from Fourier, also haunted by the dissolution of love and marriage.

20. Michelet drew on the following trips: Arcachon (1851), Pornic (1853), Nervi (1853–1854), Hyères (1858), Granville (1858), Royan, St.-Georges (1859), all in *La Mer*, and to the Pyrenees (1863) and Switzerland (1854, 1856, 1865, 1867) discussed in *La Montagne*.

21. *ME*, 409–11, 425–26, the last note added in the 2d ed.

22. Cf. M. Serres, "Michelet, la soupe," *Revue d'histoire littéraire* 74 (1974): 787–802.

23. See Kaplan, "Michelet évolutionniste," and *Michelet's Poetic Vision*, chap. 3.

24. *MO*, 55 and Kaplan, p. 50.

25. *ME*, 125, 371. The French translation of Lyell is of 1843–1848; cf. n. 9 above.

26. *MO*, 127, English version in Kaplan, p. 47.

27. *MO*, 126, English version in Kaplan, p. 44.

28. Kaplan, p. 46.

29. Michelet had first thought that Darwin's idea of "struggle" was the very antithesis of gradualism. The translation of the *Origin of the Species* was in 1862; cf. Kaplan, pp. 41–49 and n. 2 above.

Chapter Seven

1. This motto from Rousseau's *Confessions* (éd. Pléiade, 1:1024 and n. 2), also found at the head of his *Lettres de la montagne*, comes from Juvenal, *Satire* IV, 91.

2. *HF*, 4:376; *AM*, 326; cf. chap. 6, sec. 2 above, on telegony.

3. In vols. 16–17 of the *Histoire de France*, cf. secs. 7–8 below.

4. *HF*, 4:541–42, 561–62; 5:10–15 (*Histoire de France*, vol. 14 begins *HF*, 4:555) on *Esther* and other works by Racine.

5. *HF*, 4:478, 486, 506, 515, 559; cf. pp. 490, 503–8, 519–20 on persecution.

6. *HF*, 4:399, 535, 543.

7. Cévennes: *HF*, 4:533; 5:60–67; Waldenses: 4:527.

8. *HF*, 5:33, 52, 63; cf. p. 133 where Michelet specifies that half a million Protestants were to be expelled.

9. *HF*, 5:72–74; the victories were at Blenheim and Hochstädt (1704), at Ramillies, and at Turin (1706).

10. On Malplaquet (1709): *HF*, 5:91–94; effects in England: pp. 93, 97.

11. *HF*, 5:111; cf. Linda Orr, *Jules Michelet*, p. 77.

12. *HF*, 5:127; Saint-Simon is frequently cited: pp. 85, 101, 104, 118, 131, etc. Michelet prefers him to Dangeau who belabors minor issues. In the next volume he frequently cites Buvat, *Journal de la Régence*, and is proud to rely almost exclusively on writings of the time, including the letters of Elisabeth-Charlotte of the Palatinate (cited before and, e.g., *HF*, 5:51) but he has ceased making even the pretence of turning to archives. On England he cites Macauley: *HF*, 5:13, 21, 34.

13. Michelet is convinced that he is not anti-semitic but he does consider the historic role of the Jews to play into the hands of financial exploitation and tyranny on the one hand, and of the Christian dogma and hierarchy he rejects on the other; cf. *BH*, 382–83. Here Bénichou, cited in chap. 2, n. 14, corrects Monod in *Revue des études juives* 53 (1907): vi–ix.

14. *HF*, 5:134; on Spain: pp. 139, 168–69, 197; Cellamare, Maine: pp. 136, 186.

15. Saint-Simon, *Mémoires* (ed. Pléiade), 6:326–29, 363–75; on the autopsy, pp. 372–73; cf.: *HF*, 5:152, 158, 198.

16. *FE*, 56–57 and chap. 6, sec. 2 above.

17. *HF* 5:175, 203, 220–21 on gold, p. 225; on Conti, Bourbon, pp. 226, 235–36. Michelet does not mention the recall of gold currency.

18. In part I, chap. 7, for instance, we find an accumulation of rhythmical though unrhymed *alexandrins* (12 syllable verses): "Pénétrer l'avenir, / évoquer le passé, // devancer, rappeler / le temps qui va si vite," and again: "qu'as-tu dans tes entrailles? / quels secrets? quels mystères? // Tu nous rends bien le grain / que nous te confions" (*SO*, 1:87).

19. Cf. Robert Casanova in *OC*, vol. 3–5. esp. 3:476.

20. See the excellent preface by R. Barthes, reprinted in *Essais critiques* (Paris: Le Seuil, 1964), pp. 112–24, esp. p. 123.

21. Ibid., pp. 114–15.

22. L. Refort in *SO*, 2:viii–x on critics and 1:viii–xiv on the publication, the transfer from Hachette to Lacroix Verboeckhoven (Brussels) and Dentu (Paris); he gives the list of parallel (or identical) passages in the *Histoire de France:* 1:xxiv–xv; 2:x–xi. See the excellent preface by P. Viallaneix (Garnier-Flammarion, 1966).

23. Paris: Payot, 1950. Cf. E. Said, *Orientalism* (New York, 1978), but Michelet, like Quinet, speaks of both movements, East and West (p. 73).

24. B. Constant, *De la Religion*, now seems superficial (*BH*, 159, 443) while Creuzer-Guigniaut is "the basic work" (*BH*, 157–58) on Bacchus, Greece (cf. *J*, 3:243, 246).

25. P. Leroux, *De l'Humanité* (1840); Michelet distrusted his radical socialism (*J*, 1:386; 2:242).

182 JULES MICHELET

26. Cf. chap. 6 above, sec. 1 and n. 3; the article on Zarathustra is basic for Michelet's view of Persia.

27. *BH*, 167, 180, 265, 443 refer to L. Ménard, *Polythéisme hellénique* (1863); cf. H. Peyre, *Louis Ménard* (New Haven: Yale University Press, 1932), pp. 296–97.

28. *BH*, 289, cf. the *Préface* of 1869, *OC*, 4:17.

29. *BH*, 251, 257, 316–19, 333–39.

30. *BH*, 67; cf. Matthew 27:46.

31. P. Leroux, *Du Christianisme et de son origine démocratique* (Paris, 1848) p. 4, derived from the article "Christianisme," in the *Encyclopédie nouvelle* (1836). Renan, *Vie de Jésus*, chap. 21. Peyrat's *Histoire élémentaire* was one of many rebuttals of Renan's *Vie de Jésus*; others, also of 1864, are by Havet, Scherer, etc.

32. *James: BH*, 434–40; the book was edited by G. Postel (Basle, 1522); Michelet used an edition of 1832 (*BH*, 434); a recent edition is E. Hennecke, *New Testament Apocrypha* (Philadelphia, 1959), 1:363–74; its influence can be seen in the Giotto frescoes in the Scrovegni chapel, Padua, where Anne's immaculate conception is announced. Alphonse Peyrat also wrote on this subject: *Le Dogme nouveau: Histoire de l'immaculée conception* (1855) which Michelet must have known.

33. *BH*, 450; cf. Romans 7:8. Paul meant that the Law made him aware of sin which has the attraction of forbidden fruit; Michelet did not understand him this way.

34. *BH*, 454–55, 463, 480. Michelet also accuses Paul of welcoming the barbarians Tacitus describes in *De Germania* and is sure they brought only disorder (*BH*, 454, 463).

35. *BH*, 431, 447; cf. Romans 16:1–2.

36. *HF*, 5:271, 411, 515 on 1794; p. 294 on taxation *(la ferme)*.

37. St. Médard: *HF*, 5:295; la Cadière: pp. 307–9 retold from *La Sorcière*.

38. *HF*, 5:414, 464, 491–94.

39. Pâris-Duverney: *HF*, 5:278–80; Machault: pp. 361, 372, 391; Turgot: pp. 476–78; d'Argenson: pp. 272, 287.

40. Fleury: *HF*, 5:271; Maurepas: pp. 276, 412; Choiseul: pp. 418–21.

41. *HF*, 5:375. Michelet is fascinated by incest, cf. his suggestion about François I and Marguerite de Navarre (*OC*, 7:338, 341–43, and Calo, *La Création de la femme*, pp. 400–401).

42. 1778: *HF*, 5:485; 1781: p. 492; 1784–1785: p. 495. The death of Louis XVII has been disputed, cf. Jacques Godechot, *Les Révolutions* (Paris: Presses Universitaires, 1970), pp. 59, 337.

43. *HF*, 5:339–41, 380, 395.

44. Pascal: *HF*, 5:300–311; action: p. 275; Calas, Sirven: pp. 442–48.

45. Diderot: *HF* 5:275, 407–10; *Encyclopédie*: p. 481, cf. pp. 355, 395.

46. Cf. chap. 4, sec. 7 above, and O. A. Haac, "Faith in the Enlightenment: Voltaire and Rousseau seen by Michelet," *Studies in Eighteenth Century Culture* 7 (1978): 475–90.

47. Drivel: *HF*, 5:434; cf. pp. 410, 428–32, 481; Wolmar: pp. 432–33; cf. p. 415: Rousseau fears the Revolution, considers emigration, one of the most negative statements by Michelet on Rousseau.

48. *OC*, 4:19, 36, of 1868–1869. The entire text of the final version is translated by E. Kaplan, *Michelet's Poetic Vision*, pp. 147–68; the translations here are my own.

49. *HR*, 1:609; cf. O. A. Haac, *Les Principes inspirateurs de Michelet*, pp. 73–80.

Chapter Eight

1. Corinthians 15:55.

2. At Lacroix Verboeckhoven, where *La Sorcière* appeared for similar reasons; see also the new edition of the *Histoire de la Révolution*, which takes up this protest; cf. below.

3. Cf. S. Bernard-Griffiths in *Romantisme* 10 (1975):157–61; cf. *J*, 4:54 of 8 September.

4. Michelet will comment more specifically on these in *La France devant l'Europe*, pp. 27, 41. Napoleon III arranged a plebiscite in 1870. Michelet voted "no." The victory of the majority, who voted "yes" for peace, brought war! Cf. secs. 3–4 below.

5. Louis Blanc, *Histoire de la Révolution française* (Paris, 1847–1861), 10:409; cf. p. 415: "The Revolution that killed them will grieve for them eternally," but Louis Blanc considers the judgment just!

6. Ibid., 11:274.

7. Ibid., 10:395–414; cf. *HR*, 2:369–77, 791–809.

8. Ibid., 10:10; 11:114–15, 122–23, 146–47, 150–56, 279–84, 423.

9. The critical notes at the end of chapters, e.g., ibid., 7:91, 198–207; 8:476; 9:460; 10:407–9; 11:80–83, 113, 189, 192, 265–69.

10. *NF*, 364, cf. *L'Etudiant* pp. 57, 59, 163 and chap. 4, sec. 2 above.

11. *NF*, 423; cf. *La France devant l'Europe*, p. 40.

12. *NF*, 101; cf. *Le Peuple*, pp. 61-62, and chap. 1, n. 5 above: *Nos Fils* indicates Michelet's unorthodox love for Mme. Fourcy.

13. *FR*, 134; *J*, 4:263–67 contains Athénaïs's account of the critical days; cf. pp. 268–94, Michelet's notes, and *HD*, 1:4–7.

14. *J*, 4:265, 283–84, 293–94; on Herzen see also chap. 4, sec. 6 and n. 20.

15. Chap. 1, sec. 2 and n. 13.

16. Luther: *HD*, 1:6; *Gemüth: J*, 4:258; Baden: *FR*, 65, 104.

17. *FR*, 117, 153; *HD*, 1:5–6; Frederick: *Histoire de France*, vol. 16; cf. chap. 7, sec. 7 and n. 43.

18. *FR*, 91, 101; cf. 29.

19. Gustavus Adolphus: *FR*, 71; civilians: 8; cities: 100; machines: 68–70; cf. chap. 3, sec. 6 and n. 33.

20. French plebiscite: *FR*, 50; cf. sec. 3 and n. 4 above; Russians: *FR*, 121; Germans: 101.

21. Ed. G. Monod, *Revue bleue*, ser. 5, vol. 4 (1905): 582–84, 609–11; see esp. p. 611. *Nature: a Poetry of the Earth and Sea*, by Athénaïs, appeared in 1872 in Edinburgh (also London and New York), in the English translation by W. H. Davenport Adams.

22. Ségur, *Histoire de Napoléon et de la Grande Armée* (1823) which is cited; Lanfrey, *Napoléon*, 5 vols. (1867–1875), used in part.

23. Lodi: *HD*, 1:401–3; Marengo: 3:43–48; hesitate: 3:367; Masséna: 2:82.

24. Hortense: *HD*, 3:50, 156; Marie Louise: 3:327.

25. Poles: *HD*, 3:337–43; road from Moscow: 3:353–55.

26. Egypt: *HD*, 2:263, 274; lion: 3:366; atrocities; 3:374; Charles X, Louis XVIII: 3:12, 384.

27. Ferdinand: *HD*, 3:397; Elba: 3:393.

28. Quiberon: *HD*, 1:264–97; Hoche: 1:169–70; 2:55, 74–75, 221–22; cf. *Les Soldats de la Révolution* (1851 but published posthumously).

29. Goujon: *HD*, 1:218–52; the suicide was on 20 May 1795; Babeuf: *HD*, 1:23–24, 31–46, 65–70, 92–93, 104, 111; 2:146–55.

30. *HD*, 2:13–16; 3:59–65, 345–46.

31. Credo: last chapter in *Histoire de France*, vol. 16; pleasure: *HD*, 1:52, 139–47.

32. Watt: *HD* 2:11; Lyell, Darwin: 3:8; Cuvier: 3:87–88.

33. Manuscript note of 1870–1871 cited by Viallaneix, *VR*, 325–36.

34. Militarism: *HD*, 1:11; 3:2; heritage: 2:2.

35. Egypt, India: *HD*, 3:223–32, 291–312; it is typical that the historian assumes the reader knows that Wellesley is the older brother of Wellington; *Bible:* 2:232.

Chapter Nine

1. Lionel Gossman, "The Go-Between: Jules Michelet, 1798–1874," *Modern Language Notes* 89 (1974):503–41.

2. Malraux, *Les Voix du silence*, English translation, p. 619, reads: "It is not the historian who confers immortality, it is the artist with his power over men's dreams." Michelet is both historian and artist, and thus attains his objective which is resurrection.

Selected Bibliography

PRIMARY SOURCES

For manuscripts at the Bibliothèque historique de la Ville de Paris and at the University of Clermont-Ferrand, see Paul Viallaneix, *La Voie royale*, pp. 495–501; for works to 1839, the *Histoire de France* to 1855, see Viallaneix's edition of *Oeuvres complètes*, vols. 1–7. Other works are listed in the edition used for this study along with the abbreviations to identify them.

1. Editions cited in text
AM *L'Amour*. 4th ed. Paris: Hachette, 1859.
BH *La Bible de l'humanité*. 2nd ed. Paris: Chamerot, 1864.
EJ *Ecrits de Jeunesse*. Edited by Paul Viallaneix. Paris: Gallimard, 1959.
ET *L'Etudiant*. Edited by Gaëtan Picon. Paris: Le Seuil, 1970
FE *La Femme*. 16th ed. Paris: Calman Lévy, 1889.
FR *La France devant l'Europe*. Geneva: ed. du Verbe, 1946.
HD *Histoire du dix-neuvième siècle*. 3 vols. Paris: Flammarion, 1899. In *Oeuvres complètes*.
HF *Histoire de France*. Paris, Hetzel, n.d. Used vols. 3–5. These texts are to appear in *OC*.
HR *Histoire de la Révolution française*. Edited by Walter. 2 vols., revised ed., Paris: Gallimard, 1961.
IN *L'Insecte*. Paris: Hachette, 1857.
J *Journal*. Edited by Paul Viallaneix and Claude Digeon. 4 vols. Paris: Gallimard, 1959–1976.
JS *Des Jésuites*. Edited by Paul Viallaneix. Paris: Pauvert, 1966.
LD *Légendes démocratiques du Nord*. Edited by Michel Cadot. Paris: Presses universitaires de France, 1968.
ME *La Mer*. Paris: Calman Lévy, 1903. In *Oeuvres complètes*.
MO *La Montagne*. Paris: Calman Lévy, 1913. In *Oeuvres complètes*.
NF *Nos Fils*. 3d ed. Paris: Librairie internationale, and Brussels: Lacroix Verboeckhoven, 1870.
OC *Oeuvres complètes*. Edited by Paul Viallaneix. 7 vols. to date. Paris: Flammarion, 1971–.
OI *L'Oiseau*. Paris: Hachette, 1856.
PE *Le Peuple*. Edited by Paul Viallaneix. Paris: Flammarion, 1974.
Paris Guide. Vol. 1. Brussels: Lacroix Verboeckhoven, 1867.
PR *Du Prêtre, de la femme et de la famille*. Brussels: Société belge de librairie, 1845.
SO *La Sorcière*. Edited by Lucien Refort. 2 vols. Paris: Didier, 1952–1956.
Sylvine. Edited by Alcanter de Brahm. Paris: Debresse, 1940.

2. Translations

A good part of Michelet's work has been translated, from *The History of the Roman Republic*, translated by William Hazlitt, to the nature books which appeared almost simultaneously in French and English (*The Bird* was an important influence on Walt Whitman) but few titles are currently available:

The History of the French Revolution. Translated by Charles Cocks, edited by Gordon Wright. Chicago: University of Chicago Press, 1971. Contains the introduction and books 1 to 3.
————. Translated by Keith Botsford from the edition by G. Walter. Wynnewood, Pa.: Livingston Publishing Co., 1972–. Only vol. 4 (books 7–8) and vol. 6 (books 11–13) seem to have appeared.
Preface (to the *History of France*). Translated by Edward Kaplan and Perry McIntosh. In Kaplan, *Michelet's Poetic Vision*, pp. 147–68 (see below).
The People. Translated by John P. McKay. Urbana: University of Illinois Press, 1973.
Satanism and Witchcraft. Translated by A. R. Allinson [in 1904]. Secaucus, N.J.: Lyle Stuart, 1969.

SECONDARY SOURCES

For bibliography, see Viallaneix; Haac, Kaplan, and Orr; Talvart and Place, *Bibliographie des auteurs modernes*, vol. 15 (Paris, 1963); T. di Scanno, *Bibliographie de Michelet en Italie* (Florence: Sansoni, 1969); Otto Klapp, *Bibliographie der französischen Literatur (annual)*. For *JM* see Monod; For *VR* see Viallaneix.

1. Books

ALBOUY, PIERRE. *Mythes et mythologies dans la littérature française*. Paris: Armand Colin, 1969. Sensitive, suggestive.
BARTHES, ROLAND. *Michelet par lui-même*. Paris: Le Seuil, 1957. Excellent presentation of haunting themes.
CABANIS, JOSÉ. *Michelet, le prêtre et la femme*. Paris: Gallimard, 1978. Slanted, undocumented, provocative, intelligent.
CALO, JEANNE. *La Création de la femme chez Michelet*. Paris: Nizet, 1975. Highly useful list of women, from history and life.
CARRÉ, JEAN-MARIE. *Michelet et son temps*. Paris: Perrin, 1926. Excellent essays.
CORNUZ, JEANLOUIS. *Jules Michelet: Un aspect de la pensée religieuse au XIXe siècle*. Geneva: Droz, 1955. Excellent, comprehensive.
GAULMIER, JEAN. *Michelet devant Dieu*. Paris: Desclée de Brouwer, 1968. Excellent summary of religious views.

GUÉHENNO, JEAN. *L'Evangile éternel, étude sur Michelet*. 1927. Revised ed. Paris: Grasset, 1962. Excellent, sensitive portrayal.

HAAC, OSCAR A. *Michelet et l'histoire allemande*. Ann Arbor, Mich.: University Microfilms, 1961. A 1948 Yale dissertation. German history and authors in Michelet's work; complete biblography of 149 pages.

————. *Les Principes inspirateurs de Michelet*. Paris: Presses universitaires de France, 1951. Themes, ideology, historical method, shorter bibliography.

————, ed. *Cours professé au Collège de France, 1839*. *Revue d'histoire littéraire* 54, no. 3 (1954), suppl. With comments.

HALÉVY, DANIEL. *Jules Michelet*. Paris: Hachette, 1928. Biography.

JOHNSON, MARY-ELISABETH. *Michelet et le christianisme*. Paris: Nizet, 1955. The changing views of the Christian religion.

KAPLAN, EDWARD K. *Michelet's Poetic Vision: A Romantic Philosophy of Nature*. Amherst: University of Mass. Press, 1977. Excellent on the scientific background and its poetic interpretation.

KIPPUR, STEPHEN A. *Jules Michelet, A Study of Mind and Sensibility*. New York: State University Press, 1980. Excellent biography, general background.

MANUEL, FRANK E. *Prophets of Paris*. New York: Harper Torch Books, 1962. Excellent short presentation.

MONOD, GABRIEL. *Jules Michelet, études sur sa vie et son oeuvre*. Paris: Hachette, 1905. Valuable studies.

————. *La Vie et la pensée de Jules Michelet*. 2 vols. Paris: Champion, 1923. Cited in the text as *JM*. Basic study of Michelet to 1852.

NEFF, EMERY. *The Poetry of History*. New York: Columbia University Press, 1947. Nice summary.

ORR, LINDA. *Jules Michelet: Nature, History, and Language*. Ithaca: Cornell University Press, 1976. Excellent style study and suggestive analysis of images.

POMMIER, JEAN. *Michelet interprète de la figure humaine*. London: Athlone Press, 1961. Michelet interprets portraits; excellent.

PUGH, ANNE R. *Michelet and his Ideas on Social Reform*. New York: Columbia University Press, 1923. Still useful.

REARICK, CHARLES. *Beyond the Enlightenment: Historians and Folklore in Nineteenth Century France*. Bloomington: Indiana University Press, 1974. Excellent background.

REFORT, LUCIEN. *L'Art de Michelet dans son oeuvre historique*. Paris: Champion, 1923. Interesting subject.

RUDLER, GUSTAVE. *Michelet historien de Jeanne d'Arc*. Paris: Presses Universitaires, 1925–1926. Inadequacy of Michelet's documentation compared to scientific methods.

SCHARTEN, THEODORA. *Les Voyages et séjours de Michelet en Italie*. Paris: Droz, 1934. Still important.

TIEDER, IRÈNE. *Michelet et Luther*. Paris: Didier, 1976. Faithful analysis, excellent background.

VIALLANEIX, PAUL. *La Voie royale: Essai sur l'idée du peuple dans l'oeuvre de Michelet*. 1959. Revised ed. Paris: Flammarion, 1971. Cited in text as *VR*. Excellent, comprehensive, extensive bibliography.

————, ed. *Jeanne d'Arc*. Paris: Gallimard, 1974. Evolution of the text, new materials, excellent.

WILSON, EDMUND. *To the Finland Station*. 1940. Reprint. New York: Anchor Books, 1953. Suggestive, excellent evocation.

2. Collections and Catalogs Honoring the Centennial (1974)

L'Arc, no. 52 (1973). Barthes, Le Goff, Malandain, Mandrou, Mettra, Orr, Viallaneix, and others.

Clio 6, no. 2 (1977). Besançon, Gossman, Manuel, Moreau, Serres, Viallaneix, and others.

Europe 51, nos. 535–36 (1973). Cornuz, Kaplan, Madaule, Orr, Seebacher, Viallaneix, Wodzynska-Walicka, Wurmser, and others.

MICHAUD, G., and R. MOLHO. *Michelet et "Le Peuple."* Nanterre: University of Nanterre, 1975 (photo offset). Bancquet, Bérard, Crouzet, Gaulmier, Reboul, Rémond, Viallaneix, Viard, Vigier.

PAPILLARD, FRANÇOIS. *Michelet et Vascoeuil*. Paris, 1974. Catalog of the exhibition at the Dumesnil estate.

Revue d'histoire littéraire de la France 74, no. 5 (1974). Barthes, Bowman, Orr, Seebacher, Serres, Viard, and others.

Romantisme, no. 10 (1975). *Michelet cent ans après*. Bernard-Griffiths, Brisson, Govindane, Kaplan, Le Guillou, Malandain, Orr, Papillard, Seebacher, Viallaneix; also Barthes, Gaulmier, Le Goff, Mandrou, Mettra, and others.

3. Articles and Prefaces

BART, B. F. "Michelet et Proudhon." *French Studies* 4 (1950): 128–41.

BARTHES, ROLAND. "Michelet, l'histoire et la mort." *Esprit* 19 (1951): 497–511.

————. "La Sorcière." In *Essais critiques*. Paris: Le Seuil, 1964. Pp. 112–24 (cf. pp. 270–71).

BESANÇON, ALAIN. "Le Premier Livre de la *Sorcière*." *Annales* 26 (1971): 186–204.

CROUZET, MICHEL. "Michelet, les morts et l'année 1842." *Annales* 31 (1976):182–96.

EHRMANN, FRANÇOIS. "Michelet et la Grèce." *Revue des Sciences humaines* 27 (1962):49–65, 213–35.

FEBVRE, LUCIEN. "Jules Michelet ou la liberté du monde." In *Michelet*. Geneva: Trois collines, Traits, 1946.

GOSSMAN, LIONEL. "The Go-Between: Jules Michelet." *Modern Language Notes* 89 (1974):503–41.

Selected Bibliography 189

HAAC, OSCAR A. "A Spiritual Journey: Michelet in Germany 1842." *Proceedings of the American Philosophical Society* 94 (1950): 502–9.
———. "Vico and Michelet." *Forum Italicum* 2 (1968):483–93.
———. "The Literature of History: Michelet's Middle Ages." *Nineteenth Century French Studies* 4 (1976):162–68.
———. "Faith in the Enlightenment: Voltaire and Rousseau seen by Michelet." *Studies on Eighteenth Century Culture* 7 (1978):175–90.
MALANDAIN, PIERRE. "Michelet et Géricault." *Revue d'histoire littéraire de la France* 69 (1969):979–92.
———. "Michelet et Napoléon." *Europe* 47, nos. 480–81 (1969):252–63.
MANDROU, ROBERT. Preface to *La Sorcière*. Paris: Julliard, 1964.
METTRA, CLAUDE. Prefaces to the *Histoire de France* and *Histoire de la Révolution*. Lausanne: Rencontre 1964–1967.
———. Preface to *Mémoires de Luther*. Paris: Mercure de France, 1974.
PICON, GAËTAN. "Michelet et la parole historienne." Preface to *ET*.
PONS, ALAIN. "Vico and French Thought." In *Giambattista Vico*, ed. G. Tagliacozzo and H. White. Baltimore: Johns Hopkins Press, 1969.
POULET, GEORGES. "Michelet et le moment d'Eros." *Nouvelle Revue Française* 178 (1967): 610–35.
SERRES, MICHEL. "Le Tricorne et l'amour sorcier." *Critique*, January 1968, pp. 57–69.
SEZNEC, JEAN. "Michelet et l'*Annonciation*." *Gazette des Beaux-Arts*, 58 (1961):145–52.
———. "Michelet in Germany: A Journey in Self-Discovery," *History and Theory* 16 (1977):1–10.
ZALESKI, Z. L. "Michelet, Mickiewicz et la Pologne." *Revue de Littérature comparée* 8 (1928): 433–87.

Index

References to works constantly cited, like Michelet's *Journal* and *Histoire de France* are indicative rather than exhaustive.

190